God's Country and Mine

BY JACQUES BARZUN

God's Country and Mine

A DECLARATION OF LOVE
SPICED WITH
A FEW HARSH WORDS

by

JACQUES BARZUN

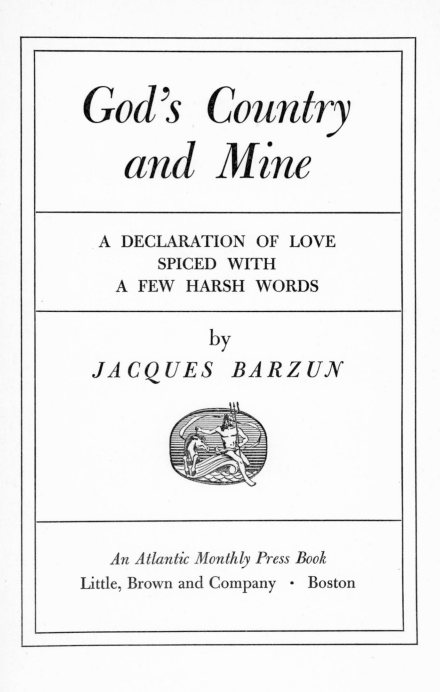

An Atlantic Monthly Press Book
Little, Brown and Company · Boston

LIBRARY OF CONGRESS CATALOG CARD NO. 53–5262

Published March 1954
Reprinted March 1954 (three times)

ATLANTIC–LITTLE, BROWN BOOKS
ARE PUBLISHED BY
LITTLE, BROWN AND COMPANY
IN ASSOCIATION WITH
THE ATLANTIC MONTHLY PRESS

Published simultaneously in Canada
by Little, Brown & Company (Canada) Limited

PRINTED IN THE UNITED STATES OF AMERICA

To
the Memory of

INGEBORG HAVGEN JOHNSON
(1905–1944)

American from Norway

Contents

PART ONE
Spring, or Getting and Spending

1. Innocents at Home

THE WAY TO SEE AMERICA is from a lower berth about two in the morning. You've just left a station — it was the jerk of pulling out that woke you — and you raise the curtain a bit between thumb and forefinger to look out. You are in the middle of Kansas or Arizona, in the middle of the space where the freight cars spend the night and the men drink coffee out of cans. Then comes the signal tower, some bushes, a few shacks and — nothing. You see the last blue switch-light on the next track, and beyond is America — dark and grassy, or sandy, or rocky — and no one there. Nothing but the irrational universe with you in the center trying to reason it out. It's only ten, fifteen minutes since you've left a thriving town but life has already been swallowed up in that ocean of matter which is and will remain as wild as it was made.

Come daylight, the fear vanishes but not the awe or the secret pleasure. It is a perpetual refreshment to the soul to see that the country is so large, so indifferent to the uses we have put it to, so like a piece of the earth's crust and unlike any map. No names on it, no lines, no walls with guns through them. It is good that in this place at least there is more of just plain territory per square mile than anywhere else in the civilized world. Europe is lovely but it looks like a poodle cut — the trees are numbered, the flat parts divided like a checkerboard, the rivers as slim and well-behaved as the mercury in a thermometer. The towns, like dead men's bones on the line of a caravan, huddle white and dry, crowded behind defenses that have crumbled. And everywhere the steeples point to remind you that you must look upward if you want space and serenity.

Here space is ubiquitous, even on the Atlantic Coast, which by the country's own scale is shriveled and thick with human beings. But even here we have space enough to swallow up the worst signs of our busy nonchalance, the car dumps. And even here we refuse to follow the ways of the citified: suburban street signs leave you in the lurch, and houses forget or conceal their separate numbers. Nearby the wilderness exists and has been kept: the Adirondacks are a paradise of woods and waterfalls and luxuriant vegetation — and yet it's only a small state preserve for city campers playing Indians with canoes and grocery-store pemmican. The sand dunes of Cape Cod are as accessible and linked with city life as any suburb, yet they stretch most of the time as empty as the desert, and they are moved by giant storms that feel like the last shaping flick of the Creator's thumb.

Starting from the greatest city in the world, almost invisible on a fair-sized map of the continent, one must push the wheels for three quarters of a day before reaching the midland seas that are the country's crown. By that point, too, one has traveled but a short distance away (as soil and spirit mark it) from America's European shore. Clock time has moved one hour back to wait for the sun, and the world perspective has somewhat changed. The doings of other men on the rim of the vast saucer in whose hollow one stands do begin to seem remote. The space on all sides dwarfs the subdivisions that are so real to the many millions beyond the seas. From America's rich gestating center south of the Great Lakes, one seems merely to overhear the world while one broods on the permanent functions of the earth. And yet that center is not central. Like the human heart, the Middle West is to one side of the median line. To really find the west there is still the Mississippi to ford, the long plains to cross, the Rockies to climb and five, six other chains to pass over, with deserts between, before going down into the last valley and reaching the country's Asiatic shore. The clocks have turned back twice again for the slow sun, and the traveler who has been drinking space is reeling.

The memory cannot hold all he has seen, for there is no common measure between the human senses and the unfolded spectacle. Quick variety — yes, we have nets fine enough to catch and retain that. But variety on a cosmic scale is beyond us. We can name the valleys, mountains, and gorges but we hardly know them. Anywhere in the world we hold our breath at moments of beauty and unexpectedness. But we cannot hold our breath for the hundred miles of endlessly renewed beauty in the Feather River Canyon. We probably give up and call it dull, but we only are hiding the truth from ourselves. Any stretch before us makes us stare and hold our breath again. Even the wastes and crags, the wreckage of the furnace days in those gray workshops of nature where it seems as if the fairer regions had been forged, are transcendently beautiful. The eighteen thousand square miles of the Great Basin in Oregon show nothing but dun palisades sloping backwards into flats of broken rocks — once the scene of unimaginable upheavals, now dedicated to carrying into the abyss, by means of its underground rivers, the broken particles of the split atom.

Magnificent, but is it art? Certainly not. Art follows rules based on our tiny comprehension. Art has to be comfortable for family men and women's clubs. None of America was made to *please*. It was made perhaps to satisfy a Worker in the Sublime, who knew that by heaping up triumphs on a grand scale he would successfully escape detection. Every region, every state, has its mystery, its defiance of probability — the colors of the Southwest, the virtuosity of desert life, the immense salt sea, the giant redwoods, the lake that won't freeze (though miles up in a crater) and that stays fresh (though without visible outlet) . . . When you think you've reached the end there is more — miles more — the source and the image of our abundance.

Only, in order to excuse so much exuberance of imagination, the Workman buried a treasure somewhere in the middle of his plot, and toward this he enticed men by decorating with small restful shapes and sights, in familiar greens and browns, the coast nearest the supply of active men.

At the same time, the artificer kept the weather congenial to his own robust frame and violent fancy. The solemn scientificos who call any spot in the United States part of the Temperate Zone are kidding. A change of thirty degrees between sunup and sundown, repeated without warning of season fifty times a year; highs of 90° to 120° in summer, with natural steam provided free; lows of zero and less in winter, with snowfalls and blizzards and ice-storms — none of these can be called temperate except in the sense of tempering. If they don't kill, they give a steel-like elasticity to the constitution.

But although the country is fertile, almost tropical in vegetation and rich in minerals, its food is bland. Everything that grows here is large but not luscious. The juices are not concentrated — as if to discourage self-indulgence through the belly. And just as there are but few delicate, man-size landscapes, so there is a lack of concentrated drama in the mountains. We have nothing like the Alps. Our bareness is diffuse, it is diluted — once again — in space. Our overwhelming masses of mountain timber are unbroken by any grassy islands that might give the scale through man's taking his cattle there. Our pure rock and eternal snows are remote, instead of rising from the midst of our daily life.

True, we can show stunning contrasts. The evergreen slopes around Lake Tahoe make a beautiful discord with the watery mass fringed by pale flowers. But the presence of man is not felt, even when you see him there relaxing from the toil of getting his Reno divorce nearby. The place keeps aloof, untouchable. The drama, so familiar elsewhere, of man master and victim of nature, is absent. Man here seems neither master nor victim but something which is at once more and less. He has not grown into and around the primal scene, but has either left it primitive or replaced it entirely by civilization. Maybe this is why he remains so innocent, his sense of struggle unembittered. The symbol of our relation to nature is the

National Park, the State Reservation, where we go on purpose to see aboriginal America, and our amusement is to play at the hunting and fishing life with all the contraptions of technology at hand. Nature is not our context or background but solely our raw material and — for recreation — our plaything.

All this has a meaning that only those who live here can comprehend. Man on this continent does not "show" because he did not start primitive with it. He came prepared. And yet the task of establishing himself was so vast that the individual man who could typify the effort did not count. The saga had to be lived so many times that the single hero, the outstanding name, is lost in the mass. America was possessed and civilized by the mass; it was a community enterprise from the start, in which the leader leads and does not dominate. Even our discoverer bears a generic name: Cristobal Colón: The Colonizer. The feats of conquest and settlement were as memorable as any in history or legend, but being commanded wholesale by necessity they grew commonplace. Who remembers the amazing life of Dr. Marcus Whitman, except schoolboys in Walla Walla? What of David Thompson, John McLoughlin, Elijah White? John Jacob Astor lives in memory not by his strenuous deeds, but by his descendants' leisure. We all know Pike's Peak because of the jingle and the slogan, but who was Pike? One in a million can tell you that this youthful hero's first name was Zebulon, but whatever history says, tradition says no more.

True, it raises haunting visions to discover from a sign outside a gas station at Murphy, North Carolina, that here De Soto and his men encamped in 1540. One can imagine the swampy ground sloping toward the river — under the present concrete and asphalt that stretches to the bridge. But for the ordinary traveler the reminiscence is barren. De Soto is a car and so is La Salle. They do not live in our imagination, for what they did many others did also, unknown soldiers of the conquest. There is no disloyalty in recognizing that by the very essence of America's greatness there can be no *national* American history as there is English or French history. What we have is state and county history rich, varied, and of the utmost liveliness and reality; complete with feuds, aristocrats, disasters, and leading roles. But on the greater scene the telling incidents and towering figures are simply not there. They may have existed but they have been dissolved away, not by time but by space and numbers.

You will say with some justice that I exaggerate. Yes, in early days, when America was still a colony of Europe, we can easily discern the great men, the chief founding fathers, but they live in us as myths and symbols rather than as flesh-and-blood people with distinct passions and errors, or cruel egos and dreadful deaths. Washington, Franklin, Hamilton, and Jefferson are wonderful legends — who will ever know or believe all that Jefferson did? — but match these names with Alexander Borgia, Henry VIII, Luther, or Napoleon, and our heroes pale into unreality. For one thing, they have no wickedness to speak of. All we can muster as villains are Benedict Arnold and Aaron Burr — a pitiful showing of borderline cases. Lincoln alone is vivid because in spite of his amazing saintliness he embodies the meaning of what happened here. He signifies not one great man, or even Man, but mankind — anonymous, humble and irresistible like the sweep of the Father of Waters.

What happened here on this enormous expanse of intact wildness is that mankind got out from under and spread out. From under what? From under the lid — everybody, from under all the lids — kings, churches, aristocracies, landlords, the military caste, the burgher class, the lawyers, the lesser nobility, the petty bourgeoisie — the piles of subclasses on top of subclasses that formed the structure of old Europe. They left an old world to stretch their limbs and spread out flat, with only the sky above them. Their goal was space. When the Eastern end thickened into layers for a new social pyramid, the under-layers slid out again to the West.

At first, a good many of the upper orders came over too, but they rarely kept their hold. The Revolution put an end to the

English and Tory ruling class. If some of them salvaged their
goods they remained as well-to-do citizens and that is all. Who can
name offhand anybody descended from a colonial governor or
bishop or major general? The connection, if known, would scarcely
affect one's behavior toward him or his place in the community.
It would be just a curious fact, possibly as funny as the "fact" that
Theodore Roosevelt, according to the chart in his old house, was
descended from Richard the Lion-Hearted. It is true that some of
our leading citizens take genealogies very gravely. It's a thriving
industry to dig them out of churchyards with the aid of a vaulting imagination. But pedigree has seldom helped any American to
get elected mayor or to sell insurance; the Fuller Brush man does
not introduce himself as a Son of the War of 1812 — ask any ten
people what the Order of Cincinnati is. Americans may love getting together in costumed brotherhoods, but these impress the
membership much more than the nation.

The same is true of the social cliques that keep their barriers
high. Movement in and out of these groups is constant, and their
exclusivism is largely convivial — who goes to whose parties. It does
not decide who runs corporations, schools, city government or anything else of importance. In fact, for all official and a good many
unofficial posts, society manners and ways of speech are a handicap.
Nor are the professions here encumbered by social pretensions as
they still are abroad. Look at the names of our judges, doctors, scientists, men of letters, and university presidents. They do not have
to be Cabot or Vanderhoof or Vere de Vere. They can be anything,
pronounceable or not.

All of which says nothing against the proud inheritors of good
old names. It only says something far more impressive for all the
rest — which is that this country was peopled by underdogs, refugees, nobodies, and that it keeps on being run by them. The noble
ancestors of the American people were, with negligible exceptions:
starving peasants, poor mechanics, domestic servants, younger sons
without prospects, unlucky youths who had to leave town in a

hurry, adventurers and shady characters of all sorts — convicts too, for that matter — any kind of man or woman who for some reason found living in Europe intolerable. That also means, of course, men of faith and education who resented tyranny of one sort or another, like the original Puritans of 1620, the French Huguenots of 1685, the Liberal Germans of 1848 who wanted constitutional government, the Irish, driven by famine and hatred of England, and young nationals from all over who fled military service.

To say all this is nothing new. We know, the whole world knows, that the American people is in its origin a sampling of the peoples of Western Europe. America began by being the haven of the disinherited — the underside of Europe — and then two providential events took place. First, the Industrial Revolution broke out and destroyed the immemorial connection of wealth and power with land. Next, the search for new wealth from industry, mining, and railroads led the American capitalists of the nineteenth century to import labor from any and everywhere, of all colors and kinds, good or bad, literate or illiterate. In doing this they made the United States the testing ground of the possibility of mankind living together.

I harp on the idea of mankind because it is a sign of the future, not an exaggeration of the accomplished past. To begin with, we have here a complete Europe — Swedes cheek by jowl with Armenians, Hungarians with Poles, Germans with French, English with Italians, Jews with Christians, Orthodox Greek with Baptists, and so on ad infinitum. No one can say that all is love and kisses in this grand mixture. In many a town there are two sides of the railroad track and on one side the poorer group, very likely ethnic in character, is discriminated against. But at what a rate these distinctions disappear! In Europe a thousand years of war, pogroms and massacres settle nothing. Here two generations of common schooling, intermarriage, ward politics, and labor unions create social peace.

Now turn from Europe to the world. The greed of the planters brought over the ancestors of our 15 million Negroes; that of the railroad builders brought the Chinese, by the tens of thousands, and the hundreds of thousands from Southern Europe, the Balkans, Greece, Asia Minor, and Russia. Not long after, at the end of our Spanish War, in came Puerto Ricans, Hawaiians, Filipinos, and Japanese. The Mexicans on our Southwestern border had long been drawn in for a similar exploitation. And the Indians we had always with us, from the days when we robbed them, killed them, and cheated them out of their ancestral lands.

That part by itself is not a pretty picture: we are only now and very slowly beginning to right a few of those wrongs. But the dark shadows are not all there is to see. We often overlook the real sweep of our democracy because we fail to add together what we know in fragments. We ignore the panorama and consider every item for our own ends or from our own tastes. We praise this and condemn that without noticing the connections and the meaning, and fail to see mankind all around us. We just read with curiosity the feature story that says Louisiana uses the Code Napoléon; that the Pennsylvania Dutch publish their own paper in their own inimitable English (this in a region they share with the descendants of their former persecutors); and that part of the ruling family of Tibet is now living in Baltimore. We never think that in loosing and mixing the masses we have all been civilized by the rubs and collisions — civilized not only from the top down, but from all parts interacting on one another, the humble teaching the proud in the literal way of the Gospels. It has proved a peculiar civilizing of the feelings for which there is as yet no name. But it is genuine and it is going on: the late war has for the hundredth time amplified our kaleidoscopic pattern of peoples, tongues, costumes, ideas, and religions.

All this has been, not automatic, but in the larger sense unplanned. How else could it have been, considering the steady dumping of the world's forgotten men — or surplus life — over here? The appearance of chaos is therefore true and important, though not in the way it is usually interpreted. We miss the central point if we think that great ideas like democracy become reality the way a blueprint becomes a car or a house, by an orderly arrangement of parts. Luck or Providence must intervene. And we must not expect the outcome to show perfect proportions frozen into place. History is movement, disarray as well as desirable direction. If the country had remained predominantly agricultural, the first comers would have taken all the land and kept down the rest of us as men had done elsewhere for seven thousand years. Once more a thin tough crust, with a deep-dish pie of human beings underneath. But every man's idea of escape to personal liberty, before or after he got here, combined with the needs of the industrial system to start an irresistible drive towards equalizing conditions. It is that drive, greater than any ideal of progress or party of resistance, that moves the world today, and we call it democracy.

This definition is no doubt incomplete. Every educated man who is a democrat at heart thinks first of the guarantees a true democracy gives to the individual — the vote, free speech, and free assembly. But most men outside the Western world are still largely indifferent to such rights. They want food, clothes, and shelter first and at all costs. Hence the dictatorships that trade on this desire by offering, say, a half-democracy, the democracy of rough equality. Here in America the thoughtful are properly concerned and most likely to dwell reproachfully on inequalities in wealth and opportunity, on injustices to unprotected persons and groups, on attempts to scoop up our individual rights and toss them to the winds of demagoguery. But while we resist being despoiled we must not lose faith in our combined industrial and emotional democracy. I call by that name our unpremeditated scheme which has an interest in pushing towards equality and fair treatment because that is the way we've learned to feel and because the scheme requires that we sell goods and keep our machinery going.

To those who decry this as "mere materialism" one need only ask when and where the world has seen a whole nation developing the habit, the tendency, of continually looking out for those who in one way or another are left out. We act abundantly on this strange motive, but let us be modest and call it but a tendency. If we had achieved the perfection of utopia and complete brotherhood, there would be nothing to talk about. Yet look at the subjects of unceasing agitation in our daily press: the rights of labor in bargaining, the fight for fair employment practices, for socialized medicine, against discrimination in Army and Navy, in colleges and hospitals, in restaurants, and places of public entertainment; in a word, the abolition of irrational privilege.

Millions, it is true, are against change. They condemn tyranny and act it out in their small, very small way. Inconsistency and resistance are to be expected. When one talks of mankind and its emergence on our soil, one must visualize men, not angels. But whatever the creature visualized one must not compare its behavior with an abstract ideal. One must compare it with the behavior of other men in the past. In the light of that contrast, it can be said that here in America, in spite of the vast problem of absorbing repeated injections of the world's peoples, the prevailing idea for a century has been, not the segregation or neutralization of these foreign bodies, but the abolition of differences, the equalizing of conditions. The reality in turn has taught the lesson that mankind is an inescapable fact. Instead of saying "Down with *them!* No, not *those!* Off with *their* heads!", we have not been afraid to take mankind out of hiding where we can look at it and deal with it as best we can, for the most part decently. There has been nothing like it since the wonderful hodgepodge of the late Roman Empire, and even there the common citizenship was theoretical and inoperative in far greater degree than it is with us.

One must immediately add that we have a thousand imperfections to blush for, heart-rending failures of justice manifested in lynchings, anti-Semitism, and racketeering; in cruelty to immigrants, to lunatics, to Indians, and to children. But before we rouse our energies to combat error we should from time to time restore our courage by taking in the whole scene, not in a detached but in a voluntarily calm spirit. The very things that upset us can be a source of strength, for aside from the effort to stem injustice and repress the oppressors, what is *the* most insistent theme of private mail and public press, of government posters and noncommercial ads, on radio and TV? Can it be denied that in a hundred different forms that theme is the fate of our fellow men? Floods break out along the Missouri or tornados in New England — the Red Cross is there and Federal and State aid pouring in. A polio epidemic — it's a rush of experts, nurses, and serum. The refugees, war brides, and homeless children from abroad, as well as our own minority groups, have not only spokesmen but disinterested outsiders who clamor ceaselessly into our ears that we help them bodily or fight for their rights: The native-born Japanese, cruelly displaced during the war, must be relocated. Farmers who have exhausted their soil must be allotted new lands and taught how to use them. We don't stop with the able-bodied. The blind, the paraplegics, the alcoholics, the insane, the sufferers from hookworm and deficiency diseases, those who lack dental care or eyeglasses, children without lunches — it's an endless round of reminders and requests. It's prenatal care for the unborn, vacations and play centers for the street boys, rehabilitation for victims of cerebral palsy or T.B., for the neurotic and sclerotic, cure for the venereal, employment for the ex-convicts, and occupational therapy for the jailed and the delinquent. You see business trucks carrying posters to say that the particular firm is ready to hire handicapped workers, and where these should apply for the names of other firms. Anyone who is hurt, anyone who feels or is inferior has a claim. One learns, for instance, by direct letter from a state senator, that there are half a million mentally retarded children in New York state alone. What is wanted is money for special schools, workshops, clinics, and camps, so that this one three-hundredth of the national population will not turn into so many unhappy derelicts but men and women like the rest of us.

This is at last moral philosophy in action. We are no longer allowed to say "Let the devil take the hindmost"; we say: "How can we bring these creatures into the fold?" No misfortune natural or acquired is any longer a bar to our sympathy or a sufficient cause for dismissal by the social conscience. We face all types of misery and misfitness and proclaim that they are equally entitled to our help, because mankind is what we aim to save. The first thing democracy has to be is inclusive. We worry about childhood, youth, the newly married, the middle-aged, the retired, the very old. We don't let God carry the burdens or the blame, *we* take them on. We don't let the kindly rich do a hand-to-mouth job of individual charity that perpetuates the evil, we try to organize the means to destroy it. No doubt the resources are inadequate and the services faulty, but the principle and the impulse are unheard-of in the only annals we have of the past, the annals of *in*humanity. There is an American Foundation for the Overseas Blind; we have yet to hear of a Foreign Foundation for the American Blind. But let us not grow self-righteous, let us rather acknowledge and thank God that there is in us a good honest selfish motive side by side with the kindly impulse, which otherwise would fester into pride of rectitude. The self-interest also shows that we have begun to estimate the waste, the loss in material output, the cost to us all, of prejudice and exclusion. That awareness is a lever to move the world.

It is clear that this amazing American spectacle has a meaning beyond our shores. Thinking about it leads us straight into the drama of Life *versus* Destruction which is being played out on our globe. What have we to offer the world beyond our despised but welcome dollars and our ability to organize the means of making more? I have purposely refrained from mentioning, as part of our way of life, on the one hand public housing, Federal credit for home building, unemployment and accident insurance, social security, and the like; and on the other hand the myriad enterprises for public education and entertainment — from the town libraries we owe to Andrew Carnegie to the free concerts and art exhibits springing up all over the land. Some of those things are traditional in the Old World; others are inevitable by-products of the factory system and the rise of labor

to self-conscious power. But the groups and institutions most characteristic of our country, and the feelings and habits that go with
them, represent something new — not an idea in the usual sense, a
deed, a practice. Our moral significance, our contribution to Western
culture, if you like, lies in this perpetual retesting and amplification
of the noblest theories fathered by European philosophers. Our spirit
is watered by three streams of thought, originally distinct but here
mingled:

> The eighteenth-century Enlightenment view of progress
> toward social reason, or what we Americans know as the
> Jeffersonian ideal;
> The Romanticist view of man's diversity, inventiveness
> and love of risk by which society is forever kept in flux,
> forever changing;
> And the native tradition of Deafness to Doctrine which
> permits our Federal system to subsist at the same time as it
> provides free room for carrying out the behests of our other
> two beliefs.

Is there then no role played by our religious inheritance? Many
an American leader, from Lincoln to Eisenhower, has said that
democracy is inconceivable without a religious basis, and it appears
from a recent national survey that 99 per cent of the American people declared themselves religious believers. They are indeed, yet it
is no less true that for the majority of Americans religion does not
mean the Church militant — we are not a crusading people; nor does
it mean the endless heart-searching of the mystic. It means the social
gospel, the brotherhood of man interpreted in the most practical way.
Only thus has it been possible to survive as a polyglot nation of
continental size: Diversity, Fraternity, Perfectibility. It is idle to report that for the last fifty years the eighteenth-century doctrine of
the goodness and perfectibility of man has been given up by serious
thinkers. (They are perhaps not serious enough.) It is idle to point
out that the faith in initiative and the conduct of life by common

reason has dropped away. Right here we see their daily and hourly application. Man is assumed to be good, for otherwise why bother about him? He is worthy of care regardless not only of his origin but of his defects. Insofar as we know how to cure them we perfect him. The perfectibility of man does not mean his transfiguration. It means his being given the means to be reasonably decent. He must have a job, or a treatment, or an artificial limb. His perfectibility may depend upon a set of false teeth, which will incline him toward proper digestion and self-respect as against the degradation of drink. We must not blink the fact that spirit and soul are entangled in humble matter — which is not the same as saying that spirit and soul do not exist or that they are "nothing but" a set of false teeth.

On all this the men of the eighteenth century could only speak out of a courageous faith, guessing at the brutishness of the creatures in the dark beneath their feet. A friend of liberty such as Edmund Burke could only call the common folk the "swinish multitude," and Hamilton was right if he said "Your people, sir, are a great beast." But we, swamped with a humanity made thus by the hands of others, have tackled the job of scraping it clean of filth and beastliness, of ignorance and superstition, and we have begun to see the thing succeed. We should not be misled by the clamor and the wailing. It is our success which is causing it. Everybody, from the youngest reactionary to the oldest happy pessimist, is judging by the self-same liberal ideal that he attacks. He finds things dreadfully bad because he has an exalted image of the good that his great-grand-father would have thought fantastic. Every protest implies that there is a standard of common right to appeal to, whereas before nothing short of slave revolts brought any change.

This does not mean that all is smooth and settled. But the complaints and heartaches do not mean that defeatism is the part of the wise. Mankind is perverse, to be sure, shortsighted, and it has a queer urge to devour itself like the snake in the fable. This self-destruction is what most sane men are forever trying to prevent, and they do it by assuaging intolerable evils. Let us bear in mind that it is not a hundred years since our brother the Negro began to be freed from our brother the Southerner. The advance is inadequate if we measure it by perfect freedom; it is enormous if we compare it with any other emancipation on record. And since Southerners themselves have taken the work in hand, the chances are good for orderly change — as order goes here on earth.

I mean by this a manageable dose of violence, bitterness, and folly. One must keep one's eye on probability and not go imagining the frictionless world of our dreams. The cry for "Order" is, on the face of it, always proper. It is a measure of our desire for decency. But how often does it spring from a really orderly set of feelings? Is it not frequently an expression of impatience, of ignorance of fact, of contempt for persons? It is too simple a view to proclaim that once upon a time there was Order, and now there is not, which is painful to all, so let us quickly return to the thirteenth century or the folds of the dress of Queen Anne. It is a pathetic mistake excusable only in youth to confuse the beautiful order of the paragraphs in Thomas Aquinas's book with the living, buzzing, fearsome society of his time. While he was writing, you could have witnessed — to take but one appalling occurrence — the Children's Crusade. You don't have to know more than its name to visualize the fate of these thirty thousand innocents who shortly disappeared off the face of Christendom by disease, starvation, and violent death — all of it at the hands of their own "orderly" fellow Christians. The luckiest were those sold into Mohammedan slavery.

And while this horror was going on with the blessing of the highest in church and state, the rest of Europe was seething as usual. The flourishing Provençal civilization was being destroyed in the wholesale massacre of heretics, while in England the fight leading to Magna Carta shows you on what terms rights were then obtained — at spear's point and only for barons at that. We are forced back to our original proposition: we are not inherently better men than our forefathers, but by dint of heeding the better men among us, and

doing something practical about it, we have developed a truer because more exacting conception of mankind.

It is because we can no longer help talking about mankind, instead of merely Us and the people we approve, that our understanding of life cannot stay a family affair confined to these United States.
We are extending it almost by reflex action to the rest of the globe.
Through Point Four providing for the development of backward
areas; through the Marshall Plan which, no matter what may be said
about it, was the blood transfusion in the nick of time which saves
the patient; through participation in a bewildering number of international organizations like the Children's Emergency Fund, as well
as through private ventures for the medical, educational, dietary, and
technological improvement of human life, we are carrying to every
part of the world our own innocently shrewd form of the social
gospel.

Once again I can imagine good judges of fact objecting to this description. I shall be told that we fail rather stupidly, that we are
hated for everything we do abroad, every penny we spend mysteriously turning into a sign of our selfish, grasping nature. A year or so
ago, all the clever "independent" minds I met in Europe kept telling me that American Imperialism was enslaving the world. The
poor souls! They too are haunted by the mirage of a perfect Eden
in which they would be prosperous, beloved, and thanked for
deigning to be alive. So they resent having to take help, work for
it, and readjust their habits to the pace of a productive century. It
interferes even with their self-pity. They cannot see that American Imperialism (let them call it that if it makes them feel better)
may be as clumsy, naïve, and "materialistic" as they say and by
that very fact preferable to any other form of meddling on record.
It has no "line," no dogma, but works for results, generally to the
benefit of those living where it works. The British and the French
and the Belgians in the heart of Africa had for generations endured
malaria like heroes, because you couldn't cover up all the water

holes and empty barrels where the mosquitoes breed. The ruthless Americans came in and covered them up.

It is attention to practice and indifference to overarching beliefs that guarantees our innocence, but our critics are sodden with ideology and cannot take this in. None the less this nonsectarianism is one clear sign of superiority over Russia. Russia is a hundred years behind us in the mere fact of being bogged down in the party pamphlet of a couple of angry men; Russia's mental date is theirs: 1848. When one forgets for a moment all the bloodshed that has come from it, there is something profoundly comic about all the quibbling and confessing and excommunicating that has occupied the best Russian brains ever since they smuggled in Karl Marx.

To put it another way, the "Russian soul" has still not raised itself to the conception of mankind as such — what a former mayor of San Francisco elegantly called "the *tout ensemble* of the whole." Russia is still playing cops and robbers, hero and villain, believer and infidel, with all the deadly religious pride of the crusader. They kill you for their good. Whatever Communism was in the minds of its early prophets, from Saint Thomas More onward, it was not this; and Russia may yet go down in history as the nation that ruined an interesting idea.

There is no doubt a good reason why Russian Imperio-Communism is so rigid and self-righteous, and the reason points to a second ground of superiority in us. Starting a century late, with a people barely out of serfdom, Russia has had a gigantic job trying to catch up with the industrialized West. The habits of a new age are not acquired in a few years. The change was dreadful enough in England and France and Belgium in the 1800's, when three generations of men, women, and children were sacrificed to the machine above and below ground. Deliberate massacre and coercion in modern Russia correspond to this wrench from the soil to the factory, and express a furious will to succeed. That fact in itself should be a warning to all other peoples who think that American Imperialism means death-in-life. We are *not* desperate. By our standards and according to our lights, we *have* succeeded. Our motives are not those of the monomaniac, but the ordinary mixture of selfishness, generosity, and pride in demonstrated ability. We may brag of our know-how and toss around phrases about the American Way, but this is half-hearted official talk. The citizen, even the leading citizen, has local pride but no crusading faith. We could not turn federalism into imperialism if we tried. Our many faults include outbursts of brag and bounce, but we may justly claim the merit that in a world plagued by the petty, deadly self-conceit of tribe and clan we have no fanaticism in our souls, any more than any doctrine up our sleeves. The continuing guarantee of all this is that we are not a nation but a people.

We are many — our interests, groups, religions keep one another in check and accustom us to many-sidedness, to pluralism. Compare the ways of unity and of pluralism through the personalities they bring forth: Mrs. Franklin Roosevelt with her modest, lifelong giving of herself to multitudinous good causes that wholly ignore creed and color, power and factional politics; and the late Mrs. Eva Perón of Argentina, who by herself controlled her country's billion-dollar fund for good works. This sum was obviously not the fruit of her earnings, but part of the annual taxes paid by the common people — two days' pay from everybody. Yet Mrs. Perón, being a devout Catholic, which was her right, would certainly not have wasted a penny on a devout atheist, nor on a political opponent of her husband's, nor on people outside her country's borders. The whole tradition of centralized control and dominant faith goes with discrimination, personal power, and fabricated glory. There is a move to make Mrs. Perón a saint, but my devotions go to Mrs. Roosevelt.

The American Way, if it means any one thing more than another, means diversity, many powers, no concerted plan, no interest in putting over on anybody else the final strait jacket of a system so as to extort the miserable advantage of lip-service to catch-

words. Not that there aren't some few million people among the
hundred and fifty of our population who would like to do just
what I deny. They may even succeed in their little corner — their
family, office, shop, or village. The impulse is age-old and will not
die in our generation. But on our soil it has a harder time thriving
than in most places.

It is to our incredible land that we must come back for an explanation of the virtues that we have but dare not take personal credit
for. We are openhanded, because we have had abundance and have
spread it wide enough to overcome the meanness of man when hard
pressed. Our first impulse is to help, because the memory of give-
and-take, of mutual logrolling in building the continent, is with us
still. To this day the outsider who settles in almost any Western
city is surprised to see a Welcome Wagon drive up to his new
house and shower him with local goods. It is publicity for the
tradesmen, to be sure, but it is none the less a gift in the old tradition — good will created in two senses, and quite innocently, without strings attached.

We are innocent because we have been — we still are — too busy
to brood. We have not sought escape from evil by mental construc-
tions of the kind that is easier to ram down others' throats than
to make real. Innocence and success together have made us calm,
not phlegmatic. The great American cultural trait is casualness.
"Take it easy." It has its drawbacks but it is also a source of pleasure, as when one travels ten thousand miles across America, through
crowded places or off the beaten track, and never once runs into
hostile, suspicious, or servile behavior.

Finally, we have no preconceived antagonisms toward foreigners
as such, because we are all foreigners to the place and to one another. Only the Indians have a right to be isolationist. We on the
contrary are disposed to take the rest of the world as our responsibility because we still feel the tug of innumerable crisscrossing attachments to other lands. The school child in the heart of Ohio
cheerfully puts her penny in the box for Greek Relief; there is a

little Greek of the second generation in her class, or a Greek restaurant in town.

We are the world in epitome and so far we have not renounced our beginnings. Here again the size and inner diversity of our regions have helped us by preventing patriotism. I mean of course the exclusive love of a narrow corner of the earth, the feeling that away from it lie unbearable strangeness and dangerous enemies. Americans love their land and are as likely as anybody else to feel particular delight in some favorite spot. But they are also a people on the move. The buses, trains, planes, and hotels are perennially overflowing; the roads cannot carry us without constant widening and extension. We move our business and families and take our vacations in a dozen different places, with no thought that to be in Arkansas is to be in exile or that The Capital is heaven. We are explorers still, and in this century's wars have shown an adaptability to the remotest soils and cultures which is one of the highest forms of intelligence. Our European and pro-European critics are pitiably at fault when they keep wailing that "man needs roots." That is just what man does not need. Man is not a tree. If the analogy were true we would now be hitting our top branches against the roof of a cave. This is not to deny the profound disturbance which has come with the means of changing our abodes, speeding through space, juxtaposing ways of life. That is another great subject to be dealt with in its proper place. But for the moment the fact remains that equilibrium in motion is possible for man — we're in it.

Europe believes that man also needs a nation and the egotistical satisfactions that go with it. Well, America could form — and in a mild sense does form — five nations; the East, the Middle West, the South, the West Coast, and the Northwest. There is Texas, too, about which none dare speak but Texans. In passing from one to the other of these vast empires, one notices refreshing differences of accent and manner, of legend and local concern. The East has its eyes glued on Europe, the Far West on "the islands," on Japan, and on Australia. The Gulf thinks of Latin America, and the North-west of Canada and our Alaskan march. Food and language reflect the different orientations. Even the currency offers surprising vari-ations — the silver dollar beyond the Mississippi, the use of mills (one tenth of a cent) in St. Louis, the "tin" penny which oddly survives in the East. And despite all our standardization, the trade marks of ice cream, beer, and canned goods never stay the same for two hundred miles in any direction. We can thus be fervent regionalists if we like, we can be fire-eating jingoes about Texas or California, or some other part of the continent, without devel-oping the sectionalism that kills — kills the heart within, first, and kills the neighbor next. We had one taste of that in the Civil War and once is enough.

Clearly it is the continent that has saved us. While it fed us, it put enough air and space between man and man to prevent the ex-asperation of hateful contacts. Blood has flowed but the land has mercifully soaked it up. We have no frontiers repeatedly marked in red, no plains and towns that are but graveyards for each suc-cessive generation. Canada and Mexico being also vast and adequate to their populations' needs, no pressure, no state of perpetual watch-fulness has been the lot of Americans for a century past.

One's only sorrow is that in saying this one seems to be boast-ing about the gifts of Providence, and indirectly blaming Europe for being less favored. It is, alas, not boast or blame but self-justi-fication. Europe and her many friends among us are the ones who boast of Europe's moral and cultural superiority, who make it a reproach that we do not come up to their standards and do not see the universe as they do. The relation is undoubtedly bitter for both. America is Europe's child, her Cinderella made to bloom by a kindly magic. The child's feelings — it is amply proved — are full of respect and admiration for the twice unjust parent. Still incred-ibly innocent, Cinderella is ever-ready to conciliate the anger that it can hardly understand: can it be true that in attempting to keep open house for all mankind, we have lost our birthright, squan-

dered our intellectual heritage, so that Americanization is tanta-
mount to barbarization?

Or is it possible that modern civilization is something new, incommensurable with the old, just like the character of the American adventure itself? One may want to give a just answer and yet
feel that, whatever the answer, the time has come when America
must no longer take scoldings with humility. And since it would be
futile to transplant the European mind so as to make it see what
is out there, beyond the Pullman window at 2 A.M., the American
mind that is conscious of the blessings and the dangers at stake must
try to redress the balance.

2. Professional European

BUT WHO AM I to speak for Cinderella — surely the boldest enterprise any man can face? Let me say at once that I have no qualifications but those of a witness. I am not even in the usual sense "an American historian"; I can only call myself a student of European history, who came to these shores some thirty-five years ago and who since that time has not ceased to observe with sympathy and wonder the civilization on both sides of the Atlantic. Though an American by law and by choice, it is not for me to say how far I have become one with the essential mind and spirit of the United States. The last thing I profess to be is a Representative Man, and if the bearings I have taken are correct, there is happily no such thing as a single American spirit or mind from which all others are deviations. There are, rather, many habits, motives, and forms of thought which we share, not in set patterns, but in endless permutations and combinations. Some of these ideas and habits differ only on the surface from their counterparts in other cultures of the West; some differ more deeply; but the mixture of what we have inherited from Europe with what we have invented for ourselves has nothing fixed, nothing final about it.

The America to which I came, in ridiculous short pants and ignorant of baseball, a third of a century ago is to all appearances as remote and irrecoverable as the America that Dickens (or Columbus) discovered. For one thing, it was physically and morally much farther away from Europe than it has since become. Its connection with the Old World was haphazard, uncertain, and strangely new. America's young men had been caught by what they had seen "over there" in 1917 and made haste to return to it, convinced that their native country had nothing to offer them but the means of making the trip. Art and the arts of living lured them into becoming expatriates and turned the best of them into excellent social critics. Babbitt was born of their new vision, and he was no sooner created than he became the means of his own extinction — at least in aboriginal form. This capacity for growth showed our corporate vigor, even when it seemed ungainly. Thus did the Jazz Age follow that of the Muckrakers who followed the Robber Barons — three Americas in fifty years, and the speed of change all unchecked.

Then came the Great Depression and with it a new knowledge of society. But the unfortunate setting and coloring of that lesson kept it from being properly digested, an accident whose ill effects have not yet abated. Still, during that decade of unemployment and emergency measures, we did learn the important truth that production is not enough, that the consumer is a tender plant which is indispensable to the functioning of our system, and whose vitaminous effect disappears when his pockets are empty. If it is ever true to say of a nation that it comes of age, it was then. We were in the midst of an adult breath when a second world war broke upon us.

The rest is recent misery; but meanwhile, over the twenty years between Prohibition and Pearl Harbor, all the surfaces of life had changed: food, drink, clothing, hours of work, hobbies, manners, secret and overt inclinations. The world was now coming to us rather than the other way around. In spite of all isolationism, the cosmopolitan touch had become natural and right. Everyone flew to the four corners of the earth and pronounced without shame the names of his landing places. The six o'clock news (and the commercials) made us worldly. Simple hearty men spoke of vintage years and the homiest home body could toss a salad. In a word, by the time I had forgotten the disgrace of my short pants and had replaced ignorance with a genuine passion for baseball, the American young were all skiing and, for city attire, wearing those selfsame short pants.

Whatever these hints may speak of or symbolize, it is also true that, within the latter half of my thirty-year span, there has been in the United States more and more expression of disgust at the world and our time, more and more yearning either to repudiate or to change what is felt to be most characteristically American — hurry, bustle, business, standardization, material increase, mechanical ability, even scientific research and the appurtenances of industrial and urban life.

This is a tendency that should not be discounted or ignored, but one may question much of the talk about it. Some of the fury is mere imitation of that European anti-Americanism, which has so little to do with America and so much to do with Europe's understandable distress. Another, more serious source of anger is that habit of over-abstracting and over-generalizing which, in other realms, produces race riots and national wars. The antimodernists among us begin by assuming that all they resent is peculiarly of this time and place, the fault of machine industry. They then equate machinery with the United States and declare war, so to speak, on their own country. They talk of "values" and grieve over dehumanization without ever making a single comparative judgment — precisely like the Europeans whose excuse at least is that they do not know whereof they speak.

It had been arranged several times that I should meet Dr. Anton Schlagobers, the famous psychiatrist from Vienna. We had so much in common — he loved travel, music, argument. "Conversation," he was reported as having often said, "is the pastime of the gods." But his American patients persistently kept him on the demigod plane of his profession, where the talking is mostly on one side. I met him at my friends' house only after he had two or three times excused himself at the last minute, telephoning apologies that could be heard from the hall where they crackled to the fireside where we sat.

When I finally laid eyes on him his appearance matched his voice and reputation. Though not very tall, he was broad of frame and

feature, heavy-boned and solid-fleshed, his head leonine above —
like an idealized Beethoven — with a powerful jaw below, which
spoiled the symmetry but heightened the impression of power. He
spoke grammatical English with a good accent that grew thick (I
discovered) only when he became excited. His handclasp was firm
and friendly. The hands, face, and person, however, suggested the
special grooming and soaping of the well-kept European, rather
than the unnoticeable hygiene of the native.

. Though obviously a great man in everybody's eyes including his
own and those of his wispy little wife, he had fine, even deferential
manners. He said he had heard much about me and was happy to
see me at last. I retorted that I had surely heard much more about
him and had moreover read several of his books.

"Ah!" said he, as if we should get this straight at once. "Which
ones?"

I named them.

"Remarkable!" he boomed — "you do not say 'Doctor, I have
read your book, you know.' Can you then really be American
citizen?"

The company laughed. My friends shot me meaning glances.
The doctor was certainly at ease and I am sure that one can spend
altogether too much time after hours working over the lifeless
carcasses of the shy. The doctor was as friendly to others as to
himself. But his sally called for an answer, so I said I was indeed
a citizen of the republic.

"Republic? No. Democracy, plutocracy, empire, if you like, republic, no!" You could see him precipitating the pastime of the
gods. "A republic it implies a culture, *one* culture. Here is no such
thing — yet, and I doubt ever will be."

At this point our hostess intervened to point out that we have
a great deal of culture. Did not the *Times* say there were over six
hundred and fifty symphony orchestras in the United States? And
haven't thousands of people gone mad about chamber music and
painting on Sundays?

To be sure, as her husband was quick to say, all that music and painting is imitative, not creative. We borrow from Europe. At which Dr. Schlagobers said, "It is so."

It is, but I'm not sure the fact of borrowing matters very much. Except among isolated primitive tribes, all art is as much a mixture as the population — no pure strain anywhere. The ancient Greeks borrowed from the Cretans and Egyptians, the Romans from the Greeks, the Middle Ages from the Romans, the Arabs, and the Byzantines. Art lives by fits and starts. In the Renaissance, Italy gave a new spurt based on the ruins of the antique. The French and English plagiarized the Italians and one another — and so it goes. Why shouldn't the Americans, who have been in touch with Western Europe from the beginning — who are mostly transplanted Europeans — enjoy their heritage? If the Philharmonic played only Navajo tunes or Negro spirituals, our critics would be the first to complain. To this it may be retorted that every European country has *added* something to that which it borrowed, and made it special to itself — but these thoughts remind me of the Doctor's words:

"Here nothing is special. All is mixed up, as you say, changing all the time and *rroshing* somewhere else. Culture is impossible because business gives no rest to people like you and me. Creatiff art is impossible because you never really think about the human life. All you think of is how to make money, how to invent a machine to do the slightest thing what can so easily be done by hand. You do not contemplate. You wouldn't know how. You want comfort, you fear pain and tragedy. Art is tragedy, the beautiful pearl is growing inside the shell of long suffering. When you get over here people interested in art, it has right away to make money. Why? Because they have not suffered, they have not learned, so they decide — no money, it's no good; they do something else. In theater, publishing, art galleries, concerts, it is all the same. Often said, I know, but it is yet so: you are a materialistic people. Doubtlessly, you and some of your friends enjoy the art *business*, it is gay to work at and brings prestige, but in the strict sense, as a nation, you have no culture *because you have no loaf of aarrt!*"

I had to confess that there was no way of disproving the accusation — if indeed it is one. And I was about to raise the question whether any ancient or modern nation loved art in the wholesale way that seems to be called for, when the doctor broke in again. "Now please don't tell me I should remember America is a young country: don't say 'Give us time!' That is nonsense. Plenty of time since George Washington, and nobody can proof anything by the year four t'ousand. And another thing you shall not say is that in Europe we have no running bathtubs, for which Rembrandts are no substitute."

The argument was in fact hopeless because, in order to set it on its feet one would have had to be excessively personal. Not that the doctor hesitated to call us materialistic, money-mad, gadgeteers and so on, but these are now such common insults they can scarcely rank as *personal* abuse. The true counterattack would have been to call him a professional European. What I mean is this. When a man has left his boyhood behind him, he begins to grow sentimental about his school, especially if it is an old-fashioned boarding school. He may have been homesick there, snubbed, bored and beaten, but on looking back it seems a happy life, filled with all that one still wishes were true about one's present condition. Youth is simply the one available place in which to jam these desires without danger of being put to the test. Now Europeans who come to the United States find themselves in much the same position. They are in distress — language, customs, people are all new and strange. Adaptation is difficult, and often the wrench of leaving Europe was accompanied by horrors that make one despair of the human race. Once safe over here, the idealization begins in order to heal over the wound. It is natural to create an imaginary world in which all unfulfilled wishes can be safely stowed. The professional European calls it culture. The truth is, he dislikes America not because we lack original poets, but because his situation is in itself very hard.

But who has landed him in it? His beloved fellow-Europeans. Their great culture has apparently not taught them how to live together. You may say that recent years have been exceptional, but that is not true. The émigré is a recurrent fact. In so-called peaceful times, rare enough in European history, the educated classes have lived in a perpetual state of cabal, envy, and bitterness. That is why, in a sense, all good Americans, early or late, are renegade Europeans. One would think it might interest other Europeans to find out why for three hundred years there has been such wholesale desertion: certain conditions of European life obviously were intolerable. The details are no secret: nation against nation, church against church, class against class, and poverty for the greater number. Now the big difference, which is also the reason we are "materialistic" as it is called, is that by good luck this country gave the former Europeans the means to divide abundance instead of scarcity. Men here are no longer trying to get a share of a fixed number of loaves and fishes, they are working like demons to multiply the total — which explains in turn the alleged money-madness and zest for machinery.

The critics of America simply confuse the principle of a civilization with a trait of character they profess to despise. They pretend that among all the peoples who have ever lived, only the Americans love comfort and seek wealth. It is truly astonishing to hear "cultivated" Europeans ignore history so brazenly. What do they suppose all the trade wars, all the looting and plundering, all the enslaving and colonizing since Alexander the Great have been about? It is no answer to say that the elite, the really refined, sensitive people, who stay out of politics and trade and loathe war and persecution, have always been a race apart, justifying the rest. The delicate tastes of the European upper crust prove nothing, because the argument works both ways. If modern Americans are to be convicted of greed and self-indulgence because they own cars and radios, then what is the meaning of the castles, statues, private parks, and beautiful objects of art that we are supposed to admire in

Europe? The same love of ease, surely, and a far greater love of ostentation. Greed is written on every piece. Half the contents of European museums are stolen goods, gathered up by military conquest. The other half has been paid for out of taxes which the common man would have spent on his own pleasures if he hadn't been kicked and coerced into paying for those of the robber barons who had the upper hand. In this country, which is called greedy and barbaric, at least none of our public treasures have been seized by armed force. In less than two generations the spoils of *our* robber barons have been voluntarily given up by them to the public — and their spoils they had paid for. It is true, of course, that in Europe, too, much that was the appanage of the few has now been made public — that is, after it was seized by the mob in revolt, made greedy at last by the example of their betters. Violence and pillage from beginning to end — hallmark of the super-civilized!

All this is but one aspect of Europe's history. One can argue that times of troubles bring about transformations of progress, and that we should not forget the model lives of the best people when all is settled and decent. We know that Dr. Schlagobers and our other European friends have never personally invaded foreign countries or exploited the heathen to pay for their cultivated pleasures. But art is not separable from society. An elite is not a flock of angels, it is a social class. Where did they get their money? They inherited it — good. But somebody had to do the dirty work at some time. Go as far back as Charlemagne, or farther, and you find a European elite just acquiring its wealth in one of three ways: the nobles by killing and seizing the land of the late owner; the upper bourgeoisie by trade judiciously mixed with plunder and swindling; the others by miserly accumulation from father to son, on the farm or in the back shop. Nothing unheard of in other climes, except perhaps the tropics.

In short, materialism, greed, the urge to survive and then to rise in the world, are nearly universal traits. And if that is so, then it is absurd and dishonest to maintain the modern (and malicious) proposition: "Materialism is a purely American trait." The reverse, if anything, is true: it was Balzac who said "At the beginning of every great fortune is a great crime . . ." and his stories are a mass of instances which make American greed look like weak-minded innocence. To this day, a European nobleman or shopkeeper will stoop to doing things for money which an American would starve rather than do. *Not* because the American is more moral, but because he has had enough all his life and hasn't got it by penny-pinching or deliberate, traditional ferocity.

Of course, racketeering and political corruption exist among us too, but those are precisely professions outside the pale, whose bearing on American life I shall deal with later on. Let me say here that their activities match the past plunder enjoyed by all the aristocracies of Europe, and let us return to the modern, decent middle class in any country and its attitude toward life and culture.

It was at this point, as I remember, that Mrs. Schlagobers startled us all by fairly shouting, in a voice trembling with emotion, "What do *you* understand of our life of Europe! In Vienn-nah, we live modestly, not like here where it cost so much for what? — for nothing but elevators and telephone and washing machine that breaks the clothes. Instead, we have tasteful home with lovely old furniture, books and books, and a few pictures. My husband has an easy doctor practice of regular hours, and a little, just a little money left over for the theater, the opera, and the hospitality. Because my husband is quite known and loves conversation, we have wonderful friends. It was the same by me as a young girl. My father was a doctor too and at the house came Schnitzler, Hofmannstahl, Max Reinhardt, Richard Strauss — all of them, and once — " here she paused as if about to pray, "once *der grosse* Sigmund Freud."

There was no denying the fervor, no disbelieving the sincerity of Mrs. Schlagobers' recollection. She was momentarily under a spell and it arose from a real magic. I have never lived in Vienna but I have no doubt it held for a certain intellectual class the same enchantment I have known in my father's house in Paris of the old days. But one has to be absolutely clear about one thing: this cultured enjoyment has nothing to do with creativeness, with furthering culture. It is consumption, not production, and consumption of storage goods. All the European artists I have ever heard invariably denounce this well-to-do bourgeoisie, this elite, for its bland neglect of *living* art. The "grosse Sigmund Freud" himself knew something of its hostility. The creative spirits are generally sons of the bourgeoisie; they know what their families think of the career of artist, they know how everybody in the fashionable and official worlds conspires to suppress their "crazy new-fangled ideas." The more art changes the more the relation stays the same. Before the Impressionist painters were ridiculed and the symbolist poets sneered at, the Romantics had been attacked for thirty years; and before them the classics had suffered persecution. Bourgeois or noble patron, it makes no difference. Under Louis XIV Racine was driven from the stage, cabals forced Poussin into exile, organized rioting by Molière's enemies compelled his widow to bribe them before she could bury his body under cover of darkness. Don't shrug your shoulders at the undisciplined French. Go to Vienna and see Gluck treated there as a servant by Maria Theresa, just as Mozart was by the Archbishop of Salzburg. Beethoven had a miserable time in that lovely city. Schubert died there in poverty, unrecognized. Wolf and Bruckner were kept down by a clique. In our day Alban Berg's operas were wholly neglected, and Bartók pined rather longer in his corner over there than over here in the Bronx.

The moral is plain: the European elite has always done what is now reproved in us Americans. It lets genius reveal itself as best it may while entertaining itself with fads. It lives on its heritage of old art after this has aged in the wood. The only difference is, the United States imports the article from a distance and Europe has it nearby. This is why I am not impressed by the claim that Europeans have for culture a natural affinity which we lack. There is not so much to choose. We are neither more materialistic nor stupider about genius than any other people.

This leaves open the question Mrs. Schlagobers raised about cultured leisure, an old-world *douceur de vivre* which is certainly unknown here. Its merits are not to be undervalued; it is one of the amenities, and it is sometimes claimed for it that this admittedly self-regarding mode of life indirectly benefits the creative minds that the great world neglects. The hardships, it is said, the conflicts and rebuffs, stimulate genius to create, and the soft life of some appreciative little group, perhaps a single family, gives that genius the aid and comfort he needs.

To this I reply that I do not believe in the supposed need to put artists on a diet of bread and water in order to get masterpieces out of them. I have yet to find any warrant for trusting the prescription. Consequently the sentimental picture of the world-beaten artist periodically nursed back to strength by a household of sensitive Samaritans leaves me cold. I want rather to examine the social basis of this artistic elegance which is undoubtedly a European institution. It is bought at a price, and the price is the endless toil, the disappointed hopes, the ignorance, the moral and physical ugliness and brooding resentments of four fifths of the population.

This is where the American conception of civilization is diametrically opposed to the European. Almost any American of the background and with the tastes under discussion will gladly, angrily shoot any *douceur de vivre* down the drain when he comes to see the poor little undersized and overworked slaveys on whose backs the whole system rests: they get up at six and sweat till ten or eleven at night to keep everybody fed and happy. Then they retire to some hole in the wall or under the gable roof, and if you ask the cultivated dragon that runs the house how much time off she gives the girls, you are stared at for your pains or obsequiously assured that they are regularly let off for early mass on Sunday. Once in two or three weeks, you will see one of them working at double speed while the other has an afternoon off with a beau.

Everybody above stairs thinks the arrangement perfect. It was laid down in the laws of the Medes and Persians.

Mrs. Schlagobers obviously had something to say to this, and she was very simple and straightforward about it: "We had three girls, all the time, fresh from the country. I looked after them like a mother. Each girl could have only one young man, which I talked to first, so there would be no trouble; and from me the girls learned all about housekeeping. I was very strict about that."

Just so. One need not doubt the lady's kind intentions or good faith. An American only feels that the system, understandable in its day, is now outmoded. He is shocked, for instance, at the idea of controlling these girls' choice of sweethearts, and for a pittance making friendless farm girls scrub floors in that desperate do-or-die fashion of a century ago. The mistress also expected them to wear her cast-off dresses, to eat second-grade food bought especially for their second-grade stomachs, and to stand snappishness and rebukes while they themselves must always behave like ladies-in-waiting to a princess. At the end of eight or ten years of unrelieved drudgery they might marry their dispirited beaux, which is to say, transfer their mop and pail to another, narrower, and noisier set of rooms, where they would bring into the world more of their kind to keep the cycle going.

The European answer to this is obvious and quite logical: why weep over the fate of plain, stupid girls and their plain, stupid men? How can one possibly match their lives and their sorrows with the *conscious* lives of people who for generations have sharpened their senses on beautiful things and trained themselves to reflect on the human condition? The American way, miscalled civilization, is simply to multiply man's actual littleness at the expense of his potential greatness. Which is why America is not a great country but only a big one — full of little people.

Nothing indeed could mark more clearly the parting of the ways, nor reveal to the comparing mind the fallacies of the modern European or pro-European view; the assumption, namely, that life is made for art, and not art for life; that the many are born to minister to the wants of the few; that beauty and philosophy can be kept in glass cases indefinitely without spoiling. For this last proposition is what all the delicate fingering of old masterpieces amounts to. It would make a European shudder or burst out laughing if you told him that one of our great artistic achievements in the United States has been to make pretty clothes cheap enough for all young women to buy; this being one aspect of our concern for good design in the products of industry. He would see in this only a weak-minded philanthropy or love of mediocrity, not recognizing the fact that the true and original artistic impulse is to embellish and refresh our lives by decorating the means of life. Man carves his wooden spoon, paints the roof of his cave, hangs beads around the neck of his mate. And he should keep doing it. It's only when the means are scarce or misapplied — as in Europe — that beauty is locked away in private safes and private houses, and dirt and drabness are out in the open. The streets are splendid but most creatures look dowdy and dejected. The last time I was in Paris I remember coming across a magazine article entitled *"La femme française est élégante."* All I had to do was go downstairs and look at my concierge to disprove it. By *The* Frenchwoman, the author meant a couple of thousand out of twenty million. But go to any village in this country and you will see hardly any difference between the farm girls and the tidy numbers swinging their hips on Fifth Avenue.

The significance of the comparison is that art, culture, and beauty in an industrial democracy are rightly applied to the common means of existence and belong first and foremost to those who make that existence possible. Our modern esthetic sense, unlike that of the past, is offended by human ugliness and degradation. As for our living philosophy, it is not the metaphysics of sorrow and tragedy but the ethics of equality. We are as indignant at the arbitrary choice which dooms certain individuals to servitude as any *précieux* may be at a misstep in logic or a *faux pas* in society; this incidentally being the very same moral principle on which Dr. Schlagobers and his friends acted in coming to this country. They resented and resisted the arbitrary choice of the master race — the *Herrenvolk* — to use them as raw material for their designs.

The only way a man can reasonably complain of injustice is to accept equality of treatment as the common rule. Otherwise it's dog eat dog, with the advantage going in the long run to the largest and hungriest pack. It must have crossed many a doctor's mind, when some poor wretch comes to him full of vice and disease, a burden on society, that if he blotted out this useless life — for whatever motive — his own would be just as much forfeit as if he had killed the Prime Minister or a leading scientist. Now if the mere continued breathing of another man is so important, how much more important his moral and physical well-being before he becomes a derelict.

To many Europeans this would seem bald Puritanism, and by its associations with America the word would sound like a conclusive argument: "We talk about culture, you talk about social organization." I can hear the echo of Dr. Schlagobers' voice: "Where Puritans are, iss no art!" But it has been shown that genuine art has always had to take care of itself. It cannot be provided for, and those who try to do so actually provide against it. In a really free market of ideas, art will take care of itself. The Puritan background has given us Hawthorne, Melville, Emerson, Henry James — not one monotonous note but several, sufficiently rich in overtones. But even had it given us a whole octave, this would not change the antiquated clichés about American culture, minted as they are out of invincible ignorance.

Most of the time we do not perceive our own clearest characteristics. We think of ourselves, vaguely, as English in our cultural descent, not only forgetting the Continental ingredients in our mixture, but failing to see that our popular culture is mainly German and our highbrow culture mainly French. The English heritage was absorbed and transformed long ago, and has vanished from our manners, habits, and tastes. Think of cricket's relation to baseball — or look for a word about it on a later page.

Our popular culture Germanic? Yes. It is not merely that at Christmas time we all eat *Pfeffernüsse* and sing "Heilige Nacht," nor that our G.I.'s in the last war found every foreign country queer except Germany. The close affinity, beyond that of the large German emigration before and after 1848, is that the German people and ourselves were the first distinctively *modern* peoples, the first to rise by industrialism and in the same decades. Here and in Germany there was no other form of national greatness to be pushed aside or destroyed. In both countries a federal government allowed social and economic change to go on under a minimum of central authority. The resulting habits were efficiency, ingenuity, organization. In both countries scientific research fitted itself identically into the academic system, for the excellent reason that American universities were deliberately patterned on the German.

One could go on forever; our appalling academic jargon bears a deep and dangerous likeness to its German counterpart; our sentimentality about children and weddings and Christmas trees; our taste in and for music; our love of taking hikes in groups, singing as we go; our passion for dumplings and starchy messes generally, coupled with our instinct for putting sweet things alongside badly cooked meats and ill-treated vegetables — all that and our chosen forms of cleanliness (every people is clean in different ways about different things) show how far a characteristic culture has spread from the three or four centers where Germans first settled. Our proper names give it away: the English ones are matched in number by none but the German. Even our currency bears a German name and, come to think of it, it was a German who named the land America.

As for the highbrow culture being French, I do not mean the new craze for cookery and wine, I mean the preoccupation with the ideas of French artists and writers who lived anywhere from a hundred to a few years ago. Open any of our intellectual quarterlies and you will find all the discussions coming back to Baudelaire, Rimbaud, Proust, or Gide. The leading poet and oracle of the English-speaking world is T. S. Eliot, and he is, through Ezra Pound, very largely a product of French schooling. His obsession has even gone the length of publishing verse in almost-French.

It might be thought that in this loud mechanical beehive of the United States, the ideas of some tens of thousands of intellectual people would not be heard at all, or if heard would not affect anything. The mixture would be strange — Henry Ford and Baudelaire! But strange or not, that is the mixture which exists, and quite logically — like the mixture of Impressionist French paintings and chrome steel furnishings in the offices of a big corporation. What does that soft, exquisite Degas on the wall do for the Senior Vice President? It gives him an antidote for the hard geometric pattern of his life. He looks at it and it's a welcome relief from the spectacle of Miss Whiteside with her enameled face and nails and her head clamped in the earpiece of a dictaphone.

In literature, the connection is even clearer, because those French writers spent their lives deploring or denouncing what the world has since become — industrial and democratic. They loathed the masses and searched the self, they feared machinery and treasured delicate sensations. For the sake of their visions, they idealized kingship, aristocracy, the church, or some nonexistent social "order," in which everybody would stay put and give them a chance to lead the contemplative life. Hence it is no surprise that today in the United States you find nearly all intelligent youths and a great many educated adults passionate devotees of these artists, and sometimes followers of the corresponding religious and social views. It's the Degas on their bare wall.

Nor is this outlook restricted to Bohemian or marginal circles. It controls great resources and justifies the catchphrase "Ford and Baudelaire." All the leading foundations established by industrial money support without prejudice or dark intent this prevailing set of ideas — call it Impressionist for short. Whatever is "new" but commercially circulated, whether plays, novels, or exhibits, belongs to that era and appeals to the mixed intellectual and business "elite" which does exist among us — Europeans to the contrary notwithstanding — and which is as active and disinterested in its search for culture as any elite can be.

Critics from abroad who come to visit acknowledge our cultural concern, and the existence of museums and orchestras where they thought there were only Indians. But they complain of what I may seem to have admitted by the phrase "commercially circulated." Our art is subjected to trade-like judgments. It has to break even or out it goes. The foundations put money into things they feel sure are wanted, as if art were a commodity like another. Nothing seems spontaneous and intimate, like Europe's little reviews and shoestring theaters.

Well, we have to do things in our own way, even when what we handle is borrowed — that is the first requisite of an independent culture. And there is an excellent reason why art costs so much in the United States, the same reason which makes the cost of living high: we pay the man power in art just as high as that which goes into making an icebox or installing a telephone. The printers of books, the stagehands, the driver who takes a truckload of old masters from New York to Chicago, are people of substance. If you ask them they will tell you they belong to the middle class.

Their reply is hardly an exaggeration, even from a European point of view: not long ago the window cleaner came to my apartment, and though I know him by sight I had never really talked with him. This time, as he climbed back in on his way to the next flat, he nodded toward an early Braque that hangs on my wall. "It holds up very well," says he, squinting at the date. "Have you studied art?" I asked. "No. I used to do the windows at the Art Students' League. You could see how everyone with the same model in front of them would draw something all different — all right, then, why not this type of thing? It's full of pep, anyhow." And as he slung his pail over his shoulder, he added, "My furniture's a good deal like yours — Swedish modern from Macy's." I do not say every window cleaner has an eye for Braques. I report a fact.

There is no need, of course, to make the cultural future of the United States depend on observant window cleaners. It would be too easy to turn the incident around and make it point to our lack of intellectual discipline, our premature sophistication — not to speak of the free and easy ways of the workman in the house. These are plausible talking points. What is more worthy of note is that the new generations in France, Britain, Italy, and Germany show much the same characteristics. One's older friends abroad tell one that "since socialism" (they mean industrial democracy), all their cherished "values" have gone to the dogs. Children in school no longer learn anything, the use of the mother tongue has fallen into barbarism, every post is filled by cocky ignoramuses. What is it they see? They see the underside of society coming up. It is the plain, stupid housemaids of prewar times with their boy friends, who now talk to the rest as equals. They were kept illiterate and now the masters complain that they cannot spell. But if the notion of the long aging that is needed to make an elite has any truth in it, why expect the masses to ripen overnight?

Democracy has its drawbacks, no doubt, and it is wise to concede in order to rectify them. But it is also important to look below the surface and not judge exclusively by the presence or absence of familiar signs. My window cleaner would cut no figure at the Sorbonne or in Bloomsbury, but surely he is a born critic. Faced with something well past the Impressionists, he put his finger on two fundamental principles — that the painter's eye is a creative organ, and that good cubist work has energy. How many professors of art can put as much truth in as few words?

Again, I do not propose my favorite workman for an honorary degree. But there is perhaps one more generality to be got out of contemplating our culture in contrast with the European — or perhaps I should say our behavior on the plane where general and highbrow culture meet, and where, even though we would not meet window cleaners, we would meet a fair range of our fellow citizens. Their callings and their conversation would remind us that like the Germans' our minds had been deeply marked by industry, making efficiency our ideal in all things and organization our forte. This, we should not forget, is a form of mental and spiritual power. The airlift that saved Berlin was a feat of intelligence and self-control, not merely of strength; and for every nondescript city across our land we can show an ordered pattern of parkways and bridges that is breathtaking with a new kind of beauty. But — this is the capital point — there is no goosestep about our discipline. We do not work through frozen hierarchies. Our organization (we call it teamwork) has no use for the barked command, the stiff neck, and the glassy eye. In short, our standard of personality is on the whole much more mature than that of any European country.

By standard of personality I mean the expectation as regards public behavior to which every type of individual unconsciously tries to conform. Take the case of an official who tells the press something about himself or his work in a general announcement. That image of the modern American is, I submit, the image of a mature man. In the first place, he does not boast about himself. Every accomplished Continental does. The European would be thought insignificant if he did not blow his own trumpet fortissimo amid the other brass. Second, the American prefers — other things being equal — to admit the facts. Just remember when the head of our Air Force proclaimed our technical inferiority to the Russians, and try to imagine the same thing happening in reverse. The daily paper provides dozens of similar examples — for instance the man in charge of sifting reports about flying saucers telling us that "if they are the guided missiles of another power, they're way ahead of us." These examples work both ways — telling and receiving. What is facing the truth if not a mature discipline? And if our people can stand it, then they're no longer infants who have to be shielded by grownups' lies.

In the third place, the American likes to hear what the rest of the crowd think. I know there are limits to this and just now our good habits are being badly strained. But in general, the man running the committee will give everybody his chance to speak. Often a majority vote will be too close to seem good even to the majority and the proposal is dropped. This happens in business, in clubs, on boards of hospitals, and in town governments, even when a certain amount of passion has been aroused. It is far from invariable but it is more common than uncommon, and it should be noted as mature.

Fourth, one may ask in what other culture individual reliability has been raised to the level of a common virtue, a matter of course. From the soda clerk and the gasman to the banker and the doctor, people do as they promise. "They deliver the goods." This is probably idiotic in the eyes of an Oriental sage, but it has its advantageous side. Not long ago, a very worthy enterprise operating abroad needed to have a long document translated into Italian, in Italy, and quickly. For speed and convenience the document was divided into ten parts, each being given to a highly recommended person. A week later, four of the ten translators had not only failed to do the work, they had lost the manuscript. *Dolce* no doubt, a sweet life; in the end it is nothing but a form of sponging on the community.

Fifth and last, we may cite the national dislike of pose. It is true we develop irritating poses abroad where we are under fire, but at home we are pretty much allowed to be as we are, too much so at times, for casualness may not sufficiently conceal individual defects. Still, our educated average often achieves the ideal expressed by the courtier of Louis XIV's time, who wrote in disgust: "The real gentleman would be he who never prided himself on anything." The best sort of college-bred, well-traveled American approximates to this. To watch him, you would never know what he was, had done, thought of himself, or wanted to seem in your eyes. He is not necessarily a great brain. You may fall asleep in his company, but you are not being prodded and picked over and marked down or basely flattered — all under cover of *politesse* — as you are by the various more or less childish types nurtured in Europe.

I concede at the outset that the best aristocratic manners are the finest in the world. But they are and have always been extremely rare. The usual middle class habits in every European country are something quite different. You can read national history in each affectation — the barking and stiff click-clack of German high society; the frozen faces and tight embarrassed throats of an English dinner party; the oratorical preening and fencing-master style of a French one; the stolid steady disapproval of everybody except the Almighty, at Geneva; the twitter of improbable lies and miniature drama in the affable Italians; the buttering agreement and perpetual seducer-tactics of the Irish; the shut-in conceit and crusader's contempt in your Spanish host — none of it is any longer functional if it ever was, and it is a bore. Why should not the human face in the twentieth century be open and flexibly expressive, the voice easy and the gestures gentle, to greet every manifestation of life? Why the prepared mask, the limbs and tones of a puppet show?

This last question I must have asked aloud at some point in my inconclusive debate with Dr. Schlagobers, for I remember his leaning forward and saying: "There, *I* can tell *you* something. The pose, the rigidity, the stiff mask — they all tell of fears. You are right to describe certain European manners as signs of neurotic attitudes. But you badly overlook your own — your American neuroses. I do not see in my office the open faces, the gentle voice and easy gestures. I see tortured people who carry the shoulders — so. They speak in harsh tones or sometimes a whisper. They tell me this life is impossible to be borne. They take drugs and alcohol to shut it away. And one pattern repeats: the strong sensitive mother, the insensitive money-making father, and the boy a homosexual. I do not want to turn conversation into clinic, but I must notice you say not a word about the forces at work in your efficient, ethical, high-wage America to destroy the man-of-the-future you have described."

He finished quietly and there was a sudden pause. He had put so concisely what we could all recognize from our own experience that he entirely deserved to have the last word. He had found out — or so it seemed — where our weak spot really lay and had enumerated symptoms that were not to be cured by recourse to art galleries.

But is it *our* weak spot in particular, or is it, so to speak, an occupational disease of industrial man, bound to recur wherever machine production thrives and people multiply? Besides, what is the ghoul or monster that we dread and hide from? Where in the American scene does it lurk? Is it within us, and if so does it correspond to anything outside? The doctor's closest answers would have to do with particular individuals and their circumstances. His general answers were, in my opinion, false — imaginary tales from the Vienna woods — and I have tried to show that this is so. Yet there must be cultural answers as well as psychiatric to the real problem he posed.

3. Statistical Living

WHEN THIS IMPOSSIBLE MODERN LIFE — as we like to call it — bears down on us too hard, how do we describe ourselves, what do we say is wrong? We are frustrated, we say, living under pressure, harried, worried, anxious. Our most observant poet has dubbed this *The Age of Anxiety*, and it is no accident that the scene of his discussion is a bar in a big city: the oppressing world and the liquid Nirvana. We have infinite wants and feel endlessly balked, in body as much as in spirit. We are pushed and compressed and tempted and deprived. Our rebellion is understandable, our indignation just, because we presumably endure the harsh discipline of urbs and factory for the sake of fulfilling the ancestral wants of man — wants of the body and of the spirit.

Incidents trivial or ludicrous daily remind us of our plight: to be pinned and held among millions of our kind, who share our lot and our complaint while we feel rejected, alienated — a paradox so gross and malicious it seems to justify our favorite view of life — "impossible." So thought the unlucky man from Brooklyn who wound up in court for having ordered six-minute eggs, under the menu's clear offer of "eggs any style." Denied, alienated, rebellious, he lost his self-control and earned a suspended sentence. (N.Y. *Times*, Oct. 3, 1949.)

What lends the perfection of true myth to this episode is not merely that it shows industrial man and his creature, the machine, refusing to change pace for the errant individual, but that the victim himself informed the court that he had "a passion for figures" and stood ready to use a stop watch on the eggs. He too was living by number and machinery — a true child of the century, *Homo sapiens* XX.

To understand this strange new creature, it hardly makes any difference whether you begin with the one or the other, machinery or numbers. We exist in large numbers because machinery exists to supply our wants. Then the machine beguiles us, frightens us, forces us into dependency. It exercises the strongest and simplest blackmail conceivable: if we fail to keep in step, the wheels jam, thousands are dismayed and turn on us in anger. In relation to the works, everyone has to sacrifice part of himself, to behave like a piece of a human being. In relation to other human beings, we can argue things out. The word BUT was invented for that purpose. In Chinese, it is pictured as a wavy fringe on some other, sterner character; it represents free play. A machine knows no *but*. It knows only its own heedless uniform motion. As machines multiply, each takes away another particle of our difference, of our fringe, of our *but*. Our individual numerator dwindles while the denominator gets larger and larger. The self (Number One) approaches zero. And long before extinction, it feels that it is nearly there. What is left of manhood kicks against annihilation and turns against the fellow slave as the nearest responsible agent. Which is one reason why an age of strong humanitarian beliefs has witnessed so much organized cruelty.

The Man with the Eggs was making an attempt to restore his whole self by an act of choice. But choices more and more depend on others' collective approval, on mass realities no one is responsible for. It used to be that short women with small feet could buy ready-made shoes size 3. No longer. Not enough feet like that. They must pay the high prices of custom-made shoes for not conforming to average measurements; we lead statistical lives. One man or woman — we say it every day — does not count; nor ten, nor — on occasion — thousands.

Privilege has passed to the crowd. This jibes with our democratic pursuit of the greatest good for the greatest number. When the President was called on by a Kansas delegation to protest the proposed flooding of their nine towns and villages by the Tuttle Creek Dam, he listened unmoved to their appeal. He remembered the great Missouri Valley ruin of July 1951. Simple figuring showed him that the real distress of six thousand people was a trifle.

What a prevailing number comes to varies with circumstance. A strike by 450,000 mine workers — roughly one three-hundredth of the population — can dislocate all our lives. But for most purposes the minimum is high — or at least our pollsters make us believe that it is. They sample opinion and multiply. The results determine everything from our diet to our amusements. A strange voice on the telephone wants to know what program is being listened to. It's Mr. Hooper rating shows, to see which ought to continue. Now a "good" program is followed by eighteen millions. Some of the great orchestras linger on the air with eleven million because — well, once in a while business has to be a sport. But supposing you sang or lectured or cracked jokes in such a way as to make two million people eager to hear you, they would not be given the chance. Your talent would not exist. If that is so, each of your hypothetical fans — I or my next-door neighbor — boils down to one two-millionth of nothing.

Nowhere more than in the United States is this lesson more regularly enforced, because as democrats we have no coign of vantage, no special power, no prepotent right to have our own way. Even money, strong and secret as electricity, meets resistance. We Americans soon learn that we cannot act simply on our initiatives to find out what they are worth. We must begin by converting, corraling, regimenting. Hence leagues, unions, and lobbies. A man gets up and says "I speak for fifty thousand active alcoholics in good standing." Who are you, all alone with your little D.T.'s? You join. We belong to a dozen groups if we want to get our wages, pensions, and medical help. Even the artist is getting to be a serial number. The composer of popular songs, the writer of books, is rated by his association as class A, B, or C. He receives, not his own royalties, but the returns on a group average of uses, rentals, or recordings. One way or another, the person is vanishing. The blunt fact intrudes even where respect is intended: the mails bring you, with an engraved invitation, a printed slip headed: "If You Should Receive Two of These." Your name is on several lists and the machinery had to grind them all out — "a factor beyond our control."

Through the connecting-rod of paper, too, the machine activates the mind. When I sent back to a chain bookstore a volume that turned out to be defective, nothing happened for a week, then I got a replacement every day, mailed from Brooklyn. Phone calls, letters, mere words were unavailing. Systems do not heed reason. They work on an *idée fixe*. No wonder people want things about them "personalized": they really need initials on the cloth cover of the toilet seat to remind them who they are.

Nor does it help to know that just as the self is sinking into oblivion, busy agencies are collecting your vital data. "May we have your name?" It is not to know you but to invade your privacy still further. You give up your phone number, apartment and office address; fingerprints, measurements, childhood diseases, and past employment. Schoolboy crimes and other privities are recorded in a dozen places to be used against you if you budge. The characteristics that you think are yourself are nothing but little rectangular holes punched in a card. To find you, a lever is pushed, and all that the world finds worth remembering dangles down, suspended from the fact that you learned Morse Code in high school. When the outfit is through with you, the common enterprise will live, not in song and story, but in figures. The write-up will be called (I cite an actual case): ".014."

Alas! The habit is catching, so that even in moments of free choice we fall into routine. The time when all this began can be given almost to the year. In a well-known restaurant at New Haven are the photographs of Yale athletes through the ages. Until about the First World War each man has his own stance. From then on the poses, down to the hands and feet, are identical. The camera is of course a great standardizer. Try, in New York, to get a professional picture of yourself that shows your face as others see it. It can't be done. You have to be reduced, by soft focus or airbrush, into the image of a plump baby whose hair is graying at the temples — what the morticians call "a real likeness." Of a girl, you get only the outline, the lipstick, and the beads.

We give up, I suppose. It happens so often and with such obvious good will, the pressure is so evenly distributed. As you set forth gaily or wearily for your holiday week end, your paper says: 480 DEATHS SEEN FOR U.S. "Seen" is very good. You read on: three hundred and one are to die on the road, twenty-nine to drown, and the rest to be miscellaneous. These statistics were laid down for our guidance last year, and you can only hope that some other body than yourself will be public-spirited enough to comply with them this year. But you are at the mercy of sixty million other people taking the same holiday on the same roads.

It will not do to think too long about such things. The record is always a depressant. What is the use of "science" telling me that as regards longevity February and March are the best months to be born in, July the worst? As everybody can see from this book, I was born on the Fourth of July and I am getting on toward the dangerous age. I'd rather think about you: you are well over forty and it is time for you to begin losing your hair, teeth, job, wits, and potency. Your newspaper has your chances worked out to a decimal. And when medicine gets hold of you, decimals become decisive. The particular week's new drug has come in on the usual wave of enthusiasm, backed by heavy advertising from the manufacturers, and the law of averages has sent you to the hospital to test it. If the drug throws more than 2 per cent of the patients into irreversible fits, it will pass quietly out of use. One way or another you will have done your bit — even though your case adds up to 1.999.

But by the same token you should not take it personally. There is serenity in very large numbers. When atom bombs begin to fly, you may rest assured your fate will be part of a going concern. Everything, or almost everything, will have been calculated. You will be wearing a blue Polaroid disc around your neck, which will tell the rescuers exactly how poisonous you have become and whether you are worth attending to. All that is needed for perfecting the arrangements is to provide one last faithful retainer to say to Mother Earth, "Madam, the Exterminator has been here."

But perhaps you have a son in the Army, which may help prevent it all. If so, he is being trained by live fire — crawling under barbed wire while machine-gun bullets streak overhead — we hope it's overhead. The Army's past experience of this drilling shows that "accidents are not excessive," and that "the number of lives saved as a result of realistic [sic] training far outweighed the hazards." It's Johnny's life for Jimmy's in a system with interchangeable parts — a machine.

This, then, is statistical living. We are assaulted by numbers in our wants, in our idea of ourselves, and in our hope of survival. Perhaps we could deal with it intelligently if we were not also preoccupied by the need to be constantly on guard, afraid — once again — of the machine. Whether we know it consciously or not, we live in fear of being scratched, caught, killed; we wear out our days in apprehension of doing the wrong and irreparable thing. We probably think we are used to it. We're alert and agile, it is true. But some part of us must register the cost. The familiar names fool us: car, toaster, automatic elevator, electric fan, and so on make our conscious thought dismiss the fact that we are surrounded by dangers. But to our bodies a city street is not what it seems to our minds. It is a factory in which the machines move and the bodies dodge. We lavish mental energy to thread our way from the kitchen to the hospital. And mere vigilance is not enough: we must know ahead of time what the powered door, or car, or lift will do. For a machine is not like a knife or a hammer. Once learn to use those and their harmfulness is nil, their good under our control. But a machine is not a tool, it is a gesture which keeps going by itself. No one saw this clearly until Chaplin's film *Modern Times* showed us how a man hemmed in by machinery comes at last to reproduce its stiff, jerky gestures unthinkingly, mechanically. The effect is comic but the real joke is that the comedy is played every minute out of sight by our nerves. The threat of every machine compels us to dance in tune with it, and the steps are so complicated we jiggle all day long.

At times we get the illusion that we have assimilated the monster. We say that last year every American family "consumed" 4350 pounds of steel. Or looking down on a busy street we see the turtle shells that man has built around himself and painted in bright colors and everything about the scene makes us think it is an organic development. Every couple of years, the animal sheds his shell and gets a new one, meanwhile feeling exposed and gangly in an unfamiliar erect position. The motion of man in his shell is entirely produced by reflexes — colored lights, symbols, and sounds that act directly on the nerves of arms and legs. Not one in twenty of the creatures has any idea of what makes the wheels go round. If this is not instinctive behavior, what is?

But no sooner does this image seem real than it is replaced by that of the creature's collapse. Again and again we hear of inexplicable crashes — no mechanical defects to account for them. The experts put it down to the "discourtesy" of drivers. Say rather sudden demonism under the goad of frustration. Everything says "Go, go, go, go" — till no inner check will brake forward motion. At other times, more often than we think, it is the mind that has given up the struggle to respond. The victim cannot tell us, but there must come a moment when it seems wisdom itself to drive head on into an obstruction and put an end to the intolerable dance of the nerves. It must feel good to drop out of the assembly line that propels and sustains us, giving every few minutes the characteristic sign or rattle of danger. The warning bell, the siren, the buzzer, the red or green light, the push button, the code number, the indicator, the color of the duplicate, the initials on the memo, the right key, the dial setting, the gauge showing full or empty, the smell of burnt rubber, the queer knocking or suspicious absence of hum, the blank to file before the deadline, the essential claim check, the credentials at the door, the baby's formula, the asterisk on the time table, the meaningless name of the product not otherwise recoverable, the weight limit for parcels, the coy reminder: "Have you defrosted?" "Is there enough oil?" "Please have exact fare," the periodic check on lethal gases and liquids, the sticker showing that you have paid, or done, or been done, the new regulations governing life — these fill our instants with the repeated cry *Qui vive? Qui vive?* till we embrace the savior death.

Short of that, the password to meet the challenge is: "Safe!" Lest we forget, it is written on everything we use, dinned into our ears by all who crave our custom. And it too is a hypnotic, mind-robbing force. The soap for your hands, madame — safe; the laxative for the children — safe; but don't buy the baby loose milk — play safe; your food in box or tin — all frozen safe; the nasty sticker on the wine bottle — a safety seal; the cleaning fluid — safe as per label; the chief device on every appliance from the layman's razor to the suicide's gun:

SAFE   SAFE   SAFE   SAFE   SAFE   SAFE   SAFE   SAFE

And the great hollow voice of officialdom on each occasion amplifies: "Safety First!" It is a chorus of voices pleading to save you, with statistics threatening in the bass: Beware! — four out of five need their chests X-rayed, six out of seven are walking diabetics, seven out of eight should watch for cancer symptoms, and nine out of ten will die of some unknown disease. What impudence in us to keep saying that, unlike ourselves, primitive man walked in fear! That, lacking science, medieval man was frightened by every unusual phenomenon of nature. I say, "Give me a comet to be afraid of — it comes only once every fifty years!" In fact, the truth about us can no longer be covered up. It came out a while ago when one of the New York bus companies plastered its vehicles with the nth Commandment: SAVE YOUR LIFE BY SPENDING YOUR TIME BEING CAREFUL.

Meantime the mechanic pace installs itself inside the bodily signal wires and tries to coerce limbs and viscera that refuse to learn, and to deaden a mind that revolts. Body and mind both withdraw as the nervous system takes charge, sending out messages like the lone, demented telegraph key in the railroad depot — *tuckota, tuckota, tuck-a-tuck-a-tuck-a-tuck-ota.* Anything rather than ignore the message. To run from it or because of it is all one. I am compelled. Breathless, I reach the lobby of an office building with five minutes to spare. The conference is important. None of the express elevators is on the ground floor. I fret. Thirty seconds' wait. It comes and disgorges. Inside, my number said and duly punched, I catch myself tingling with anxiety. When will the starter signal my car to go? Shall I be late? Who cares? Still. . . . Forty-five seconds. Nothing logical or discussable about these antics, or else why, sitting in the stalled taxi, did I want to push? The muscles of my legs are sore from heel to hip — or is it nerves? The idea of the machine — the going on . . . on . . . on — has got inside and is fighting the live self.

The struggle jerks me about and makes my heart pound — or is it yours? It ulcerates the stomach and tenderizes the colon, gives facial tics and a compulsion to be smoking cigarettes. Not that tobacco dulls the pinpricks or clears the giddiness, but the creature wants to be doing something with hands, lips, lungs, that isn't dictated by the rhythm of the iron gesture. To light a cigarette is to be deliberate. By tacit agreement, no one will hurry you or command your attention. And at five o'clock you may have a cocktail, more than one. The taste is sour but the hour is sacred, a respite from little fears. The alcohol will even allow your gentler traits (I mean mine) to regain the upper hand. This isn't just because we are Americans harried by climate as well as industry. Old Europe is fretting too. West Germany alone reported in 1950 150,000 alcoholics. Britons, who never will be slaves, must have that cup of tea, they will turn vicious for lack of it; and the whole world is now tobacco-stained. By 1945, a year of shortages, cigarettes had become European currency, the object of fraud, crime, and prostitution.

In ordinary times, all over the Western world the saving vice is gambling. Stocks and bonds for those whose trained minds can fly high in the abstractions of the financial page; cheaper and more concrete risks for the workingman, yet no longer casual either, or connected with the prowess of one's own horse or dog or fighting cock, but organized on a nation-wide basis. Bought excitement, it entails scientific study — horses' records, weather conditions, and the mathematics of probability. There are learned journals on pink or green paper. Or else the gamble is on policy numbers and the hidden workings of a pinball machine — making, out of the twin blights of numbers and mechanics, uncertainty and drama.

The solace need not always be illegal. There is music — popular, danceable, with its short repeating phrases and tom-tom rhythm. The daytime mind, which cannot fasten for more than a minute on its own thoughts or anyone else's words, can refresh itself in the evening by taking in pure, brief sensations of sound, noting with pleasure tiny variations of harmony, beat, or timbre. Homeopathic thrills bring out all our lust for surrender. We run to hear a trumpeter and his one note, a pianist's left hand playing tenths. It is pleasure, yet it has the same form as the rhythm of the day — short, insistent, repetitious.

The stronger types, who boldly subject themselves to classical music, elect the exquisite, the eighteenth-century, to which they deny the meanings of real life. The full orchestra reminds them too much of its industrial origin. They want the delicate in form and scoring — a few strings are best. They turn maniacs about nuances of tone grooved on discs. They listen with the fury of self-murder, they soundproof their souls. All the arts, if they are to succeed with the likes of us, must show a break with reality and carry a potent dose of the anodynes — flattery, nonsense, sex, fantasy. In vain. The patient still needs his sleeping pill; he fears insomnia even at parties.

From the absence of it in our work we detect in our vices the need for self-regard. Going the whole hog in this craving, we call a breakdown. It is almost as good as a head-on collision. It draws upon you all the solicitude of your entourage, with doctors and nurses to boot. Part of the world at last takes its tempo from you, *waits* on you. You have won, if only for a time, the seventeenth freedom, the freedom to be stupid or slow without suffering immediate penalty.

Apart from the sickroom, the efforts made to give the ego the attention it desires are most inadequate. A million words of advertising can say that YOU have become the object of somebody's special care; you remain listless. Somebody also hopes that the receptionist in the front office, the hostess or coat girl in the restaurant, will revive you by giving you her goo-goo eyes for half a minute. Alas! She too looks like something made in Detroit. She has read and believed the nylon ad that says: YOUR LEGS CAN BE YOUR MOST ATTRACTIVE ACCESSORY. "At a little extra cost" she has added that accessory to her machine where you can see it. You can almost smell the bright varnish on all her shiny surfaces, Cadillac trimmings on a Chevrolet body. But you doubt even her individual existence. How can you be sure of anyone these days, when blood is being poured in and out of people promiscuously and strangers' eyes and lungs turn up in your best friends? Talk of interchangeable parts — the young lady was probably assembled by the management. At any rate she can hardly be expected to show some self on the job, on her assembly line of customers. Where everything is done, nothing happens. So we remain anonymous to each other, each imprisoned in his silly woe.

It must be silly: have we not proved by counting noses that anyone is safely negligible? Hasn't the TV screen shown us the size we really are? In vain do we try to publicize facts and print pictures to suggest importance and apartness: "Rubber Figure Dies," "The

Man Behind the Menu," "Wins Annual Award." Who is he? Who are they? Unrecognizable. There are too many of them, and we expected them to be there anyway. They are lucky if their families take notice.

This is the point of hopelessness where self-contempt, growling beside the whine of self-regard, swings into the cycle of aggression, guilt, and further aggression. When aggression is uppermost scapegoats crowd around us. They display as if by magic all the hateful intentions we fear and know so well, for self-contempt and self-regard are thorough students of the self. When guilt is uppermost — well, have you noticed how many men and women on our streets wear dark glasses? They are not in the desert, they have no cause to fear Australian sandy blight. They are in hiding, watching, unseen. . . . In bad cases cancer starts, or some other secret suicide. Having lifted the load of living from our minds and muscles and settled it on our nerves, the loose unharnessed energies go into making useless cells — a wild hypothesis of course: I have no rats.

There is only one cure for the conviction of worthlessness to which we have been brought by so many strong currents. That is work, real work involving drama and difficulty overcome. Have you ever seen a sorrowful plumber? No, he works. The rest of us have jobs. A good many years ago, students of factory work found that if you put workers in new surroundings output increased. They changed them again — more increase. On they went, getting more and more. Finally they put them back in their original surroundings. Output jumped again. It is new worlds to conquer that we all want. Wages may be high but dullness can't be redeemed. The garment girls who run up sleeves at a hundred and twenty-five dollars a week want a five-day week instead of another day's pay. They live for the two days' release that they hope to enjoy. And so do the clerks by the million, who miss even the pleasure of stacking up piles of clothing. They live in utter abstraction in a world of colored slips of paper. Where is reality? They must at times pray for a holdup.

We are back at our starting point. The machine that feeds us so abundantly denies us our life. The machine is strong with the powers of nature and man's mind; it is our muscle externalized and rendered tireless. But what we want as persons is the chance to keep objectifying *our* power, the skill of our hands and the forethought of our minds. We want, in addition, the unexpectedness of matter resisting our efforts, so that we can conquer and complete. That is the play which like children we never tire of acting; we run through it on the slightest excuse, provided the occasion is real and the stuff handled directly. We need not pretend to be Michelangelo carving Moses. Carpentering or shoeing horses will do. We may grow weary and even a little bored with it, but we will not become exasperated into self-destroying futility and sadistic contempt.

What then are we to do? Do we choose between the physical means of life for all mankind, machine-made, and the fitful chance of humane handiwork in the midst of scarcity? Who could call that a choice? Rather it is a puzzle for practical philosophers, for scientists, and for the nameless worker and citizen — the same men who have made the machine and now live by it. It can be solved. Great civilizations have been ransomed before, provided they knew and wanted what they were paying for.

4. Philosophy of Trade

I HAVE SAID THE WORST, I hope, that can be said against the characteristic tempo and tremor of American life. I do not know whether the analysis would satisfy Dr. Schlagobers, but it seems to me satisfying on one point, which is that the true cause of complaint we or our critics may advance against our civilization is inseparable from our ability to produce goods and the consequent supremacy of large numbers. Test the grievances, common or petty, that make up anti-Americanism and the stereotyped hatred of the age, and you will find most of them due either to the forcing of the pace by machinery or to the balking of the will by the presence of the many.

Hence anybody who merely damns us or our machines is by implication accepting, preferring, scarcity and hierarchy in place of industry and democracy. But on our view it follows also that most of our other troubles, emotional, political, and what not else, have causes that must be sought in their own spheres. It is childish to heap the blame for every evil on the largest, most obvious fact in the neighborhood and think something has been accomplished. Individual and collective misfortunes happened before America and the steam engine were discovered, and they will continue to happen even after all machinery has been rusted away and the world's work is done by proxy atoms.

But before we get there, and once the worst has been said about our present pains, we should see ourselves, without favor or disfavor, as a people trying to fulfill a far from unworthy role in the mysterious march of man through time. Civilization is not one thing but many; and even though man and his woes remain, the aspect of each successive epoch that he creates is a fresh form of his spirit, not to be recaptured and even less to be yearned for. We may admire the old Egyptian order and be glad there are pyramids, but we should not want to build them again, or worship cats.

Speaking once to a man of science, I was told that even though each age could be justified in the eyes of history, it was also possible to measure different civilizations on an exact, objective scale. For civilization, said he, is just heat, and we have unquestionably the hottest civilization on record. From the day when man first domesticated fire, he went on, we have been multiplying its uses. Beginning about two centuries ago, Western man has made combustion give him not only light and warmth, but an infinite variety of powers and pleasures until today, surely, our civilization can be called the highest, categorically and calorifically.

This started a discussion (for I was not alone with the physicist) which finally led us into the heart of the question: what the American system is, and whether it justifies its existence. We had with us a visitor from Oxford, a young don from the side of the humanities, who objected with scornful banter to the physicist's measuring rod. "You forget the shoe," said the Oxonian. "Your own test is too provincial. Civilization has been hot before, and elsewhere than in America — take farming on the slope of a volcano: the winegrowers on Vesuvius, for example; they're hot as blazes — and happy as larks. But they don't wear shoes. The deformation of the human foot by the shoe is the test of ripeness in civilization — not heat but feet. That is how we know we have passed beyond the perfection of the Greeks. Socrates, we are told, stood barefoot in the midst of battle, and on a frosty morning at that. You couldn't do it under modern facilities of war. The Romans wore sandals, which was one step ahead, but you couldn't puddle iron in that gear. The wooden shoe of the medieval serf marks a further stage, but it only suits a leisurely agricultural life. Civilization began to ripen fast, to turn up its toes in fact, about the time of the Renaissance — in the West, that is. A footbound Chinese woman obviously cannot do clerical or factory work — "

"No doubt," broke in the physicist, who was taking the irony in good part, "but then what do you make of our women, who wear on their feet a tight sloping case of leather and cardboard, which lets the toes protrude, and by means of a three-inch spike raises their heels so they can hardly keep their balance?"

"Oh, that's so we can tell when they're at leisure and ready to be pushed over."

But all this was visibly making one of our group rather restive. My old friend George was far from being the least able man present. In many ways, he was probably the best citizen there, the most generous, even-tempered, and truly representative American of us all. He was a businessman who had made his way quickly and brilliantly, though neither from the gutter nor from a position of means and pull. Well-traveled, he knew much about many things, but was seldom articulate about them outside the business occasions requiring him to tell what he knew. It was only my long friendship with him that had given me glimpses of his resources, and that enabled me on this particular day to interpret some of his ideas.

If I give them here in a form resembling a dialogue, it is to allow room for the others' objections, rather than to give a speaking likeness of George. His thought was more coherent than his remarks, and yet they lose something in being recast.

"It's really in the figures," he began abruptly, "output and distribution, unit cost and percentage profits — volume of trade, if you like. Show me how much a civilization produces of what people want, how efficiently they distribute the goods, and I'll tell you its place on the scale; the biggest at the top. Nowadays I'd include services among goods, of course. But you can imagine getting on without them — or some of them — and if you ask me about fundamentals, I tell you it's goods, solid tangible things to clothe you, feed you and put over your head when it rains."

"Aren't you just converting my heat back into matter?" asked the man of science.

"I'm converting useless matter into useful products," retorted

George. "Or rather, I'm seeing to it that it gets done. If we had only people like you around, we would all be listening to the mathematical implications of boiling an egg, but we'd never see one on our breakfast table."

"We don't see them much now in England," said the Oxford don, "and yet we're the ones who invented that grand philosophy of living for trade that you're advocating."

"I don't have to advocate it. It's here and here to stay. England's trouble is — and I have the greatest admiration for her people and her inventors — that you hadn't the resources and you lacked the essential ideas. You still make a machine as if it had to last a hundred years and were going to be the only one of its kind. So it costs a mint of money and it's only fit for a museum of science and industry. You don't love cheapness and you don't understand the human value of speed. Now our great men were differently conditioned and — "

"Just a minute," broke in the don again. "Who are these great men? Do I know them?"

"You should if you don't. I have three in mind: Eli Whitney, who invented the cotton gin and got the idea of making corresponding parts identical so that they could be quickly replaced; Henry Ford, who had the idea of making a cheap car; and Charles Sorensen, who had the idea of the assembly line. No doubt you think that these three men are nothing compared to Shakespeare and Lord Tennyson — "

"You do me an injustice. I abominate Tennyson!"

"There you are. But you don't have to love or hate Henry Ford. You don't have even to *think* about him and his kind. Their ideas have become facts in your lives. Every time you pull out a fountain pen to write a poem — or a formula — you accept and embody the mechanical modern world. You may despise it in words but that means nothing. I'll believe you when you pull out a goose quill and sharpen it in front of my eyes."

"All the same," put in the man of science, "you can't expect us to take your estimates at face value. When you say 'ideas' and then mention your captains of industry, you are obviously confused. Edison was not a man of science in the proper sense of the term, yet he was a man of ideas in far higher degree than your Fords and Eli Whitneys. You can for all of me put them ahead of Tennyson, but I will not let you rank them as thinkers and benefactors to the race on a par with Newton or Lavoisier or Darwin."

"Darwin, Darwin!" cried George. "You and I aren't talking the same language. You speak of ideas in a hushed, funereal kind of voice. You talk of benefactors to mankind. You want to give out medals. I don't. Business has nothing to do with all that. The virtue of business is that it sticks to business, whatever it is. Put yourself in my place for a minute: I want razor blades so my wife can kiss me in the morning without displeasure and injury to herself. A packet of five blades is a quarter. I have a quarter. I get the packet — it contains five blades, no more no less. They're identical. They fit my razor. The steel is just good enough for the purpose. My cheek is inviting and I get my kiss. Can you say as much about the efficacy of a poem? Can I shave with an equation? Please don't misunderstand me. I'm not saying that poetry and science are worthless. I read books, even European ones; I've always loved Kipling, and now that T. S. Eliot has approved him, my taste is permissible. My own business employs scientists, people like yourself, and couldn't get on without them. But none of that is any reason for your saying that my business — any business — is some foul enterprise that the world could do without. I'm not saying an assembly line is better or greater or nobler than Shakespeare. I'm saying it's a damn good thing. You're the people who want to carry off a prize for everything you do. But I notice that the Poetry Professor here thinks very little of nuclear physics, and you think less than nothing of verse techniques. So the laurel wreath might start a tug of war, except among us stupid businessmen. Meantime, you join forces to call me names. I wouldn't dream of reminding you that my work contributes to your comfort more steadily and modestly than yours does to mine. That argument wouldn't touch you because you think nothing of comfort. You just enjoy it thoroughly for the sake of higher things. Still, you compel me to point out that if my activities are vicious and criminal then both of you are living off the earnings of vice and crime."

"I don't know whether you are referring to my Rockefeller Fellowship or not," replied the poet, "but I admit my purpose in taking it was not to glorify its source but to redeem it: my aim in life is to show young men that there are other livable lives than the businessman's, other standards of judgment than whether a thing will pay. All that's best in the world, art, music, poetry — even science — notoriously *doesn't* pay!"

"It all depends what you mean by 'pay,'" said George. "The people who print Shakespeare's plays and put them on the stage make money out of him. He's a thoroughly salable commodity. You will say that Shakespeare pays three hundred years after his death and that some modern poet is starving. I grant you the fact. But what does it prove? It proves that the demand for certain luxury products is very slow to grow, and has to be organized — like everything else."

"That is beside the point. I am not interested in seeing poetry and philosophy make money, now, later, or at any time."

"Well then, what is the complaint? Seems to me you're taking the wrong line. You should tell your students on the contrary that since poetry is of great value it should fetch a high price."

"The young are sufficiently corrupted by your business culture without my adding sophistries. I am interested in what poetry and philosophy tell me about the real worth of things, which has nothing to do with their price. You, on the contrary, care nothing about real values. Your mind is so obsessed with money that all you believe is what the ticker tape quotes about meaningless pieces of paper called stocks and bonds, you gamble on farm futures that haven't even been planted in the ground — or else you devise tricks to make the gullible public buy things they don't need and wouldn't want if they knew what was good for them."

"Well, we do see things differently. But your account overlooks what I consider fundamental in my business and — I thought — in yours too. I mean Demand. It may be a demand for a poem or for a pair of shoes. Now your last remark suggests that you think you know what is good for people — what shoes or poems they will want. I, on the other hand, don't know what they'll think good, and to me Trade is simply a practical method for finding out."

"Nonsense!" put in the man of science. "You are constitutionally incapable of describing your products objectively. According to you they're all miraculous and indispensable. So you waste millions of dollars repeating this lie *ad nauseam* through advertising, and that is how you 'find out' — you fool them into buying what you've made, with the object of filling your pockets — nothing else."

"Yes," added the poet, "one would suppose that people would forget to eat and drink if you didn't remind them."

George sighed. "All I can say is that your life has obviously been easier than mine — perhaps because I, or someone like me, has stood between the real difficulties of surviving economically and your own efforts to do the same. I don't mean this personally, it's your profession. You both live indirectly off the profits of trade. It's no disgrace. What else could you live off of? If you decided to grow your own food and make your own clothes, you wouldn't have much time for the things you care about, and it would be a loss to the community.

"So let's get back to what trade is, what it does — that you wouldn't do. My notion is that it starts with a demand, somebody's need, which somebody else is willing to supply. Very well. You've both had college courses in economics, so I can skip five thousand years and come to the present to meet your accusations. It strikes you as dreadful that businessmen advertise their goods, put prices on them, and think continually about money. Well, the world of business has to keep going incessantly. When it stops or even slows down, disaster is right around the corner. That's a crack of the whip you fellows know nothing about. As professional men you can take two years or ten years for your experiments or your publications. The world won't stop revolving if you're six months late. But a business goes bankrupt in half that time. Why? Because you and all other human beings are subject to daily needs, a daily pressure you pass on to us as suppliers. You want three meals a day and expect the grocer to have food on his shelves. Your ladies want hats and coats in the latest fashion twice a year. And because you are men of established reputation you expect your salary or stipend on the nail. Now the businessman is the poor devil at the center of the whole machine. He has to deliver the goods you clamor for and he has to fork out the cash you want to spend."

"Meanwhile being grossly overpaid for his trouble!"

"Perhaps so. But how would you like his kind of trouble? You professional men speak of rivalry and competition, but you haven't any notion of what real struggle is like. Facilities are put at your disposal and you're left alone. The businessman, on the contrary, has every man's hand against him, besides being at the mercy of fashion, climate, foreign goods, movements of stocks, legal decisions, unscrupulous competitors — "

"That's tautology, isn't it?" asked the poet. "Or else every man's hand wouldn't be — "

"Competition," went on George, "seems crude and wasteful, but no one has yet found a better way to direct production. How can mankind know how much something ought to cost — not so much in price as in goods and labor — unless all those who make it are constantly trying to make it with least amount of trouble and materials? You were complaining of our obsession with money — forgetting of course your own obsessions with the details of *your* undertakings. You naturally think verse meters and millimeters are very important things, whereas dollars and cents are just a crude way to tell one butter-and-egg man from another. But that's a cliché, not a true description. In our imperfect world, money is a test of technique and the measure of accomplishment — crude and sometimes dishonest, but still the only one, and indispensable. Take the supermarket, which I consider a really great American institution. How is it that your wife can get the week's groceries there at a considerable saving? Because after computing all sorts of costs — in money, naturally — somebody found that it was possible to get a large volume of business, a rapid turnover, and reduce the price of each item accordingly. Every minute that a loaf of bread stays on a shelf there instead of being seized by a customer and tossed into her little pushcart adds to the total cost, which ultimately comes out of your pocket. That is what I meant when I said the English — and the Europeans generally — don't appreciate the human worth of speed — time. Our standard of living in the United States owes everything to our thinking of time and space in these ways — the assembly line and the supermarket.

"Now as to advertising — "

But the scientist grew indignant again. "You don't really expect us to fall prostrate with admiration over ways to knock two cents off a package of corn flakes by making it fly faster down our gullets. If I thought my life had to be justified by such triumphs, I'd — "

George shook his head. "It is easy to be taken in by conventional distinctions between what is trivial and what is important. There was a time when medicine was looked down on because it dealt with that disgusting and trivial thing, the human body. Now that doctoring has become the leading profession, we think none of its details is trivial. But how do its results differ from what the grocer does? Doctors patch up people so they'll go on living. The grocer feeds them for the same purpose — "

"Indeed," said the don, "the two professions play into each other's hands."

"What is very significant," went on George, "is that neither doctor nor tradesman asks any questions. They both help along life for its own sake. The doctor's oath means just that. Like a good tradesman he never inquires: Is this client worthy? Does he believe the same as I do? Would he admire Tennyson if he knew who Tennyson was?"

"In short," broke in the poet again, "a tradesman has no principles."

"If you want to put it that way, yes. I happen to think it is a principle, a very high and difficult one, to stick to business and forget a man's looks and his schemes and his opinions. Has it ever occurred to you that the very things you're interested in — art, science, new ideas of every kind — would never have been widely distributed had it not been for the tradesman's interest in the commodity and *lack* of interest in what it's about? Leave it to the philosophers and artists, and each fanatical sect will suppress all the rest on grounds of principle. Your trader is your only impartial man. He would sell pitchforks to the Devil if he saw there a big account and a steady sale. What else is the principle adopted by democratic peoples under the name of free trade in ideas? Competition, with the Devil in the running, shows what is best. How would you like it if Blackwell's in Oxford refused to sell you books because they had heard that you 'abominate Tennyson'?"

"So you've been to Oxford?"

"Oh, we traders get around. If you remember, it was for trade that America was discovered and Asia awakened and Africa explored. Others swear by their clan and parish pump, but the trader is a citizen of the world."

"And a pretty mess the trader's made of it! For every boon to humanity that we men of science have produced by patient research, greed for markets and monopolies has unleashed a thousand evils in the form of slavery, disease, and war. Imperialism — "

George was being driven from pillar to post, obviously, and no matter how straightforwardly he met objections, another would be advanced from some foreign quarter, as if trade and traders were the only forces shaping the world. The discussion certainly proved

Philosophy of Trade

how wise Socrates was to ask all the questions and not let anybody say much beyond "Yes, indeed, Socrates." But I wanted to hear what George had begun to say about advertising and I forced the discussion back to that point.

"It is true," he said, "a businessman tries by means of incessant advertising to make people buy things they don't want. It may be too bad that it has to be done but there it is. Suppose I come to you and say, 'Look, you fully understand that our modern economy is one intricate web. When purchases decline, workers are laid off, dividends go down, factories shut, and the downward spiral leads every other man to the breadline or the dole. Now since you are one unit of purchasing power, I come to ask that you go out and buy something — anything. Spend fifty dollars, spend a hundred. It will get back to the producers, and from them to the machine makers, whose work keeps the wheels rolling and the people employed. Your buying means that goods are enjoyed also by others, and at the same time it insures your security.' If I came and said that to you, would you do it — would you go out and spend fifty dollars for the good of your country? Or would you suspect me of being cracked, shut the door in my face and say: 'What I spend is my own business — and anyway, what good would fifty dollars do?' I thought so. And that's why instead of ringing your doorbell, I advertise. I wheedle you, cajole you, jockey you — you and millions of others — into parting with your cash."

"Just so you can stay in business and get fat — "

"Yes. Don't ask now whether it is right that I should be fat and others thin. The point is that when I stay in business with your money, that business is not mine alone. It is much less mine now than it used to be and it hangs together with nearly everybody's business, your own included — which justifies my making you spend on things you do not need."

"But it doesn't justify your practicing on our ignorance, vanity, sexual instinct, and fear of disease with idiotic slogans and pictures of girls' legs."

"A great deal of what we do is low, no doubt, but to complain of that is to complain of people as they are. You yourself have just now admitted that you had faults, otherwise the advertising man couldn't practice on your 'vanity and ignorance.' A moment before you tacitly agreed that you would answer my personal plea by saying 'What I spend is my own business.' A bit selfish, perhaps? Anyhow, that leaves only two ways to make you support your own economy — coercion and cajolery. Advertising is cajolery, and I should think you'd like it better than coercion. It is curious how the question of advertising, of business — the whole philosophy of trade, in fact — comes down to the moral issue, What is selfishness? Or in other words, Why should I exert myself on behalf of others? Whatever monopoly businessmen may hold, they haven't a monopoly of selfishness. The poet, too, consults his self-interest, and rightly so. But it will not do to compare businessmen in business situations with poets in nonbusiness situations. You might as well argue that I am a bad businessman when I give my wife a birthday present free of charge. The commercial greed people speak of is not a pathological trait. It is self-interest organized and made productive. What unselfish motive could make thousands of men go and build a railroad across the continent and thousands of others give them the materials to do it with? Can you imagine yourself persuading one man after another with good reasons — civic duty, the lure of the West, healthy outdoor life, and so forth? It was self-interest all along the line, from the coolie who couldn't get a bowl of rice in China to the speculator who formed the company in hopes of becoming a millionaire. No one pretends it was a smooth or edifying performance, but the railroad got built. It was a good thing when legislation caught up with the practices of buccaneers, but good or bad, now or in future, the world's work is going to be done by organized self-interest — or under coercion; one or the other. Why do you suppose the Russian world is full of labor camps? Even under self-interest, getting things done is no bed of roses. Nor is it just a matter of watching the ticker as some people seem to think: I could tell you of actual experiences of mine . . . But they would probably bore you. . . ."

He had done his best. The discussion trailed off, we went our ways. The next thing that brought our thoughts back to George was the announcement in the papers that he was dead — a heart attack — only fifty-two. . . The obituary was nearly a column long, for he had done many things, but as usual it told little that anybody wanted to know.

George came of what is called in this country a good family — that is, his people were nobody in particular, but known for good business, good nature, and good works in their community, out in the heart of Indiana. They had connections in New England, of course, and the first distinct memory I have of George goes back to the summer before we entered college together. We were about sixteen, and having met a few months before at the interview which settled our admission to the school, we had been invited by an uncle of George's to the Commencement coinciding with his class reunion. This uncle, I learned, was the first man to sell dried fruit in packages. He had regimented the loose, individualistic prune of our ancestors and made a fortune out of it. For years I considered George's uncle the best living joke I knew.

The spectacle of George's own career made me change my estimate. He might be pathetic but he was no more comic than Man, who has to have prunes or perish. In college, George was never outstanding though always popular. Like so many of his fellow Americans, he had the small, almost girlish features of his very pretty mother, which made him attractive as a youth but undistinguished when middle age thickened his face. He was a fair athlete, like his father before him, and was also like him in build. His head rose out of powerful shoulders without much formal neck, and his co-ordination was remarkable. Regular in looks and behavior, he got elected to various class offices, never the highest, but always the positions of trust.

George's studies were economics and psychology, which he had a vague idea would combine into a formula of success. For George made no bones about wanting to succeed. His father was well-to-do in a modest, regular way, and his mother had of course been married for love, without a penny to her name. Long before any of us, George knew what he wanted and did not want to do. For business he thought he should know some law, and he had chosen the combined course that would bring him to Law School in his fourth year, but halfway through the first semester of law he gave up in disgust.

He had a rooted aversion to agility of mind, verbal fencing, and abstract discussion. His final condemnation of any point of view he distrusted was "Words!" for he never really distinguished between words that led to imponderable realities and words used to quibble or conceal. He deplored the need to advertise — as he had shown in our last conversation — for the same reason that he distrusted all poetry but Kipling's. This defect became a quality in friendship. George was not one to evade possible obligations by fair words. He would say: "Here, you'd better have some money," and give somebody the means of taking a vacation, or a sanatorium cure, or a quick trip to see a dying relative. The goods of life, he thought, largely depended on economic goods; he was determined to carve his reputation and his income from tangible and useful matter.

At the same time he had confidence in his ability to know what people felt. He did know. That is why they trusted him — he was somehow plugged into one's emotional system and could sympathize even when he did not understand. His tastes were sure to be those of any average person, which was another bond that made words and calculation superfluous. Sensing all this, he realized that the only obstacles he would have to meet would be those of contrary interests — money interests — and there he was equipped by his football pugnacity, ruthless without rancor.

After dropping out of Law School he was at loose ends, impatient to get started. Before the end of the year he had entered into partnership with an older man — an outsider we didn't know — and, with money borrowed from his uncle, had started in business for himself. I have a confused recollection that the stock was machinery and materials to make mayonnaise, and that finding the market pre-empted, he switched production, with the same ingredients, to facial cream. But this may have been subsequent gossip. During those first years George was trying his wings organizing and promoting a succession of small businesses, all of which proved profitable. His generalship was instinctive. I remember how one summer, when we were spending a month together in the country, he organized and put on its feet the one dry-cleaning establishment where we took our suits to be pressed. He liked the incompetent couple that was mismanaging this village business and showed them how, by using their car and the telephone book, by having regular rounds and paying a little attention to details, they could make money and serve a summer community of twenty-mile radius and sixteen thousand inhabitants.

In his own ventures, George was soon bored by success. He would sell out and begin again. He soon had a very sizable working capital, and by that time he had met Sally, wanted to get married, and what is more, to have children. Of all our friends he was the first of that generation remarkable for the reversal of traditional roles — the men wanting children and learning how to cook; the women wanting careers. But that is another chapter. To have a family and keep Sally from working, George must settle down to a good thing — or so he thought. There was a great deal of industrial unrest in that decade and George's only view of economics having been very conservative, he was strongly anti-labor. Yet class war did not jibe with the humanitarian tradition he had inherited from his deeply religious mother. He grew irritable when this was pointed out. He had somehow persuaded himself that the use of tear gas to break up labor riots was both humanitarian and sound economics. With a chemist friend, he organized Lachrymose Products. Unfortunately, being addicted to concrete experience, he hadn't any more begun to expand his business into profitable sidelines when he made the mistake of going to see his gases in action at Terre Haute, in his own state. What he saw horrified him. His ready sympathy made him feel with the workmen who looked like good fellows while the strikebreakers looked like the thugs they were.

He was mulling over this and a cup of coffee in a "quick and dirty" outside the town, when he was joined by a worker who had had enough and wanted some coffee too. That talk finished George's ready-made ideas of economics. He continued to fear unions, especially when he saw them employing all the tactics of fraud and force first used by business, but he knew once and for all that workmen were people like himself, Americans who should have everything in life — if it could be managed with profit and credit to the producer. Having no social or intellectual snobbery, George could accept the brotherhood of man much more easily than some of his highbrow friends. He really believed the only difference between man and man was a difference of income, and he was absolutely sincere in looking for ways to pull up the lower — again, if it could be done without changing the game he was good at. But now he hated the idea of beating people over the head or choking them with gas in order that he — George — would have enough to marry on. He was in fact pretty well off already. So he sold Lachrymose Products, in two parts — the works to a munitions maker and the name (which had been his own idea) to a self-scorning movie producer who was never heard of again.

At that point George had a kind of second birth. The world suddenly seemed unfamiliar. He wanted time to think and recast his lines of life. He began to read books on current affairs and turn the talk to questions that apparently obsessed him. Finally, he sold some securities, shut up his house and took Sally and their first child for a six-months tour of Europe.

George did not miss a thing. His memory was strong and he loved sights. Nor did he miss the significance of Europe as a civilization.

He accepted its seduction of the senses and deplored its class structure and practical backwardness. What one could do, say in Italy, if . . . Yet he was not taken in by Mussolini, which was then an unheard-of feat among American businessmen. He was all the more repelled by the Duce's "high ideal tension" when he saw that nothing thorough was being done about malaria, irrigation, fertilizers, and George's pet operation — "tooling up." Everything was for show — dust in the eyes.

The stock-market crash brought George back in haste and very poorly off. The bank that held his trust fund had failed and his other assets were anything but liquid. He would have to start almost from scratch like the college boy he had been eight years before. But he was just under thirty and his energy always rose to a challenge. It was boundless, exhausting to everybody, even to Sally, who looked upon him as the greatest American since Chauncey M. Depew, a distant connection of her mother's.

Everyone was saying that the cause of the crash was an overextension of credit through installment buying, and many businessmen said "Never again!" But George "figured differently." He thought installment buying the cornerstone of democracy, giving the common man a stake in the economy and the producer a corresponding grip on purchasing power. George made up his mind to do what he could to bolster the system even before he knew what he would make or sell. The question was, who would buy in a depressed economy? Only those, he argued, who had fixed incomes as yet untouched by the business lag — civil servants, middle-aged clerks, teachers, holders of pensions and annuities. That meant little money — the article must be fairly cheap. But what would these people want that they didn't already have? What was new, desirable, and likely to appeal to these generally cautious people?

After pondering, George set out to make cheap radio sets. From the start he intended to set up a research unit and exploit all the possibilities of the talking machine — gramophone, dictaphone, sound equipment for movies, public-address systems, and intercom.

Almost the first "crybaby" device for single-handed mothers was George's own notion. But it would take from five to ten years to get beyond marketing simply a semiportable radio at twenty dollars. Meantime he would scrape along. He raised the capital and corralled the talent, and with his last few thousands bought a farm in Jersey, cheap. A few chickens and what Sally could raise of corn and vegetables would see them through if the new business failed.

The program of work was no effort for him to conceive and he enjoyed carrying it out. But the approach to the public, the right names and slogans — all the verbalisms that he loathed — were to him a source of annoyance and worry. After endless conferences, the ideal name was found for the as yet nonexistent "superhet": Lincoln-Vocal was born. The name was arrived at by reasoning as rigorous as any Aristotle dreamed of. "What," the managing board asked itself, "is this thing doing?" . . . "It's talking, talking to *you*." . . . "But who is talking?" . . . "Why, Lincoln is talking to you." There was some floundering for a while over the possibility of calling the firm "Gettysburg Address System." But danger lurked in the initials and a masterly retreat was made to the more dignified and resonant Lincoln-Vocal. How reassuring, friendly, democratic! The proof is that out of one thousand different makes of radio sets marketed since 1930, Lincoln-Vocal is high among the 186 survivors.

In less than ten years, George was a millionaire. Of course, like his peers, he did not confine himself to the one business. He could make anything succeed, and it became impossible to follow all his interests. They proliferated out of each other, though some grew out of his fancies. For example, he became something of a gourmet and started to import coffee; then he backed an intercity chain of restaurants where his coffee was served and sold. After his uncle's premature death — a family failing, it now seems — George bought the fruit business, soon converting it to marketing frozen foods generally — a little ahead of the rush. And as you might expect, he was the first to take a flyer in plastics for household utensils.

"Everything we use around the house," he would say, "is too

heavy, costs too much, and lasts too long. It's all wood and metal and looks ancient. I want light, colorful things that are so cheap I'll be glad to chuck them and redecorate my surroundings with different ones. I want every room to resemble the children's nursery. Besides," he went on as we gaped, "it means business, work for more people, opportunity for new capital and a chance for young men."

As I try to put into words the reasons why some of us nonbusinessmen were devoted to George, I find myself reporting his phrases, which I should not do. They are easily turned against him because they imply something to the hearer that was absent from George's mind. He sounded like those great artists who happen to use the clichés of revolution or of reaction. Moreover, there is a whole range of accomplishment which words automatically belittle. Describe the one and only purpose of a bridge and all you can say is that it brings unimportant people to the other side of the river. You can of course call it "a triumph of the engineering imagination" but that is covering up emptiness of thought with stale metaphor. One of the loftiest spirits that ever walked the earth set it as one of the goals of greatness "to make two blades of grass grow where only one grew before." But we detect in the image the poet's instinctive avoidance of a discredited association of ideas. Change "grass" to "beefsteak" (which is the next step toward what is meant) and we recoil from the maxim: "Is that all he wants genius and statesmanship to perform? To feed us better!" We will have none of it, or such is our pretense. Fortunately, men are found to whom the praise of poets means nothing, and the making, exchanging, and messing about with vulgar goods means a great deal. If their activity helps life more than it hinders, it justifies itself without a single word.

This is not to say that George was not at times a nuisance — I almost said a menace. His compulsive love of organizing and money-mongering got the better of his easy good nature. Since he had made it a rule, when a child was born to him, to enroll the baby in a savings plan and increase his own life insurance by a calculated amount, he would challenge you to do the same. He joined every sort of protective association except the Elks. It was not fear of penury or love of pelf. It was an article of democratic business faith. Unless you did these things according to your ability you were not pulling your weight, you were not helping to make the edifice solid and impregnable.

Similarly with new products — fluorides for saving teeth, raw carrots for dark winters, fruit juices for every function — till he got a rash and his doctor told him to give a chance to Chance. Fortunately, gadgetry is relatively harmless and George could revel in its incessant novelty. The first ballpoint pen ever made shone from George's vest pocket, a gift from an astute sales manager who knew the free advertising he would get. George could not let a new industry down. The rest of us could live without pencils that sport four colors of lead or memo pads that spring up at the desired letter; but George would give us no peace. We had to buy the earliest nylon shirts and only managed to hold out against experimental sweaters made from potato. Once, as George was leaving after lecturing us on the theme that the future would see nothing but synthetics, "made by man expressly for man," one of his subordinates muttered something that sounded like: "I wouldn't put it past him; his bowels are plastic!"

Rightly interpreted, George's love of gadgets, like his love of money, was abstract, philosophical, not sensual. It was the paradox and the greatness of his character that although he considered himself a plain man in love with solid material things, his principles of action were ideal and abstract. Money is one of the greatest abstractions. It is everything and nothing, and in modern business, where it is not even handled as money but as signs and symbols, it is less than nothing, an endless algebra. George's indifference to what he dealt in, his ability to deal with anything, his detachment from the collector's lust to touch and possess, approached that of the ascetic. This gave a purity to his motives that was unmistakable even at his worst moments of stubbornness or pugnacity. He was an innocent. He never hesitated to give himself away before anybody, dimly sensing that their conventions were probably more arbitrary and shifting than his — as he showed in his ironic comment about Kipling and T. S. Eliot.

When he came back from Europe, one of his first remarks was: "They say we Americans are a greedy sort of people, but, my Lord! We don't pamper our stomachs the way they do and no American will ever want to live in rooms the size of Grand Central and gilt all over!" This was sound observation. All it needed to make it profound was to add that Americans' lust for possessions satisfies not a physical but a metaphysical need. The pleasure is in having the instrument that works, in fitness. Efficiency is after all an artistic criterion — economy of matter and sufficiency of form. There is nothing carnal about the search for order in action, for organizing, as we say — except insofar as every gratified desire may be said to please the flesh. It could in fact be argued that we Americans do not wallow enough. Some of our bitter novelists keep accusing us of neglect in this regard. They say we caress our cars too much and our women not enough. It was certainly true of George that he never gave the impression of taking enjoyment through the body. His taste in coffee was technological — a thing of grinds and filters. He played golf for business and for exercise. I doubt whether he enjoyed it. He did not even like play of mind. He was serious about all his occupations, and his love of fun was simple friendliness. His many charities showed his good nature and impartiality. He gave to whatever he thought would enhance life, no matter how. His favorites were his own college, where he endowed scholarships and renovated the plumbing, and an Apprentices' Trade School in Indiana, which he kept supplied with the latest machine tools.

The one thing about which George was truly down to earth — or as he would have said in his jargon, "realistic" — was the infinite needs of men. His cult of business went with an awesome regard for individual desire. He never judged or questioned it; it was as if he saw a great chain of being in that first link of a felt want. A man going into a soda fountain for a hamburg on roll made George visualize the entire industry of the United States, from the cattle ranging the plains to the flour mills of Minnesota, to the steel foundries of Pittsburgh and the marble quarries of Vermont. Uninteresting to you and me, that clerk or messenger boy filling his stomach was to George a Customer, and therefore sacred. He could see that humanity's survival in a double sense depended on the marvelous, ever-renewed mystery whereby, at periodic intervals but out of sight, there arose within that living being a slight discomfort which made a thought float up into the mind and shape slowly as the demand: "Hamburg on roll." Next to the Deity, the universe's mainspring was the Customer.

George was a trader.

The true record of achievements such as George's is necessarily buried in the lives of the beneficiaries. We can never measure the achievement and nowadays we are likely to get a distorted picture of the lives. Because democracy exhibits its tradesmen with pride instead of despising them and forcing the richest to marry blue blood, the impression is given that everybody (especially in the United States) is in business, making or selling things that others will consume in order to make or sell in endless round.

For the same apparent reason Napoleon called the English a nation of shopkeepers, and his saying so puts a certain choice very clearly: are you for Athens or Sparta? Athens was rich and civilized, a nation of traders, for trade brings surplus, and with it all that we regard as the sign of high civilization — leisure for art, science, and thought. Socrates or Plato cannot subsist for very long on an unfavorable balance of trade. Add if you like that where trade is king we also find cheating, lying, and war, extremes of riches and poverty, and a rooted conviction that everything can be bought and sold.

Were the Spartans better? Principled, possibly, but not pleasant

— aggressive boors, in fact. Where shall we find high civilization and complete integrity? Among the consuls that Rome sent out to govern the provinces she conquered? They robbed and pillaged the populations under them so as to return wealthy to Rome. They didn't have to be businessmen to do it. What of the soldiers who had first taken — that is, stolen — these territories? Men and therefore looters. And what of the kings and noblemen whom we are asked to deem superior to men of trade? Their simple plan for keeping or enlarging their possessions needs no description. Where then was big business and the modern corporation?

To this it may be said that imperialism is no more agreeable in one form than another and that, with our improved means of seizure and exploitation, we can wreck faster than any Roman consul the few untainted spots left on the earth. The record of the white man, wherever he has brought trade and "civilization" within the last hundred years, is something that Heliogabalus might envy.

Yet the fact that we shudder at this record is something new. In that alone one might say that industrial civilization is superior to its predecessors, for the old scheme did not change one iota in three thousand years. And there is something else. With all its opportunities for corruption and even violence, modern big business has come to think of wealth as production for consumption. "Dollar imperialism" may be greedy, wasteful, ruthless, but it creates wealth and cultivates the customer. It does not kill him in order to rifle his pockets and simply move wealth from here to there. Cortez came to Mexico to lay hands on the portable goods of a conquered people. The worst of our traders were there to do business. Any "conquest" was metaphorical.

Concede all the sharp dealing involved in oil concessions and the like. What is the result? In a relatively short time an industry grows up, ideas penetrate, and soon the outsider is sent packing without thanks. In the very beginning, the change is painful. The population is exploited, but the new industrial life must be compared with the previous conditions of life on the same spot. Saudi Arabia lived under a feudal catch-as-catch-can in desert country. The new oil industry takes the youth away from marauding and in a few years makes them into skilled mechanics on regular wages. Is that such a dreadful, immoral transformation? We talk loosely of the idyllic spots dotting the Pacific, where our ugly civilization has brought its blight. We should ask about the pre-existing blight. If we put down an airstrip there, the first thing we do is to abolish yellow fever, malaria, yaws — whatever it is that has plagued and racked these inhabitants of paradise. The next thing is usually to teach them to read and maintain some personal hygiene — "destroying," I can hear someone say, "their lovely native culture in the process." Quite so. A living civilization is dynamic, heedless, it seldom makes the most of its resources in men and raw materials. It gobbles up forests, ruins scenery, and exhausts mineral deposits. We know this from our own fair land where we did it to ourselves. Civilization is waste, there is no question about it. Where there is nothing to waste, neither men nor resources, there is no civilization, for mankind has never learned to be exact and economical in the housewife sense.

But side by side with waste there is organization for certain accepted purposes. When the Romans built roads through Gaul, down went the beautiful oaks that the Druids worshiped. The lovely culture of Gaul, which included human sacrifices, went down too, and all you had in its place was a Roman road with a Roman legionary directing traffic with his spear. You can take your choice, but mine is the road, the police, and the abolition of human sacrifices, whether natural or supernatural.

To be sure, nobody openly favors human sacrifices. But sacrifices can take different forms, and we are all complacent enough when it isn't a question of setting a maiden afire in a wicker basket. One hears a good deal nowadays about the inherent superiority of "the East" over "the West," because the East has learned the wisdom of contemplation in place of our busy activity. Those of us who go there — if lucky — are handsomely received by a wealthy and cultivated Hindu who, when he is not contemplating, directs several publications that denounce Western materialism as the enemy of civilized life. But as his guest one cannot help noticing that the palace he lives in and the jeweled marvels of his private museum are fairly material goods, balanced by the abject degradation of the naked paupers outside.

In various forms, the situation repeats itself in many places east of Suez, in Europe, and in Africa, wherever feudalism persists. Our sentimental friends deplore the "Americanization" of those regions. It is Americanization only by an accident; actually it is modernization. And what does this replace? Invariably, the utter domination of an impoverished people toiling for a few nabobs who are generally to be found in Paris or on the Riviera. Now nothing will budge *those* exploiters except modern industry. Industry routs them out because they are sitting in a pool of oil and the population can be turned into customers for our ready-made shoes and inimitable movies. It is far from a heroic aim but it has long-range results we need not be ashamed of. For where industry takes hold it isn't long before a kind of democracy begins. The most hopeful event in Egyptian history since Cleopatra hugged a serpent was the recent strike of factory workers in Alexandria. It may take years to undo centuries of abuse, and it may have to go on as it has begun, under army control, but it is unquestionably the direction of civilization. Look at our own South. Planting industry there has been a hard, ugly struggle. But if there is today a Southern movement for the emancipation of the Negro and the rehabilitation of the poor white, it is due in the first instance to machine-made wealth and the natural democracy of the factory.

As regards the rest of the planet, it would be stupid to say that the present painful emancipation of the masses is an attractive spectacle. The new nations that have sprung up in the last half-century have exchanged some of their ancestral habits for the worst of the new ones. They are blatantly nationalist, their government is frequently corrupt and seldom orderly. It is easy to argue that Westernizing and trade plant the seeds of barbarism and war. But if the evolution of the Western powers in those same fifty years is indicative, we may expect stabilization to come with power and responsibility. Practical forces have gradually purged us of the worst abuses of imperialism. A scandal like that of the Belgian Congo — the handiwork of a king, by the way — would be unthinkable now. The recognition of national rights, of minorities, of access to raw materials, is an established principle struggling to become a general fact.

There is still in the former colonial world an enormous amount of fear and hatred, but much of it is accumulated grievance over things that will not recur. This backwash may destroy us yet, but in the face of such danger governments have certainly grown more mature. In the last half-dozen years there have been enough "incidents" in Europe, Africa, and India to set off a hundred world wars. The old Kaiser must turn in his grave at the thought of so many swashbuckling opportunities lost. The difference in temper is one of economic conscience, so to speak, based on a knowledge of the unity of the globe — a tradesman's idea. And to this, America has added its home-grown idea of welfare, of sharing, unconnected now with religious propaganda.

We may have acquired the name of Uncle Shylock over the debts of the First World War, for to the trader, a debt is a debt, and this fact heightens the value of a gift. But President Roosevelt's handling of the second war loans as lend-lease was as delicate a pooling of resources as was ever made to look like business. Since then our private and public welfare services have been at work all over the globe, fighting a world war against disease, malnutrition, and ignorance. I remember meeting in New York a young Hindu doctor from Bombay, who had spent two years at the Rochester Medical School on a Rockefeller fellowship. He was going back, not to a Bombay hospital, but to some backwoods community where, he said, even the hardened physician experienced a daily sense of horror at the sores and miseries of humanity. We were talking about life in the United States (which he admired but did not like), when it occurred to me to ask whether all his new knowledge would not be rendered useless by lack of equipment. He gave me the smile of a child on Christmas morning and said: "I have forty-two cases of your equipment coming by freighter."

It is easy to say that such a gift is insidious American propaganda, buying India's good will with X-ray machines in order to offset Communism. Rather a roundabout sort of propaganda, but if so, it is of the ideal life-giving kind. One healthy thing about it is that it is a charity that began at home, when all the millionaires of the Gilded Age began to disgorge, from Carnegie onwards. No one held a knife at their throat. Wanting love or fame or both, they established a tradition and attached to it the businesslike principle of giving aid in exchange for effort, so as to strengthen and not destroy independence. Their scheme goes on. The millionaires are gone but the tax structure of the country is such that the modern equivalent of the Merchant Prince, the corporation, is busy devising ways to become the public benefactor — the ways are already codified in the *Manual of Corporate Giving*. In a federal country, local latitude to give is better than a single stream of bounties from the central government.

To these practical props of learning and good works, it may yet be objected that they fall short of recreating Athens, or Civilization in the honorific sense. The American world is no doubt less coarse than Sparta, more generous than Rome, but does it not look as if all our doing and all our frustration might in the end go up, as our scientific friend says, in mere heat?

We come back to the problem of measuring civilizations, for there is no guarantee that any type of activity or achievement would convince all men at all times that a given nation was civilized. Even, or especially, in the realm of Culture with a capital C, the widest disagreements prevail as to what constitutes worth. I happen to like music and I find that this mechanical civilization of ours has performed a miracle for which I cannot be too grateful: it has, by mechanical means, brought back to life the whole repertory of

Western music — not to speak of acquainting us with the musics of the East. Formerly, a fashion would bury the whole musical past except a few dozen works arbitrarily selected. Now, thanks to gadgetry, business, and — God save the mark — plastics, we have at command nearly everything from the Greek Hymn of Apollo to the *Ionisation* of Varèse. Neglected or lesser composers come into their own and keep their place. In short the whole literature of one of the arts has sprung into being — it is like the Renaissance rediscovering the ancient classics and holding them fast by means of the printing press. It marks an epoch in Western intellectual history. . . . But it is only fair to add that neither this nor a dozen such contributions to the life of mind *prove* the merit of our civilization. Not to us, at any rate, precisely because we are so self-conscious and aware of the diversity of men's tastes.

Remembering that the recognition of diversity is a spiritual act (since we ascribe it to the Deity), we can perhaps measure our day-to-day civilization by using the two pointers of Waste and Fulfill-ment. Waste is inevitable. But the accepted purposes which our society fulfills offset or redeem the waste. Our society fulfills more and more purposes, recognizes the desires of more and more differ-ent kinds of human beings. It gives me music, others cyclotrons, and still others camping sites or football games. It allows half a thousand different churches, a vast variety of schools, a profusion of styles in art, clothes, and modes of life, putting each material or spiritual opportunity at the absolute disposal of the citizen and even urging him to multiply his interests. This is not without danger — the more abundant the life the greater the danger; but this, if anything, is what must be meant by human liberty — choice. Nor does it detract from the moral value of choice that it is involved in material things, and thus rests ultimately on George's respect for the consumer. Your dollar spent this way or that is a vote to which the trader re-sponds, however clumsily or greedily; and your choice of a prod-uct, a pastime, or a President alike manifests the variety within the communal life that we call democracy.

5. *Last Best Hope*

It is hard enough to believe that buying a can of soup is a vote that influences the economy; it is even harder to believe that a ballot-box vote, a slip of paper marked with an X, dropped in the proper place at Aspen, Colorado (where one feels nearer the stars than the earth), can influence American history and also the lives of people at Omsk, Tomsk, and Magnitogorsk. Government is a mystery, a miracle, and the most miraculous is the one we call democracy. For we know what men are, what *we* are, when we mean to win: we hate to let slips of paper stand in our way. Energy, daring, and self-righteousness are right there at our fingertips to tear up paper and even stouter bonds. We think we know the way to put our opponent in the wrong, if not simply laugh him to scorn for believing in a mumbo jumbo designed to fool fools.

And yet in our sober moments we recognize what solid advantages depend on abiding by the rules, on believing in them with reverence and awe. Our vigilante tradition tells us that government is indispensable. Even on the frontier, men are creatures of habit and want assurance that tomorrow will be like today. We want to feel that we can go out on the street unarmed and unsuspicious, to carry on the business we have in hand. The ultimate aim is always business — feeding and clothing and sheltering. But political means are endless, from the state of siege under martial law to the ceremonial by which we inaugurate a President or induct a Supreme Court judge.

To get to that point is no easy road. Many men, many minds — or rather many wills. They must be bent to a common aim but not broken. No nation of disheartened derelicts could survive, much less achieve civilization. When we recognize this, consciously or by instinct, two paths open out. The many wills can be united and kept strong by being given a single direction — through ideology; or they may be brought into working unity as well as kept strong by the free conflict of purposes, by agitation. Our century seems to be dedicated to finding out which path mankind prefers. Totalitarianism is ideology, unity engineered and enforced from the top. Democracy of the American brand is anti-ideology, diversity, and minimum cohesion achieved by haggling. Our politics without doctrine matches our philosophy of trade — every man a customer (and a voter) regardless of color, religion, or political opinion.

It is a paradox, but the truth nevertheless, that our absence of ideas, the exclusion of ideas from American political life, gives us a superior kind of public morality. In New York some years ago a German refugee, who was just beginning to breathe freely our sooty but impartial air, was attacked and robbed in broad daylight on First Avenue. The young muggers looked to him like the stuff storm troopers are made of, and he said to himself, "There it goes again!" But there was a vast difference, a difference, as he told the court, that on reflection he was able to appreciate. In the first place, the attack had no idea wrapped around it, it was just plain greed. In the second place, the police had no ideology either. They were for the victim whoever he was.

You may say that the impartiality of the law is an idea in itself — the idea of human equality, served by the policeman who makes equal the weak and the strong. But that is not the sort of idea that goes to make up ideology. It is far too old and too simple. Ideology nowadays has to look special and scientific. It is bookish medicine for sick nations. True, any government has to reckon with the fact that people in the mass are more like children than they are like the "reasonable man" assumed by the law. And this defines the appeal as well as the danger of "ideas." Children and the common man outside his business think in abstractions, in words mostly. Their experience of the world is limited and they ignore details and distinctions. Their heart is in the right place but their mind wanders.

This is not a criticism of the common man, it is a social fact easily tested. Prepare some simple announcement and make it to a group of twenty people. The chances are that most of them will understand and carry out the instructions. Make it to two thousand people and the outcome will show that half of them have got it wrong or missed the meaning altogether. To forestall this, drill into them by repetition an abstract idea connected with their country or religion or supposed rights, and you are surer of results: you have tapped a tremendous source of unused energy. The dogma, though, must first go through a deadly simplification for the childish mass mind. It becomes a parody of reality. Among the more intellectual it makes hypocrites and martyrs. For the rest it becomes a mad catechism. Ideology is to genuine ideas what process cheese is to the real thing.

Being a cheap substitute, it spoils real work and obstructs the proper business of men and women. News from Argentina tells us that only "politically indoctrinated" doctors and dentists will be allowed to practice. The needed courses in "political formation" will be given by the government-controlled University of Buenos Aires. Imagine the dull nonsense to be learned and repeated. Think of the trained inspectors who enforce conformity in the consulting room and in the tip-back chair. "Open a little wider" will seem like a dangerous allusion to the closed mind.

Now the United States, as part of the human race, is also a great producer of nonsense — some have said the greatest producer of it, as of nearly everything else. We have thousands of mad cults as well as the only political party that offers the flatness of the earth for a platform. But we seem to know just what to make of ideas. Most of them being hot air we let them go up out of sight, as nature intended. We wait and see. We are all from two states: our own and Missouri. And yet for all this skepticism we are not unresponsive blockheads. We are quick (often too quick) to see danger in our neighbor's views. At the same time we have the best machinery for agitation. Our press is multitudinous and loud; our pulpits, lecture platforms, radio and TV stations pour out a steady stream of opinion, debate, and argument. Almost everybody who has learned to sign his name can somewhere print what he thinks. It will not do to underrate the role of modern mechanics in making this kind of democracy possible: TV can arouse the people to awareness of nation-wide crime as well as block the rigging of a Republican Convention. Nor is our popular intelligence channeled only through nation-wide hookups. All things considered, the greatest instrument of our political life is probably the typewriter. With five dollars a month and a few sheets of carbon paper, any man, woman, or child can air his views, start a movement, defend his liberties or ours. As for the mimeograph, it is the mechanical equivalent of Paul Revere's horse.

Sometimes the din of shouting and the confusion of counsel gets on our nerves. We wish we could have quiet or else a smooth unison. But we wish wrong. Even Russia has discovered that "the suppression of critics is damaging to the welfare of the state." (*New York Times*, August 27, 1952.) But it is one thing to say it and another to know how to take off the lid. The people have to learn the ways of agitation, that is to say, the techniques of self-government. It is with our lungs and our ears that we carry on self-government — the true kind, which does not mean the government of everyone by himself, but the government of each by all. Its formal side is legislation, as everybody knows, but before a law can be passed and enforced we must be waked up to the need for it, made to understand it, coaxed to accept it. Which we do by pleading, denying, groaning, and waving indignant arms at one another till reason and fatigue combine to make us say, All right, all right, let them have it. The great value of a two-party system is that after the progressive party has taken a step forward in the face of agonized yells, the conservatives come in and — true to their platform — change nothing at all. Such is the way dangerous innovations turn into glorious traditions.

So described, democracy sounds anything but noble. It is as vulgar and higgledy-piggledy as trade. But there are things about which man has no right to act noble. Pretending that the need for agitation doesn't exist means concealing the necessary mess behind a false front. The people are kept gaping at a puppet show of ideologists. But behind these stretch the concentration camps and torture chambers. It is the part of maturity to take the mess in stride and suspect all quick disinfectants.

My barber Giuseppe is the living proof of all I say. He is hardly what could be called an educated man. He left Sicily at the age of eleven and has had no schooling since. But he reads the papers, listens to the radio, and talks with his clients so intelligently that they find his conversation instructive and elevating. Democratic agitation has sharpened his mind to the point where I am never tempted to give him the answer of the ancient Roman whose barber asked how he wanted his hair cut: "In silence."

But Giuseppe is often troubled by things that trouble me too about America. Rackets and corruption, lynchings and denials of minority rights, evasions of the income tax and connivance with organized crime, bureaucratic incompetence and a floundering foreign policy, make Giuseppe shake his head and say, "Maybe the other fellows are right." He means the waiters of Italian extraction who work in the same hotel and who try to destroy Giuseppe's faith by hinting to him of dark and unerringly clever conspiracies. "It's all fixed beforehand: big business . . ." or "The tough guys nobody don't hear of . . ." or: "Just you wait, when the so-and-so's take over . . ."

One reason he is disturbed is of course that he hears very thoroughly through the press and the radio about our local and national misdeeds. The ruthless scandalmongering of journalism, which we deplore when it lays waste private life, has the redeeming virtue of exposing public crime. But see the result: Giuseppe being a man with a conscience, he takes in all the reported evils as if he ought to be doing something about them. It seems to be the price of living in a republic that all good men feel they're in the Augean stables but haven't the strength of Hercules.

"I know," says Giuseppe, "it's better to have scandals come out. But you and me, it's not our business to enforce the right thing, josstice. It's the gover'men', and they doan' do it. They doan' care. They take-a bribes. The President, he is allri' but he can' do ever'-thing."

One can only nod agreement with Giuseppe, and at the same time learn something from our joint feeling of confusion. When it comes to trouble, Giuseppe thinks first of the President. He thinks of him as the little father, the king, the source of power that would set everything straight if he could only attend to it all. The people naturally compare the state with the household, where order and justice prevail under a kindly ruler. But *do* they in fact prevail? Have not we improved our individual and collective lot by getting rid, first, of the father who had the power of life and death; and later of the king who could do no wrong? The price of self-government is that in our fatherless state many things go visibly wrong. Yet we dare not tell ourselves that they are inevitable. We must protest, denounce, clean up the spot where we are, be constantly rebelling against purposeful or accidental evil. That is what makes democratic life arduous, unresting: it frustrates our child-like wish to be taken care of.

In America especially we have to work like beavers, and in addition we have to temper our indignation at wrongdoing by bearing in mind some disagreeable facts about ourselves. We should not use these facts as excuses, but know that they are real reasons for some of our political shortcomings. We must know, for instance, that our size and our wealth magnify all problems except that of wealth itself. Take corruption: it has existed the world over since the dawn of history and in the highest places. Julius Caesar was a gigantic grafter as well as a political and military genius. But we have got at least as far as to make corruption no longer proud and elegant. It seldom reaches our top men; it thrives in the dark basements of the edifice. It is still true, as Henry George said half a century ago, that it is easier for the mind of man to design and build Brooklyn Bridge than to keep a shipment of condemned wire from going into the construction. There is such wonderful co-operation over a piece of graft!

The form of corruption that fastens on business — racket or monopoly — is also a universal phenomenon. It has roots in the common human drive towards power and enjoyment, and it is a rare person who is not guilty of some form of coercion, blackmail, or graft in the course of leading what is called a blameless life. Even little Peter, aged six, nags his mother into giving him what he wants, and Aunt Agnes uses her weak heart to dominate the entire family. Organized racketeering sets in wherever the same relation of strength and weakness exists, either because some illegal activity gives a blackmailing hold (remember Prohibition) or because the honest business is small and divided. Monopoly is the thing done in the grand style for the same reason — greed and laziness, one might almost say weariness of the competitive game. How good to control a market and grow fat on it! And how close that is to living off income from capital, or slaves, or a downtrodden population! The differences are subtle and important; they justify our destroying rackets and controlling trusts. They do not justify our regarding these menaces as purely American evils, proofs of our crassness and immorality. Read the papers even more thoroughly, Giuseppe, and see what happens where cash accumulates. Financial aid to Europe produces: PSEUDO-AGENTS ABROAD TAKING CUTS ON U.S. ORDERS. In South America: TIN-MINING INTERESTS BACK TERRORIST PLOTS; in Spain: ARMY PAYMASTER MISSING WITH FOUR MILLION. We haven't all the swindling talent over here by any means. And the late war showed in every nation a pretty turn for looting machinery and art treasures — always our good old friend Man-in-Society.

Let us remember, too, that the United States is not in the old sense a nation but a people, and an epitome of the whole world.

What we cope with when it comes to graft, crime, vice, disease, illiterates, psychopaths, and the hundreds of technical offenders under the regulations governing our complex economy, resembles what the world conscience is trying to do to clean up the globe. I say "resembles" because I still see some differences — amazing ones, sometimes — in our ways of being crooked. It seems likely, for instance, that part of our political corruption comes from our love of being a good fellow. Logrolling is a national tradition, and now that the log cabins have all been built, we roll frigidaires, an expensive camera or a dozen cases of whisky out of the public pocket into that of our friends. The feeling is, "There's plenty of everything, it won't hurt anybody." In local government this has long been known to American historians: the party machine is an unofficial welfare agency; it buys Mrs. O'Leary's vote out of what might be called roundabout public charity. Did not a notorious Mayor of Boston get re-elected on the ground that when *he* was in office, someone at least knew where the graft was going, and since he split it fairly nobody complained?

Our black markets, too, are not altogether what they seem. The motive is half mercenary, half loophole-stretching. For we are by tradition a lawyerlike crew and we love to be ingenious, smart guys who can beat the game. Showing off is not confined to us and our criminal classes, but I wonder in how many countries you would find holdup men like ours who have been found keeping scrapbooks of clippings about their exploits.

But it's no joking matter, says Giuseppe, when this traffic in other people's money goes on within our tax system. A decent American who thinks at all should feel reconciled to, if not wholly enamored of, paying taxes. They are his dues in the best club on the face of the earth, which come to about five hundred dollars a year for a single taxpayer. But two thirds of the taxes paid come from people making five thousand a year or more. The American citizen can truly feel that such a proportion is fair, even without counting the returns to himself in public services. But he also

wants to be sure that equity prevails as between one man and the
next, and that the government gets the full benefit of his contribution. With graft on the one hand and condoned evasion on the
other, he begins to feel duped, he thinks himself a fool not to work
the racket in his favor. In short, he has been given a strong inducement to become a criminal himself. As for the government, local,
state, or Federal, it falls under public odium at the same time as
it has to exact revenue by oppressive new taxes. As my news dealer
once put it: "If they spend it like water, and let their friends get
away with not paying, you and I'll have to be squeezed harder and
harder till we're reduced to Mexican peonies." Obviously a good
many of the conversions to Communism by sincere young people
who have since recanted had their origin in the belief that everything was rotten — business at one end, government at the other.
The hope of getting clean government, honest trade, and full minority rights all in one operation, overnight, was a powerful bait.
That hope was naïve, of course, and the failure to appreciate our
steady exposure of corruption to daylight was bad judgment. But
this much truth remains in it, that without the faith in equity and
equality — a faith sustained by facts — democracy might as well
shut up shop.

It is because we are the world on a smaller scale that our minorities problem is so serious: it shows us up. Our critics take the point
of view of humanity, whether they have a right to or not, and
from that point of view minorities do not exist. They are fictions,
errors, blindness. The world is just a billion or two of diverse men.
But when these cluster in haphazard but recognizable groups
trouble begins. Here again the habit of abstract thought is our undoing. I once caught my sister in a typical instance. She had taken
a cab driven by a Negro, and on getting out found her dress stained
with grease. Being annoyed she generalized immediately: "One
should never get off the train at 125th Street. All the taxis there
have Negro drivers and the inside is filthy." So easily does the love

of finding a cause for everything fasten on human differences. A dirty cab driven by a white man is just a dirty cab; one driven by a Negro becomes a racial cab, dirt being the sign of race and vice-versa.

In the South, the prejudice is clearly an abstraction, as Southerners themselves admit. They feel no personal animosity toward Negroes. They live with them, entrust their children to them, eat the food prepared by their hands. Jim Crow is an idea, a fetish. The lobby of the main hotel in Athens, Georgia, is full of Negroes. They're wearing bellhop uniforms and carrying bags, so nobody minds. In business suits and wearing straw hats, they would turn into enemies of white supremacy. What goes on then in Northern hotels with white porters? Who is supreme over whom? Nobody, or else it's an individual affair. The collective abstraction does not exist.

But knowing this does not end the problem. It is unfortunately true that when a group has been kept enslaved and degraded, its members bear the characteristics of slavery and degradation. To emancipate them is difficult because there appear to be good reasons for denying them equality — they are ignorant, irresponsible, unhygienic. So it takes courage and long sight to behave as if they were what they will become — men like the rest, good, bad, and indifferent. America today is just passing through the stage of making that effort. We no longer babble about an unchangeable slave race: too many of its members are, for all to see, persons of intellect, wealth and manifold distinction.

But the hardships on both sides are not over. The uphill struggle of a minority breeds in them fighting traits which turn the supremacy idea inside out. Some at least of the oppressed want their chance to domineer too. This can be seen in trivial ways in New York's public vehicles, where handsome and expensively dressed Negroes — usually women — will arrogantly elbow white people out of their way and shout down expostulation. It is almost the only instance of bad public behavior one notices traveling in America but it is significant. The world over, subject nationalities have almost invariably used their newly won independence to put down some lesser minority at their mercy: not a sign of strength — on the contrary, it is weakness of nerves, lack of imagination — but devilish all the same.

It seems there is something in man's irritable make-up that reacts violently to the extremes of sameness-in-difference. I came home one day to find the colored cleaning woman still there, talking on the telephone. I gathered her niece had just returned from a trip out West. Bessie was saying to her: "Yes, dear, I know. You gits so tired of hearin' nothin' but white voices." It was the first time I realized that I must have a "white" voice, but after the first shock of recognition, I could see that Bessie was right. If someone's little tricks of speech or face can get on one's nerves, the repeated mannerisms of a segregated social group can do the same. One gets unreasonably fed up with Bronx whine or Alabama bleating, and one can understand (without in the least condoning) the border feuds which have racked Eastern Europe for a thousand years. Language, custom, costume, diet, are so many provocations to mutual contempt and mass murder.

Some people draw the conclusion that we must therefore give every group its orbit and be very tender of peculiarities and touchiness. I disagree. Legal and social equality throughout, yes. To every individual his niche for the sake of the richest diversity, by all means. But to set up group difference as a *virtue* is to perpetuate the struggles. It is a re-enforcement of the "pure race" idea which is inseparable from the idea of a master-race — hence of slavery for others. The game of "outs" and "ins" is a tribal and primitive sport, ridiculous and passé in a century when man can travel faster than sound and is thinking of colonizing the moon. We must on the contrary dissolve particularism, vary the mixture indefinitely, disseminate all traits, enriching ourselves by permutation and combination. Anything else is the vicious circle of neurotic irritation and neurotic fear.

And this applies as well to the absurd habit which has grown up in the United States, side by side with the sincere advocacy of equal rights: the habit of finding threats to minorities in critical remarks and even in harmless jokes. You cannot say anything in fun "against" lawyers or plumbers or any other profession on the radio. *The Merchant of Venice* is banned from certain schools because Shakespeare is "unfair to the Jews." A while ago organized Negro groups made a most illiberal attack on one of the finest textbooks of American History — Morison and Commager's *Growth of the Republic* — by perversely misreading the words of two men who have certainly done as much for social justice as their accusers. Self-pity and suspicion of this kind know no rational limits. The Wildlife Federation will want to ban "Little Red Riding Hood" for being unfair to wolves.

We are also asked to protect and preserve minority cultures. This seems a harmless demand, but what price are we willing to pay for the pleasure of seeing movies of Breton girls in their native headdress? In other words, can we any longer afford separatism? The "cultural" side blinds us to the political emotion. No one objects to local cookery or basket-weaving. But cast your eye over the globe, beginning with the "settled" countries of the West: the Welsh and the Scots agitate for separation from England; the Bretons and Alsatians make trouble in France; the Walloons do in Belgium, the Catalonians in Spain. If we listened to their demands, they would all be sovereign states speaking their own dialects; all of them unable to support or defend themselves, a trap and a temptation to the bigger powers.

Turn eastward to the iron curtain. It is a hodgepodge of would-be nations whose pride, in inverse proportions to their puniness, has unleashed every war since Napoleon. Balkans and Baltics, the populations are not to blame so much as their incredibly grasping and stupid ruling classes, over whose broken remnants we in America shed many undeserved tears. Farther south, the same spectacle: a broken-up Asia Minor where mutual injustice goes back so far that there is not enough time left in all futurity to pay off old scores; Egypt in eruption is just beginning reforms long overdue, while South Africa is in the grip of a fanatic bent on whipping up a racial war on his own doorstep; the Far East is bursting with a myriad nationalist groups wherever the Westerner has given up control; and India has faced civil war ever since its liberation: such is the score for nationalism to date.

With human material no different in essence and just as varied in cultures, the United States has managed to create a livable society. What does our experience suggest for the world in its present explosive state? Some say world government, which is still an abstraction floating in realms above. Politics is confined to the realm of the possible. I think in our absent-minded blundering way we have gone about dealing with this particular world problem as well as could be done within our means. The lesson of American unity in diversity is "feeding and easing up," giving people reasons to live and work rather than fight. The formula is no great secret: fill their stomachs and save their children from rickets, at the same time as you enhance self-respect by granting equal citizenship with the rest.

That too is an abstract statement, but it tells you where to begin: relief, sanitation, CARE, Point Four and similar going concerns. They may not catch up with famine and fury, but practically and morally they are the true path. The problem of Asia is not to reconcile Karl Marx with Confucius or Confucius with Thomas Jefferson but to distribute the rice. If success along this line means cultural intervention, the extirpation of taboos and prejudices and suicidal ignorance, so be it.

What is the alternative? The nationalisms are so many dead ends filled with dead bodies, whereas American federalism asserts the principle that no ideal is worth a second thought if it is not anchored in a real possibility of humane fulfillment. Empty stomachs make bad philosophers, let alone bad neighbors. The first thing needful, then, is goods, machines, and organizing ability. When we shrewdly and generously organized the "Moslem Airlift" to take pilgrims to Mecca, the Mohammedans were suddenly quite glad of the speed they usually blame us for. They thanked us for our "spiritual aid." We see what they mean and we say "You're welcome," but do *they* see that it was first of all a *material* aid? They themselves had enough spirit to take them to heaven, but not to Mecca. And we acted from motives as good as any preached in the Koran.

The task is staggering. So much so that it often seems best not to think of it but just do it. With our common way of assuming that a man's a man for a' that, we are shocked daily to discover how the other half lives. It was only yesterday we learned that India had liberated its "criminal tribes" — several million people dedicated by the British a century ago to a life of crime from birth, without choice but with full penalties. We learned a while ago that the illiterate chief of a remote clan, who had been sent to New Delhi as member of Parliament, had been kept a slave and a pauper by an absolute overlord whose word was law. The poor "M.P." could not even speak any language known to his colleagues. In twenty-two other kingdoms, the peasants are serfs under masters with the power of life and death. In the face of these and a thousand other instances, who can extol cultural autonomy as a boon or a right? Who dare ask us Americans to defer to "civilizations," whether European or Asiatic, in which the rudiments of social reason are only now beginning to be heard of? When our visitors throw lynchings in our teeth, ignorant alike of the restricted area and the dwindling number of their occurrence, would we not have every excuse to remind them of such wretched symbols of their "philosophy" as are now emerging under the pressure of democracy? Not that we have the need or the right to become holier-than-thou. We have enough to do at home making democracy a reality. But sober comparison should help us to go our way confident that our tradition of government by discussion and distribution is today the straightest road to a civilized world.

·   ·   ·

The temptation we Americans are exposed to by our know-how, and also by our "materialistic" belief that economics do more than creeds for good government, is the temptation of what is called the "welfare state." I think it would be better named the "well-run state," with the accent on *run*. The urge behind it is to become finally efficient, to eliminate waste — the waste which, I tried to show earlier, is inseparable from civilization. The technical talents we use in organizing our foreign aid programs or in rehabilitating our own backward areas are of the exact, perfectionist kind. Those in charge are naturally drawn by the lure of still more complete organization. They may be caught, too, by certain examples of planned economy in Europe. We tend to forget that the continental nations are by and large used to monopoly and centralization. The state there has for centuries taken a hand in dividing a limited income among the classes and the masses. Their areas and resources are small and not to be compared with our continental spread. The doubling and redoubling of our production is a phenomenon unknown to them and culturally as uncongenial in its demands as our habits of community enterprise are alien to their fierce individualism.

All this leads to the conclusion that we do wrong even to consider the well-run state in the abstract. Those who are for it skip over the means and ignore the quality of the results. And by reaction those who are against it resist the many Federal controls that we do need, seeing in them the first girders of a dreadful, rigid superstructure. Both the "principles" appealed to are inimical to our real welfare. We should stop talking about "free enterprise" versus "socialism," and the rest of the bugbears. The jargon may mean something abroad. It has no meaning here. Every day some manufacturer "proves" that Roosevelt made this country socialist, and every day some labor leader "proves" that big business has an iron grip on all our lives. The facts brought forward may be true, but the general conclusion is false.

The common man judges the goodness or badness of the government as he goes about his own business. For an American there are half a dozen tests that he has every reason to think reliable: (1) Does carrying on our affairs require endless waiting in line — for rations, for permits, for being safe from control by the authorities? (2) Does every move for pleasure or profit entail enormous paper work and public prying into private concerns? (3) Are the regulations we are compelled to observe counter to logic and common sense? (4) Do our necessary dealings with government officials take inordinate time and depend for their outcome on pull or whim? (5) Do we as law-abiding citizens live under police surveillance? (6) Do we dare, in law and in fact, to speak up for or against our officials, our laws, and matters of beliefs generally?

If the answer is Yes to the last question and No to the other five, we have a tolerable government of the kind our forefathers left the Old World to bring forth upon this continent.

All are agreed that side by side with this ease of mind must go a sense of relative security about the means of life from birth to death. It is on that account that the managerial minds among us would like to make everything come out even. Their intentions are of the best though their imagination is a little stiff. Every evening at the rush hour the subway disgorges its millions. Suppose that suddenly, instead of each individual's finding his way home, the entire crowd lost its will and had to be distributed by some appointed agency. The first results would be: a quantity of errors, apprehension in the citizen's breast, and possibly friction between him and his guardian. The elaborate system of tags and numbers, the changes of address and verifying of identities, would engross the energies of a monster bureau beyond the wit of man to render efficient. Yet this machinery would be designed for a relatively simple purpose. Enlarge the purpose to include the economic, medical, intellectual, recreational, and spiritual needs of the whole population and it is clear that the first rule for carrying out the plan must be "From here on, don't let anybody move!"

The very essence of a plan is co-ordination. Each function in turn gains importance out of all proportion to its worth, simply because it connects. Free play must be curbed. "Deviation" becomes a crime because it endangers not only the state but the credit of those who have assumed the task of making the plan work. So far, luckily and wisely, this country has kept in its bureaucracy a generous attitude toward the citizen. Dates for filing applications are wonderfully elastic, the interpreting of rules is seldom picayune, appeals from decisions to a higher authority are nearly always possible, personal kindliness toward even the most bewildered petitioner is almost invariable. An American taxpayer can say quite literally that the officials he pays for are his civil servants. The Army itself has caught the spirit. When a private on furlough missed seeing his girl owing to an error in dates, he got sympathy and a second chance. Why should he? Why should he *not*, is what Americans like to think of first. It means extra work, irregularity, precedent, yes, but the bother is in the right direction — letting another man have his reasonable will, not keeping him in line just because there is a rule to do it with.

Our tendency is re-enforced by the fact that the citizen and taxpayer has a life outside the orbit of authority. Remove the independence and the leverage is destroyed. Favoritism becomes the rule instead of the exception, and the great majority step down from the level of people to that of populace. To the bureaucrat there comes a flattering unction in his superior role. He is special and indispensable. Gone is the sort of tutti-frutti society we now enjoy, where almost anyone has been or can be a government employee: lawyer or businessman to begin with, then appointed official of an agency; three years in charge of a foreign aid program, then president of a college . . . in and out like elected rulers, instead of a caste as in the nominal people's democracy, in which to be a ruler is to be privileged — until the purge.

But none of this can serve as an argument against specific Federal functions and controls. They have proved necessary again and again ever since the first union of the states under the Articles of Confederation nearly foundered for lack of funds. It may be the duty of a conservative party to resist change, but how many Republicans today would repeal the Federal Reserve Act which "interferes" with all business? Wherever local or state enterprise does not take the lead in matters affecting the general interest, the central government is bound to step in sooner or later. After 1929, no sane man would want to see the control of the Stock Exchange removed, or Social Security, or the insurance of bank deposits. Some utilities, like the airlines or radio and television channels, are of necessity controlled from one center for the whole country. For others it is optional. Social medicine, for instance, could be organized on a state or even local basis as easily as were the state and city universities. It is clearly the next service destined to fall into the public domain, as it were, and if the doctors want to avoid Federal control, they had better take the lead in shaping the plan — as the Medical Associates have begun to do in Boston.

For the amazing thing about the United States is that in spite of our backwardness in social legislation, in spite of our beating the drum for rugged individualism, we are by instinct a very social, sociable, in fact, a "socialist" lot. We love a crowd, we work and play in gangs, we go from the church social to the committee room. Gertrude Stein was right to say that the true America was a camp meeting. More recently the American banker and man of letters, Mr. Lewis Galantiere, aptly generalized when he said that "America swarms with thousands of self-critical and self-inspired organisms." In the words of one of them, they "embody the belief that men and women can assemble from different interests and occupations, from different racial stocks and religions, from different social and economic conditions, and, by subordinating special interests to general interests, can achieve a richer, fuller community life." (*Foreign Affairs*, July 1950.)

We see there the fusion of two American arts: self-government and teamwork. The religious utopian sects that settled here by the hundred during the last two centuries have not survived, but they have left a heritage of feelings which animate us still. Even in our leagues of self-interest, in our lobbies, unions and promotional groups, the underlying idea of our government, which is the idea of mutual checks and balances, is apparent. Every conceivable interest has its voice. They talk all at once and counteract one another. They are restrained by the publicity given their words and their financial outlays. They operate internally by democratic process (as one can tell from the howls of the minority report). They run the gantlet of criticism in their own nation-wide campaigns of lectures and meetings. The war of attrition tests their stamina, rising and falling with the needs of the time. And parallel with this, we see the flowering of government boards and agencies supplementing constitutional departments, and injecting into the very heart of central authority the fresh blood of personnel drawn from business, journalism, and the academic world.

It is Babel, yes indeed. It is pluralism, and so far from system and plan that it may well drive blueprint minds to distraction. But the very waste itself oozes political virtue. It feeds and tests democratic strength. It produces American civilization.

PART TWO
Summer, or Sitting and Thinking

6. Policeman Within

It seems a long time since the morning mail could be called correspondence. A couple of genuine letters, soon read and reread, then a wad of moral suasion from perfect strangers: you ought, ought, ought; you must, must, must. I am summoned to love my neighbor as thyself and to do it in a way that requires a change of heart and of bank balance.

On closer examination, I find that I approve of most of the practical objects urged on me by our kindly, worried, fervent leaders of social welfare, and I only wish I had the means to help them all. But some of the appeals involve moral and religious issues as well as physical welfare, and as regards those I find myself getting more and more impatient with the so-called ideas that accompany the plea — usually a string of clichés of the unsettling sort, a kind of dull sensationalism on a high plane.

These clichés are in fact an echo of the larger debate outside — in the pulpit, on the platform, in the serious magazines and books. All arguments there follow one of two predictable lines, which, by dint of repetition, crop up in people's talk as accepted truth. The first comes from what might be called the Lost and Found Department. It gives and also answers a kind of public notice: "Lost: a complete set of moral values, at the corner of Modern and Secular Avenues. Substantial Reward. No questions asked." The second group are not shedding tears over any loss. They side with the builders of the development out on those new avenues. They want to reclaim any moral swamp with the aid of modern engineering, with psychology, sociology, group dynamics — some kind of expert help. The two groups naturally denounce each other, and as a recent writer to the *Times* says, the constant recrimination fills the bystander with despair. Each type of moralist is perpetually indignant, frothing with violent condescension: his opponents are wrong-headed — or wrong in the head. At bottom, neither school offers much of a choice and both, I think, misrepresent what today's moral situation is.

The central cliché of the engineers' party is: SOCIAL SCIENCE LAGS. "Whereas man's knowledge of the physical world has made gigantic strides, his knowledge of ethics and philosophy of life has not kept pace. It is backward and uncertain. In these days of crisis, therefore, we must, etc. . . ." Statement and attitude are equally absurd. *What* "days of crisis"? What imaginable "keeping pace" with nuclear physics? All days are days of crisis and have ever been. As for invoking science, we should be a little humble and take thought of what we mean. Science is general knowledge of measurable things. The units of matter are so small that taking them in the lump gives a high probability of accurate prediction. As against this, ethics must be as particular as possible: what is right for *me* to do *now* in relation to *him*. And it deals with nonmeasurable units (men and women) moved by imponderable forces — affection, loyalty, anger, lust, peace of mind, blessedness, and so on ad infinitum.

To this the stock rejoinder is: "If we had spent as much time using scientific method to find out what makes men tick [the delicacy of these moralists!] as we have in splitting the atom, we would know by now what to expect from the nature of man and how to control him."

Worse and worse. Measuring may tell us the incidence of suicide in a given population, but it can no more demonstrate that suicide is right or wrong than it can stay the hand of those about to kill themselves. The scientifico-moral complaint is therefore a piece of self-delusion which could easily turn dangerous, as we can see from the typical sermon or commencement address proclaiming: "The need today is for thinkers who love their fellow beings better than themselves and understand completely the whole human organism." What I should like to know before we come any nearer to this "moral science" is Who will control Whom by means of complete understanding; and what kind of moral world it would be in which the knowers used their knowledge to make their neighbors "tick" more regularly? Loving others better than oneself seems no guarantee against error, much less against absolutism. Meanwhile, it is important to take care that we shall not be used as guinea pigs in the search for a science of human nature. Man has no nature in the scientific sense; he has a culture and a character. And what is more, he knows thoroughly well what moral conduct is, has known for thousands of years, when he still knew relatively little about astrophysics and the behavior of electricity.

The great difficulty of the moral life is that our knowledge of right conduct, as embodied in the Decalogue, the Sermon on the Mount, or the Analects of Confucius, is abstract — like the articles of a constitution. The concrete application of the rules cannot help being difficult because we find ourselves in complex situations in which we usually are required to act on the spur of the moment. The Constitution states that a man may not be deprived of property without due process of law. What is "due process"? To answer this there are millions of words defining circumstances which the courts have studied at leisure. A comparable question in ethics cannot be similarly studied and defined to fit every case. For example: should one tell the truth, regardless of consequences? Ask any intelligent, responsible person you know and he or she will say: "It depends. Some consequences should be disregarded. Others not." Just so.

Like the scientific moralists, the seekers for lost values believe in applying formulas from outside. They think "the values" should be strongly in evidence, like prices in a shop. They assume that men cannot possibly have any valuing power in themselves. And this suggests that they do not really understand their own times, do not rightly interpret the morning paper or morning mail. For the very messages I spoke of as accompanying breakfast show that

ours is an age of great — perhaps excessive — moral sensitivity, nowhere more so than in the United States. We Americans are flayed
alive by the thought of the evil done and suffered throughout the
world. We have become superrefined in those matters, and do not
hesitate to reprove others who may be a little thicker-skinned.
"Countries receiving refugees," says a report of the World Federation for Mental Health, "do not sufficiently concern themselves
with the adaptation of the immigrants to their new circumstances."
Suicides, it appears, were too frequent among refugees in Britain:
an earnest American pointed it out.

On the face of it, this deserves our praise; but it also is a reason
why the selfsame earnest people cry "We've lost our values." The
cumulative effect of the calls for help is in itself demoralizing.
Every minute our attention goes to some cruelty or neglect. Help
is always behindhand, and as we are incessantly told, it falls short
of the needs. We end by feeling that we have undertaken a hopeless
task; would it be so hopeless, so gigantic if our age were not gigan-
tically wicked? We want to see progress, make the spring-cleaning
last forever. Says one of our influential leaders of thought: "Our
need, our desperate and terrible need, is to impose upon the world
of chaotic phenomena an order of understanding, a moral order, a
humane and human conception." Another writer, completely mis-
taking the philosophical meaning of the concept he attacks, bids the
United States give up "tough-mindedness" — as if most of us were
moral gangsters and not the Caspar Milquetoasts we are. Symposi-
ums in literary magazines discuss the question whether intellectuals
ought not to temper the search for knowledge with the practice of
love — spiritual love, of course, nothing rude. Meanwhile a banker,
subsidized by a research foundation, studies the possibility of averting both revolution and reaction by promoting in our midst what
he calls the City of Love instead of the City of Reason. Love has
gone to our heads and yet we ache, calling piteously for a humane
moral order.

We have only to compare this state of mind with the hearty

ages to see how far the current has carried us. Anyone who has
visited Lisbon and seen the burial place of Henry Fielding, the
sound moralist of *Tom Jones*, is probably reminded of the journal
Fielding kept of the voyage that ended with his death. The most
striking incident is the account of his boarding ship in England. He
was a broken man, palsied, visibly dying, and he had to be carried
in a chair. This proved a horrible experience because he had to run
the gantlet of the assembled stevedores, who jeered at him and in-
sulted his weakness with guffaws, confident that he could not chas-
tise them. Now stevedores today are not exactly leaders of ethical
thought, but I doubt whether in any port of the Western world
such an incident could occur or would be tolerated by the bystand-
ers. There has unquestionably been widespread moral refinement
since 1754. However bad we may think our age, no one would want
to restore the conditions of that time, when the young George
Washington ran the risk of having his eye gouged out in a quarrel
with another "gentleman."

Yet it is probable that the roughness and moral indifference of
those days was in one respect healthier. Kindness, when it occurred,
proceeded from strength. Acquiescence in the brutality of life left
the survivors capable of resisting it. Today, much of our goodness
proceeds from the conviction that we are weak, that others are
weak, that self-assertion is wrong and vindictive impulse guilty. We
are bottled up inside and enmeshed outside. We owe something to
everybody. Equality, the rights of ever larger numbers, the increase in technical offenses and technical duties, make us supermoral
creatures taking ethical quizzes every minute of the day: Should
I have scolded my child? Should I give my cleaning woman a paid
vacation? Should I cross the picket line at Rosencrantz and Guil-
denstern's? Should I write to my Congressman about the cut in European aid? Should I boycott caviar and help bring Russia to her
knees? Should I be a foster parent to some D.P. child? It goes
round and round, appealing endlessly to the most dangerous human
emotions — pity and self-sacrifice.

The by-products are there for everyone to see: a continuous seething of indignation and hatred, a profound urge to find enemies and outlaw them, a desire to join some authoritative sect which sharply divides the sheep from the goats, thus restoring the justification for animus without pity, while exacting strong discipline from the elect. One of the appeals of Communism when it flourished among the good-natured was that it simplified life by showing the one thing needful. The claims of loyalty, friendship, generous impulse, intellectual honesty, and even common civility were canceled.

That kind of philosophical farce is not new. It was the fascist scheme as well, and what it offers is escape from our intricate bourgeois morality, together with the comfort of a rigid external code and the pleasure of "imposing a moral order on the chaos of phenomena." We know what that "imposing" leads to — the Warsaw and Buchenwald phenomena. Yet many who shudder at Communism or Fascism would be surprised to know how closely their routine complaints of the present day answer the emotional drive in both. One even wonders whether our century's literary passion for Dante does not owe something to the fact that one third of his poem inflicts gruesome torture on the damned and the other two thirds depict various aspects of an ideal order.

Mankind is readily carried to extremes, but we Americans are especially liable to the temptation of sudden moral rigidity. We like to prohibit. It springs from innocence and the belief that compromise belongs solely to the world of interests. About other things "There ought to be a law," for although we wish other people well, we mistrust their pleasure. Over large parts of the country laws passed by local option restrict the sale and consumption of alcoholic drinks. Ordinances in many Western and Southern cities prevent hotels and restaurants from serving liquor — sometimes only *mixed* drinks — on Sunday. Why may we sin freely on straight rye, and on week days? A moral mystery. And why the correction of a single vice? Surely the Sunday dinners served in the selfsame places are incitements to gluttony, public exhibitions of unbridled appetite. The wide-open consumption of candied sweet potatoes alone amounts to what a Methodist classmate of mine used to denounce as "fornification."

Under many names, poor Frederick Jefferson West, though long since dead, seems to be with us still. A nice, very nearsighted boy, he came into our ken in junior year. We heard that he had had to leave his denominational college back home for "radicalism." In the mid-twenties the word had no clearer meaning than it has now; it turned out that Fred's only crime was an irresistible passion for dancing. He had gone through agonies before deciding to grieve his parents, leave town as a black sheep, and slip away to the lascivious East. In our crowd he was of course a moral martinet, an intense prohibitionist. He tolerated cards because in his original creed that was on a par with dancing, which he had come to accept. But betting (small or large amounts), "walking" with more than one girl at a time (let alone kissing two or three), drinking the horrible "red ink" of the period, were deeds of shame from which he tried to restrain us, qualifying them in his peculiar Biblical English as I have qualified the eating of yams.

As a result, when it came to moral speculation about birth control or divorce his vocabulary was spent and he became physically violent. He could not endure the idea that morality *in toto* was not recorded in the Scriptures of his church. When we retorted upon him his liberalism, indeed his radicalism, as regards dancing, he argued from the silence of the Gospels. When we pointed out a similar silence about wine bibbing or birth control, he brought up the stories of Noah and Onan. He was entirely unscrupulous about interpreting texts. But fighting as he did, one against five or six in protracted bull sessions, he would use a last-ditch argument which used to give us considerable trouble: if, he said, the common rules of moral behavior are not all written down and enforced by social pressure backed by the law, why then, anything goes. You don't

know what your neighbor may not do, you don't know where to
have him in order to expostulate and gather public sentiment behind
you, so that he will restrain himself the next time.

Fred had a point. He was saying that society could not take care
of all offenses after they occur and cannot afford to set a policeman to watch each citizen. Society must therefore plant the policeman within. This it does by incessantly dinning the rules into people's ears and from infancy onward penalizing the transgressors.
This is the argument we hear again today in the growing agitation
for moral strictness. The feeling is abroad that the generations since
1914 have been too lenient, that the breakup of the family, the increase in contacts with alien peoples, the "relativism" taught by
cultural anthropology, have destroyed our moral fiber. The discipline needed to stiffen it, we are told, is the traditional one of Biblical moralism, supported by churchgoing and the particular absti-
nences of the given creed.

Undoubtedly this return, this home-coming, is for many people
a personal solution. No one would begrudge it to them. But it can
hardly serve our general purposes as a people. For one thing, a
new-found moral concern seldom ends with the individual. It turns
into a crusade and begins to create ill will and miseries that offset
the gain in the original quarter. Each convert thinks he holds the
truth but forgets that he lives in a country numbering some two
hundred and fifty religions. And this total leaves out of account
the variety of beliefs held by unaffiliated persons, some of whom
may well be self-disciplined and moral by their own lights. The new
passion and proselytism of former backsliders is a threat to the tol-
eration that men waded in blood for three centuries to establish,
here and in Western Europe.

On our soil, we must not forget, the most conspicuous moral
achievement is the quiet charity which enables us to seek our
friends, business associates, and public officials without regard to
their beliefs. So far there is not with us a left and a right, a Church
party and a body of dissenters. Our wisdom goes even farther.

Most of us tacitly agree to consider actions in certain realms as none of our affair. No man of moral discrimination would knowingly associate with a liar, thief, killer, or false witness. But he does associate with people who smoke, drink, play cards, have been divorced, practice birth control, or disbelieve in medicine. The difference is significant. By the force of tradition we have, morally speaking, all been Christianized. But Christian and creedal do not mean the same, and it would be a moral loss, a relapse, to put creed ahead of moral unity.

And what I call Christian behavior in the United States is now typically ours in the sense indicated by all our good works. An American of today is appalled to see a devout Italian peasant beating his horse, a group of Frenchmen stand by while a very old peasant woman draws a cart, or a church-bred English boy or schoolmaster caning another boy. This shows that morality is not fixed in all details. Like the earth, she do move, whether ecclesiastical authority recognizes it or not. And if change is right in certain regards, the question about change in any regard is and remains open.

What Fred would not see was that the bent of his impulses shaped, in fact warped, his moral judgment. The particular desires which he lacked or could easily dominate he would compel everyone else to subdue. His one irresistible urge to caper about in tune to music — and he never wondered whether dancing might not be a compensation for other pleasures he suppressed — he rationalized as well as he could into his creed of morality by the book. It was impossible to make him understand the superior morality of doing right with ease, from inside out instead of outside in. He thought it impossible that some of the virtues he admired might be false fronts for egotism, aggression, and lust. And he accused us of being Pagans who believed with Aristotle that moderation was true morality. Well, Aristotle's formula did not satisfy us, either. It tells the ethical man to find his road by keeping away from the ditches on each side — not to be rash or timid but courageous, not gluttonous or abstinent but temperate, and so on. But the words beg the question, and the space analogy is useless for beings who live also in *time*. The real question is rather *when* to be rash, *when* to be completely abstinent, *when* to be scared to death, as well of course as when to be courageous, temperate, and self-controlled. The man who saves another's life by a rash act is the man we want, not the prudent man who plays safe. Nor do we want moderately intelligent, moderately loyal, moderately honest men. We want the extreme of those qualities.

A tenable ethics for this century must take account of the fact that standardization in many things has been accompanied by the release of millions whose circumstances are infinitely varied. Any modern morality must substitute a dynamic equilibrium of the passions for the static one of former days; though it must aim, as before, at enabling people to do right by instinct and habit, not by self-scarification according to a list of DON'TS. Perhaps the reason thousands of people in this country are now going to psychiatrists instead of to philosophers and clerics is that earnest minds want knowledge that is really applicable. Psychiatry has its errors and superstitions but it at least inquires into human motives under actual conditions. As we no longer live in tribal tents and farming villages like the peoples from whom most of our ancestral morality is derived, we need new forms, new symbols, new interpretations of the traditional code. It is no accident that psychiatry arose in the eighties of the last century when industrial and democratic life began to cause large-scale maladjustment. The so-called Victorian morality crumbled, not because of Darwin, but because of its own inadequacy. And if some seekers feel lost today it is because genius in morality is as rare as in any other art. What we have usually is convention leading the conventional.

I receive a church bulletin where not long ago I read some remarks about the "psychotherapy of prayer." If this is not just bait to catch the innocent modern by a show of "science," it should imply a revision of the Victorian ideas upheld by that clerical writer and that church. But the words stay put while the world spins away beneath. To this day, well-meaning Americans utter plaints about "the family" and shake their heads over divorce statistics as if any family was *per se* a moral good and any divorce a moral evil. They should open their eyes and look about them. If that is too frightening, they might remember that it was a deeply religious Victorian thinker who said a century ago: "The dark places of the earth are the happy Christian homes." Through him and others, the recognition grew that family affection might conceal great tyranny, but "the family" did not change because people revolted; it did not change because of the mere whim and looseness of its members. What broke up the old-style family was factory work for women and children and the subsequent emancipation of women from legal slavery — an obvious moral good. What transformed the institution further was a pair of world wars which took the men away for four, five, or more years and effectively broke millions of marriages, for that duration at least. In the same period, vast populations were shunted about like cattle, with little regard for family life though in the full view of the unprotesting clergy. Many found their feet again at home or in new lands, for men are creatures of habit. But to expect after two such hurricanes a round of family reunions like those described in *Pickwick Papers* is to lack all social imagination and to disqualify oneself for assisting in any moral reconstruction. What is cause for surprise is that so much stability and loyalty to old forms has survived the last fifty years.

Similarly, if today many men and women are seeking and floundering, it argues a genuine moral preoccupation. The relativism complained of in the press, so far from being the cause of the floundering, is the chief instrument for finding the right moral relation to a changed and ever-changing society. With our strong sense of community, we in the United States have acquired the habit of asking about any act or move, Is it antisocial? This is a relative, anthropological way of going about things which is most encouraging, for it retains the fundamental aim of assigning the labels right and wrong to acts and their consequences, and not to the mere names of things. To take an example once more related to the family: It is in general true that to keep husbands and wives together is desirable, for them and for their children if they have any. But it was recently found in Ohio that to talk couples out of a divorce was no solution to their problem or that of the community. They re-applied to the courts after more misery. In other words, the union of two or more human beings in a family is not an absolute but a relative good. It is a good when, like national union, it denotes loyalty from within, continuing consent and desire to work toward a common goal.

But if the community wants to support this ideal of the family, it must also give heed to material conditions. Affection and compatibility are not irresistible forces, and the wretched cramped housing of recent years has much to answer for. This is shown by the increase in the number of people who run away from home, by no means all children escaping from their parents; it is the extra sister, or the mother-in-law, or some other relative who feels in the way, possibly a hindrance to the overworked wife, in a household where everybody is too incessantly in one another's path. At least from the tribal tent one could step out into the solitude of the desert, lunch on fresh dates, and return home at evening a restored, sociable being.

To what I have been saying a good many millions of my fellow citizens would reply, in sad or angry tones, that I was undermining civilization by considering marriage solely as a practical, earthbound enterprise and other moral questions as arguable. To be sure, by another of our wise precepts, we Americans have banned the discussion of religion from polite conversation. This is a sacrifice, for there is hardly a more engrossing subject, but the rule is good — or should one say *was* good? Of late, inevitably, the outspoken restlessness about moral questions has brought back religious faith into the arena of formal and informal debate, with the kind of result exemplified above. Religious discussion in itself poses anew a long-forgotten paradox: If a man's religion is true, he must bend all his efforts to see its commandments respected. But if ideas differ about the true faith and what it enjoins, then it becomes antisocial to militate for this or that creed. In a tight little world such as we now have, who can cry "Sinner!"? We are in one another's pockets and in all probability living off the wages of the sin we impute.

But few, apparently, can see Christian charity in this view. The successive attempts at unity of the World Council of Churches show that even within the small part of the earth's population calling itself Protestant and Christian mutual concessions are unobtainable. "We have reached a point," said a recent report, "at which our divergences stubbornly resist easy solution." When one looks at the Monday page of sermons preached the day before, one is vividly aware of the distance between men in one church and those on the next street, though all profess and practice a common morality, speak the same American speech, wear the same ready-made clothes, and view workaday life in much the same way. How fortunate that most of them never discover in themselves a talent for theology, and that they can commune in the spirit and scriptures of Judaeo-Christianity without analyzing the divergences found by the World Council.

I consider myself a religious man and in the course of my travels I have stepped into many different churches to recollect myself — which you may translate as pray or worship. But I must confess, without attaching to it any but a personal sense of deprivation, that what the professed experts offer us by way of aid, anywhere in the world today, is scant. Cathedral, synagogue, Greek basilica, mosque, chapel, conventicle, meetinghouse and — no less instructive — basement gathering of "new thoughters" or fashionable summoners of spirits to the tune of banjos and table rappings — everywhere that I have been led by curiosity or friendship, I have found myself thrown back on my own slender resources.

I say this neither polemically nor with the slightest wish to wound or attack, least of all to convert, in token of which I shall use the egotistical pronoun for as long as this subject lasts; it should then be clear that I am reflecting, not dogmatizing, speaking for the small and feeble thinking reed designated by the letter I, and not for any group or party of my contemporaries. It is in fact impossible to represent others' awareness of faith, and perhaps the defining of one's own by differences and negatives is still the best description of theirs. At any rate, I find that the current language of devotion in this country, when it departs from scriptural phrases, is virtually incomprehensible to me. It seems to allow no gap for faith itself to bridge, but rather fills it with quibbles or business arguments. I confess to being equally baffled by GOD's OMNIPOTENCE A PURE ACT OF LOVE and by JOINING CHURCH LIKENED TO TAKING GOLF STANCE — REQUIRES FOLLOW-THROUGH. The latter especially is dispiriting in its refusal to see modern man as a creature whose moral and esthetic senses have been, for good or ill, refined beyond those of his ancestors. "Do as we say," drone on the men of God, "and it will profit you. Rewards and punishments worked out by the Great Bookkeeper on your individual balance sheet." Another warns: TIPPING OF GOD DECRIED . . . "in the last analysis our sense of values is reflected in our use of money." This is traditional. One of the most successful religious books in the Western world betrays it plainly in its title: *Hell's flames avoided, Heaven's felicities enjoyed*, by John Hayward, D.D., 1733, Thirty-fifth edition. Such was the vaunted religion of our ancestors.

True, in the modern homily the same argument is sometimes recast and, as it were, psychologized: "You will feel better here below for having all our answers." Indeed I find in an actual sermon: "The world is built on such a pattern that if we do not love our enemies we will get stomach ulcers, and if we do, we will thrive in our own personalities and know the deep, satisfying experience of the presence of God." Small wonder that the true religious passion, especially when matched with intellect, prefers either the vast and complex systems of the medieval schoolmen or the plunge into incomprehensibility. The effort in either case does seem capable of pleasing and glorifying a worthy God. But placating, investing in future gains, and avoiding perplexity by any means alike fail to meet the need for a religion at once social and personal, at once comformable to Western thought and developing with Western life.

The conclusion follows that there does not exist a single creed which a religious temperament educated in science, art, and democracy can accept. By democracy here I mean, once again, the vision of all mankind considered as candidates for equality; a vision to which I feel committed by my Americanism and which, strengthened by the testimony of art and science, I find no reason not to find again in my religion.

Reflection on this lack has sometimes suggested to me that the idea so glibly praised as a great spiritual advance — the idea of one God — might possibly be the stumbling block. Certainly, whoever says one God says *my* God. HE is revealed to *him*. The believer becomes possessive, exclusive, elect. God is on our side, we saw Him first. In theory, the theologian admits his human fallibility, but with sword or scimitar in hand his modesty falls away, and he lays about him to centralize once for all the divine government. Now to a federalist by instinct and training, it should seem that the true spiritual advance was not from many gods to one God, but from *local* gods to universal, ubiquitous elements of Divinity.

Taken as a whole and historically, the world *is* a polytheism. One may say that every church worships the same God — "you in your way and I in His" — yet there remain the "divergences" that church councils encounter and that make a fact of multi-divinity. Moreover, several of the great religions enfold within an abstract monotheism a concrete polytheism. They have prophets, apostles, saints, and incarnations of the one God, all of which inspire varieties of religious devotion. This many-sidedness obviously corresponds to something in us and in our experience of the world. Doctrine is not at issue here and I speak from baffled ignorance. Moreover, I freely confess that as I look upon the wonders of the world, I am tempted to worship not one but many manifestations of divine power — as billions of men have done before me. The figure I shrink from, when I call myself a humble polytheist in the great tradition, is that of the desperado for whom only his mother is sacred. All other women are vile and all lives forfeit to his frightened will. As against this, a will at peace and a mind unafraid has reverence for many beings and for many principles in divers things.

If I am asked what I make of the evident order prevailing throughout the whole, I have to reply that I fail to see it. I see beside the wonders the horrors of the world, and am driven to resist them, believing that the divine is at work in us to first reveal and then abolish evil. This brings down on my head the curse of a well-known heresy: "You're a Manichaean!" Possibly, but I cannot resist pointing out to my orthodox, monotheist reprover that his reason for promoting his particular explanation of the universe is to *make* it an order. He does not find it ready-made. So there is at least a doubt whether all hangs together as perfectly as imperfect creatures tell us.

One of the grandest passages in the history of faith confirms my doubt on this point. "To consider the world in its length and breadth," says Cardinal Newman, "its various history, the many races of man, their starts, their fortunes, their mutual alienation, their conflicts; and then their ways, habits, governments, forms of worship; their enterprises, their aimless courses, their random achievements and acquirements, the impotent conclusions of long-standing facts, the tokens so faint and broken, of a superintending design, the blind evolution of what turn out to be great powers or truths, the progress of things, as if from unreasoning elements, not towards final causes, the greatness and littleness of man, his far-reaching aims, his short duration, the curtain hung over his futurity, the disappointments of life, the defeat of good, the success of evil, physical pain, mental anguish, the prevalence and intensity of sin, the pervading idolatries, the corruptions, the dreary hopeless irreligion, that condition of the whole race, so fearfully yet exactly described in the Apostle's word, 'having no hope and without God in the world,' all this is a vision to dizzy and appall; and inflicts upon the mind the sense of a profound mystery, which is absolutely beyond solution. What shall be said to this heart-piercing, reason-bewildering fact?"

Two things can be said, the one — which is Newman's answer and that of every orthodox believer in a personal God — is that an omnipotent divine intelligence does superintend the seeming chaos, which exists as chaos because of man's disobedience to His law. This answer represents the leap of faith from "reason-bewildering fact" toward an unseen source of hope, and in those who can reason and recognize fact, this leap is an act of courage. For it is manlier to hope and obey an invisible lawgiver than to mope in self-pitying idleness. But in those who conceive the divine otherwise than as an absolute, single-minded Power of Benevolence, the leap of faith is no less real and at least as courageous. For they give up any shadow of ultimate guarantee that all will come out right, and at the same time they involve themselves in the responsibility for any and every outcome. "All deities," says Blake, "reside in the human breast."

Whoever agrees in this with Blake, our modern publicists of religion will charge with the abomination of worshiping man, self-worship, "the fatal Humanism that has landed us in our present plight." No need to ask what caused the previous plight, when Christendom or Islam or any sterner theocracy suffered evil, though untouched by secularity. There is not time enough to argue with those who do not see at a glance that there has always been a present plight, man-made and clearly man-remediable since its character changes. Let this answer suffice: worshiping the divine in man and in nature is not self-worship; it makes one humble, not arrogant; it spurs the energies to second the forces of order emanating from divinity. The great difference, as I conceive it, comes down to this: whether one takes the moral and material universe as finished or unfinished. If taken as unfinished, then the divine is not one and absolute but scattered and emergent. This is an evolutionary way with no guarantees — which redoubles in me the spirit of effort and gives value to the slightest spark of what I hope we would agree to call divine.

I am orthodox enough to attach great religious value to effort, to works, but I know from my own experience and that of others that it is impossible to predict what beliefs will yield the most or the best effort. When one reads of a sermon, for instance, the point of which is summarized as ULTIMATE REMEDY SET FOR INJUSTICE: ACCEPTING CROSS WILL RECTIFY ALL ON JUDGMENT DAY, SAYS PREACHER, one may be tempted to suppose some listeners weakened in will or discouraged, their effort postponed. But that is demonstrably not so. It is not the bare proposition that determines action but the way we take it and how it meshes with a myriad subtle forces within us. I think that if doomed to extinction within a stated time, I should work like a beaver. But I might equally well be paralyzed by the too sharp focusing, as it were, of my last opportunity. Those we know well continually surprise us by their actions under stress or when inspired by a new idea. Artemus Ward was surely right, in his inimitable American way, when he said the issue in the Reformation was whether to be damned by faith or damned by good works. Which being interpreted means that one cannot but seek the belief that best fits one's best knowledge of both outer and inner worlds.

But this self-made, self-propelled, all-too-American view of religious choice (I can hear saying this the confident of all the orthodoxies, from the Greek to the Yogi) allows no place to revelation. Your so-called religion is entirely spun out of your own weak, blind, solitary, and temporary little mind.

As to my limited capacities, I don't know what we can do. Any religion, however revealed, has to enter the small receptacles that are our minds and be cut down to size for this purpose. History shows us few examples of total awareness, and those examples — the experiences of the mystics — were not only temporary but also incommunicable.

Nor is it true that the view I have tried to sketch here, crudely and with the serious omission of its emotional tone, originates in me and ignores revelation.

On the contrary, it is built on continuous revelation, and from every source. As a believer in widespread divineness, I cannot afford to neglect any message. It is also true I cannot heed them all. The world has kept the memory of many seers, and in their poems much is confused and contradictory. I do as the rest have done — interpret, understand, sort out the credible from the foolish or merely spectacular. And being humble in the face of tradition, being aware of development, I tend to think that the later revelations are the richer and truer. They have caught up and distilled what went before, refined it to present uses, broadened it to take in more and more of what God's multitudinous witnesses have said. To particularize from among the authors of modern scripture, I find four most persuasive because most revelatory — Blake, Nietzsche, William James, and Bernard Shaw.

This implies no rejection of the writers of certified scriptures. But reading their words, one surely learns that in all times prophets and saints have been self-appointed. The founders of religions are seldom bishops to begin with. And in church scriptures also, the latter tends to be the truer — the God of Jesus is ampler and more loving than that of Abraham. Here too is confusion and contradiction that requires sifting — Ecclesiastes, for instance, preaches a doctrine of hopelessness that the story of Job refutes and that I cannot share. I think "vanity of vanities" applies to Ecclesiastes himself — and in a sense he did not mean. Isaiah would have made short work of him. Farther on comes the divine Jesus, who speaks like no one else — often as difficult to understand as impossible to imitate. Yet who would not own Him as a Master?

No less evident than truth throughout this treasury of revelations is the carelessness of those who have transmitted it. Wrong meanings from bad translation, garbling and mixing of texts, arbitrary decisions taken in sectarian ages about what is scripture and what is not — all this should permanently cure the most eager believer in a fixed canon of doctrine. These flaws are not the inventions of infidels, they are the scholarly findings of the clergy itself after years of devout study. We are told, for instance, that one of the most beautiful stories of Jesus' life, that of the woman taken in adultery, is a late interpolation. This does not make it less beautiful and wise but it does render it more permissible to find beauty and wisdom in revelations of all epochs.

Others of the gospel stories are so profound that they seem to transcend moral teaching. Take what seems to me the most haunting of them all: the account of the respective fates of Judas and Peter. Judas committed a horrible act of betrayal, ostensibly for gain. But he was himself so horrified by it that he took his own life. Who does not feel stirred to the depths by compassion for such a man, so like Everyman. And are there not moments when his self-execution makes him seem a more conscious being than Peter, who thrice repudiates his Master, and then goes on to found a church and receive the Keys of Heaven? Peter's fault too is like Everyman's. But recanting allegiance and then finding prosperity makes the offense twice abhorrent. Perhaps we are meant to understand that the way to expiate a sin is not to seek a scapegoat, even in ourselves, but to become a different self through better deeds. The story does not preach or assert; it is for pondering and recollection.

But one thing all sources of revelation do hint or tell of is that faith impulse action, to be good, must form a single natural power. "Grace" is the fit word for the unforced working of the divine motion within us. When we do not possess it, that is because it does not possess us. Hence, as I think, the grave error of describing another's misdeeds or one's own as springing from original sin. They seem to me to spring rather from subsequent sin, that is, from complication of mind and dulling of imagination, excess of striving and superfluity of righteousness.

Which is why, when I open the morning mail, I refuse to be drawn, even in imagination, into the many gaseous crusades against "these times of crisis." Good work has to feel familiar and spontaneous, and this implies that we must begin by accepting ourselves. We shall conquer and be saved if the divine energies suffice. The highest social morality I can find in my world today, and my religion such as it is, alike forbid me to engineer salvation by plotting to control man through devices that will work *de haut en bas*, whether force or superstition or the science of his supposed "nature."

7. The Eye on the Needle

FOR EVERY WELL-INTENTIONED MORALIST who wants to save us by scientific method (and who usually obtains support from foundations for anything that comes under this head) there lurks somewhere in our country if not an opponent and decrier of science, at least a thought which tends that way. The scientific front is as yet too imposing, too popular, for many people to risk attacking it — even supposing they had the knowledge of its weak spots. But one notices none the less a good many indirect expressions of doubt and disenchantment. The respect as well as the lip service being paid to general education and the humanities, to religion and moral feeling, to self-cultivation and the arts, tell of a rising suspicion that all knowledge is not science, and that perhaps science is not the friend of man that a more trusting age took her to be.

This fresh view of the matter seems to have been made more vivid by the palpable consequences of atomic fission, and the first to be affected by this new notion have been the men of science themselves, or at least the most sensitive among them. The time was ripe for a little self-consciousness to spoil the complacency of the guild and awaken it to some of its grave errors of omission. Having been praised and petted for a century, they had come to take their absolute superiority for granted and to enjoy their moral isolation as a privilege — the nobility of the lab: not an exclusive caste, to be sure, since one could enter it by hard work, but one which acknowledged no obligation to the rest of mankind except that of "giving" its inventions and discoveries outright. Few recognized how difficult it is to "give" anybody anything, and how dangerous it may be to him who takes when no real communication exists between donor and recipient.

Men of science who recalled the time when their subject had to be justified to the world — the time when scientists were suspected as workers in black magic, or as wastrels shirking the common tasks, or as mechanic minds unfit to associate with educated men — did make some effort to explain themselves to the public. But the explanations were as crude as they proved easy to credit. The layman was told that the scientist alone has method, judgment, intellectual virtue; he alone pierces through error and illusion to fundamental truth; he alone is not swayed by convention and sentiment.

The people, who had to have some ideas about science, swallowed this superstition and stayed under the spell. There is a powerful appeal in authority that asserts itself. Our subjugation was made complete by the virtual bribe of new products, new cures, new mumbo jumbo. Do we not still speak, in relation to science, of "the layman"? What he sees most clearly of science, quite without re sentment, is its arrogance and boasting and lust for power. The policy of purism, by which science courses make only practicing scientists, has created a sort of cultural neurosis about science as powerful as science itself. A great many scientists are themselves subject to it, with the result that by and large the profession shows an amazing ignorance of practically everything worth knowing — their own branch of learning to begin with, then the essential facts of modern civilization and their own characters as human beings, in short, the rudiments of the good life.

I speak, despite superficial appearances, as a well-wisher of science, and an admirer of scientific genius who has taken some trouble to understand what there is to admire and who feels no professional animus in offering criticism where it seems due. In fact, we are all responsible (as in every serious imposture) for the strange and false position that science and scientists hold generally in the twentieth century and more particularly in the United States. If a little while ago a Scottish scientist named MacBeath could accuse his American colleagues of being authoritarian, it is no doubt because we have all condoned the usurpation. We have forgotten that every profession without exception is a natural, unconscious conspiracy against outsiders, and that it must constantly be criticized from outside (aptly or not) so that it will keep criticizing itself from within. The spectacle of the American Medical Association trying to stifle its own rare critics from inside the ranks is a model of how *not* to have the best medical association in the world.

It is not by incapacity but by ignorance that the ordinary man of science is ignorant. He thinks and works in an intellectual vacuum that he has consciously or unconsciously prepared. The profession at large gives little or no thought to the generalized effects of science on the world, only to some of its physical effects. And individuals pursue their own results often with no thought of their science as a whole. They work and extend the techniques they have inherited. They are like a gay lady with a fast car. They turn the switch and press the pedal and they're off — nobody dare cry halt — freedom of research, to be sure. But the friendly onlooker cannot help wondering about brick walls. I am not thinking of social responsibilities alone. A number of scientists, beginning with Einstein, have warned the world about this or that menace implicit in their own previous work. Some have even undertaken not to work on destructive projects. Others have been, as college and foundation heads, conspicuous leaders of nonscientific thought. "Conspicuous" is, I hope, the proper word. For it corresponds to the noncommittal character of the moralizing we have lately heard from scientists. We have yet to find them engaged in the kind of mutual criticism that has long been familiar in the world of letters and politics, to hear them warn us against the tendency of one another's assumptions.

In a very strict sense they do not, most of the time, know what it is they *are* doing. Take the cliché about "our increasing control of nature." Everybody repeats it and takes more or less credit for the fact. But is it fact? Is it not possible that the amazing machine has switched itself into reverse and is heading toward the opposite of control? Science toils until it has freed the energy of the atom. We cheer and discharge the force in others' faces; they do the same to us. What has happened is that mankind sees written ever larger: "Here is nature unleashed, see what you can do with it." And there is nothing in our repertory to tell us what to do. In a lesser way, the same is true of the drugs, gases, engines, and synthetic foods that we have subjected ourselves to. They are nature enlarged rather than quelled. The question is not whether to go back to a simpler set of unknowns, but of how to describe correctly what it is that mankind has been receiving at the hands of science. As a plain straight fact, cars are more deadly than horses. We destroy with the same hands by which we save, our freedom limited by our power.

But I should be the first to point out that we must not let engines and bombs monopolize our imagination of disaster. Let us turn rather to the opposite quarter and consider some of the cultural effects of science, beginning with the lesser ones. I spoke of mumbo jumbo. I had in mind the invasion of every language by hundreds of empty noises like Bab-O, Duco, Rinso, Kodak, Kotex, Kleenex, Vapex. Why is X so impressive and O so reassuring? It is the echo of science. With this goes the would-be technical compounding of names (Hydramatic, Hooperating), and all the verbs in -ize suggesting that some secret process has transformed the commonplace into the miraculous. Do not suppose that you wash your hands with powdered soap; not at all: it's "a specially formulated skin cleanser." And you dry them on an "Aqualized" paper towel, made by the "wet-strength process." The strange thing is that a few things are still left called simply Scotch tape and stainless steel. The effect of so much nonsense should not be underestimated. It maintains the popular mind in the semihypnotic state. Here is a magazine advertisement showing a young woman wearing some new form of brassiere. The containers are strapless, separate, and designed to make divergent the axes of her breasts. "Fashion and science," says the caption, "bring you this modern marvel . . ."

Why blame Science? There is no blame. Science is an abstraction. But when we come to describe the present, when people say "this is the age of science," we must take in all its manifestations, including those outside the laboratory. That is what an age is — the whole composite mess. This is certainly the line scientists take when they describe with disfavor the ages of superstition. They throw in the witchburnings and inquisitions, the fear of comets and faith in wonder-working relics. The saints were undoubtedly not responsible for any of those, but the whole formed one culture, and so are the symbols of trade and advertising one with the scientific culture of today.

This does not contradict what was said in a previous chapter about Trade, which has to exist, like the rest of us, among circumstances it did not shape. But occasionally it is good to seek the reasons behind what we live by, and what then emerges most clearly is the duty of each profession and branch of learning to amend itself. The scientists are not called upon to improve Trade, but neither should they be so quick to dissociate themselves from its contemporary doings. Historically, science owes much to trade. The scientist's habit of exactitude and measurement, like his interest in material things, is probably an offshoot of the trader's love of regular procedure and intense search for the odd penny. We know that algebra's plus and minus began in warehouses to mark the weight of bales. This was six centuries ago and, ever since, trade and science have played into each other's hands. If Trade now sells brassieres in the name of science, it is obviously because science is what people will be impressed by. Unless scientists protect us against the misuse of their sacred calling by a truly scientific education, who will give it to us? We are all in the same boat. The advertisers are hardly more foolish than the scientific editors of newspapers who printed on the front page the "key formulae" (note the *ae*) in Einstein's new theory of December 1949.

One step above mumbo jumbo, which disfigures our language, comes jargon — which disfigures our thoughts. And modern jargon is "scientific" whether in social science and literary scholarship or in the talk of the man in the street. Nobody says: "What do you feel? What do you think?" But: "What's your reaction?" After fifty years of this, an experienced observer writes: "I am convinced that American readers are looking for the truth that man is not simply a puppet twitched into love or war by his unconscious which pulls the strings . . . they are seeking for integrity and dignity."

The use of the single word "reaction" does not account for the trouble, but it points to the acceptance of the puppet feeling. A million repeated instances of jargon all tending the same way end by establishing the belief that we are all automatons. In the last few years the public has been able to follow in the daily press the career of the electronic digital computers miscalled "mechanical brains." Their superiority to man has been impressed upon us. Recently, one of these machines "learned" something, and in a little while we should begin to watch the back pages for news of its "marriage" and "obituary." So far there have been quotation marks about the metaphoric words, but in our present frame of mind this only increases their authority. Yet a machine is not a brain, if only because the brain (or mind, rather) invented the machine and not the other way around. A mechanical brain could not invent an egg-beater; it works because the knowledge we expect from it is first put into it: to forget this and be in awe at its processes is like worshiping the biceps of a steam shovel.

In man's mind, however, dignity, integrity, and self-respect depend on what he imagines about his life. Let him be told often enough that he is a machine and that some other machine is his natural superior and he may come to believe it. For fully seventy-five years now, it has been dinned into his ears (often by scientists) that man's gradual loss of self-respect was inevitable. "When Galileo and Copernicus displaced the earth from the center of the universe, they started a movement that must logically end in man's feeling absolutely insignificant. Later Darwin, then Freud . . ." This old rigmarole has of course no validity whatever. It is the one bit of fiction given to science students in college. There is no evidence that any great mass of Western men have ever said to themselves, "Dear me, if the earth isn't where Ptolemy thought it was, then I am less than nothing." Sometimes in that same lecture the scientist will try to have it both ways and will exalt man (meaning himself and his colleagues) for mastering the secrets of the cosmos. This only makes the advocate of religion rise up and say that man is far too bumptious nowadays and ought to return to the medieval conviction of his nothingness.

Why not pair off the votes and return to facts? No one lives by abstractions such as these. Actual feelings and beliefs are formed by silly little words and metaphors, by multitudinous little blows and frustrations, by little successes and powers that come directly out of life. The unpleasant self-consciousness and self-abasement of today is a cultural result of raw science undigested — pseudo-science, if you like — and not of any philosophical generalizations about Darwin and Freud, whom only a handful have read and understood.

Indeed, we have not even begun to master science for general purposes, either emotionally or intellectually. True scientific study discloses elements and relations in a defined situation. But if human beings are to be the better for the new knowledge they obtain, it must become a part of their habitual, spontaneous actions. They must get over the conscious awareness as fast as possible. In riding a bicycle you begin by thinking of your feet, but when you really know how to ride you forget them. Science applied to society, though, keeps us perpetually self-conscious, at the wrong time and the wrong place. This is expressed in the Parable of the Shin-Kicking Hour: "Science" having discovered that young children kick each other in the shins, time is set aside for shin kicking: it is more scientific than the old haphazard way. We are beset by studies and experiments and results. The puppet's strings are jerked every instant. A study, a survey, a controlled experiment, "It's been found that . . . ," and we worry accordingly: Is prayer psychotherapeutic? Can music lengthen my life? Has this bread been irradiated? Have I drunk my fluorides?

At the same time, the convertibility of everything into something else robs familiar pleasures of their comfortable qualities. A chemist in Hamburg has extracted a protein from human hair to serve as food. He makes a powder that he says can be taken straight "or mixed with other food such as cheese." I suppose this cystin, or whatever, is clean enough and lets one forget its origin, but it does suggest in the maker a sort of mindless cannibalism, a symbol of man going around in circles feeding on himself.

That product is not so objectionable as its maker. I suspect that if he ever exchanges ideas with a man of another calling, he says something about "science as a way of life." Now science is not and cannot be a way of life, any more than art or war or maritime law. Nothing is quite good enough to be made into a way of life, and all attempts fail. The true character of life is that it is miscellaneous — our recognition of this in America is the sign of our political genius — and all disciplines, professions, "ways of life," try to destroy miscellaneousness. The more nearly they succeed the more they cost in deprivation of life. Supposing a scientist to have a friend, it is clear that he can hardly keep him as a friend if he greets him by saying: "Why, if it isn't Tom, that old bunch of cells! How are you replacing them? Not too many in one spot, I hope — or any of that nonrecommended brand called cancer? They say it doesn't do you any good — though of course it hardly matters — most of your proteins and nitrogen keep going regardless of what happens to you — as a scientist, you know, I see things differently."

This little fantasy is feeble compared to what we have come to accept from some who are not even our friends. A would-be social scientist trained in biology proposes in print to unite the world by submitting propositions all can agree on. To find them he starts from the simplest postulate he can find — that "Cells must eat." Overlooking Voltaire's famous demurrer, he goes on to say: "The path that food takes to the alimentary canal is along the axis of an unbroken zone of sensation shaped like a funnel." So be it. Ten lines farther on, listing man's distinguishing features, he suddenly calls the face a "food funnel." It makes one want to take the veil — not because one refuses to acknowledge the act of eating but because that act is not the whole of life and that description is not even the whole of gastronomy. Call the statement scientifically true just for the sake of argument and you see why science cannot be a way of life. On every subject it has mastered, science is correct but incomplete. It is always less than life, much less, and from its very nature cannot stretch to embrace it all.

This is no new heresy; it is an old observation. Its importance is that it goes counter to the prevailing pervasive dogma that scientific method is the only path to assured truth. Americans especially, but more and more other peoples every decade, believe that every mode of thought outside science has been tried and found wanting. What is not science is subjective, emotional, "inspirational," illusory. Science is trustworthy because the method of patient, exact observation, measurement, and verification builds on bedrock to erect a harmonious edifice of reliable knowledge. Any man who is satisfied with less must therefore be a fool or a knave.

There is enough truth in the dogma to make it impregnable, and in fact no reasonable man wants to dislodge it, but merely to reduce it to tenable size. Possibly this is easiest accomplished if we once recognize that science, meaning modern physical science, is a reduction of all experience to the one sense of sight. Without the eye science does not exist. Only with the eye can science take in accurately the simple marks or points or lines by which it measures. All its work depends on visual discrimination — the height of the mercury in the thermometer, the reading on the slide rule, the needle quivering on the dial, the hairlines in the eyepiece of the microscope, the dots or streaks on the photographic plate, the curves on the graph, the interference bands on the spectroscope, the angle of the beam in the polarimeter — the eye is the sole witness because it is the most generally exact of the senses.

This general, widespread accuracy of the eye is what permits us to define objectivity. Some people have sharper ears than others, but it is difficult to compare what they hear; you cannot put lenses on dull ears. Chemistry makes some slight use of taste and smell, but they are inexact senses; people disagree about sweet and sour. What we call objectivity rests on the common agreement of normal eyesight. What you can see, I can be made to see — and argument stops. The diversity of opinion that is so mistakenly scorned in other branches of learning disappears, and we arrive at the two fundamental principles of science that have affected our culture: Seeing is believing, and Seeing is agreeing.

No doubt the latest conceptions of science have gone far beyond the stargazing and substance weighing with which physics began. Clark-Maxwell changed all that. We live in a world of waves and electrons invisible to the eye, and the modern scientist no longer constructs models of his ideas as Lord Kelvin recommended everybody to do. We put our unseen and unseeable conceptions in formulas, and make our way forward by mathematics.

But this only shifts our use of the eye. Even the unseeable conceptions of modern science began some sixty years ago with the famous Michelson-Morley experiment which disproved the existence of any light-bearing ether. This was done, quite literally, with mirrors. The observers wanted to see any perceptible difference in the time of flashing of two reflected beams, one going with, the other across the motion of the earth. The eye settled the question: they *saw* no difference to correspond with the assumed drift. Jump ahead to 1920 or so. Einstein has completed and published his general field theory. What does the world of science do? They wait till the total eclipse of the sun in January 1924 for verification. They expect to see or not to see the bending of light around the sun. They see it. Whether it comes to the naked eye or through lenses and tubes with a camera plate at the end is a detail.

As for the use of mathematics, it is but another application of the same faculty humans have of agreeing by using their eyes to compare the simplest possible things — simple and easily visible. In mathematics as in experimental science, the method is sure because every step is made as minute as possible. A child could check it without understanding it. Does it say plus or minus? Is the needle at 12 or at 12.5? Mathematics works with symbols that are kept clear and distinct. A 5 is not a 3. You may make a mistake but you cannot stick to it once it is pointed out. And in the laboratory, what is seen at the end of the experiment another must be able to see also.

Nobody, it is true, has ever seen the square root of minus one, any more than Euclid's circles or triangles, yet to deal with them takes paper and pencil. The essence of the objective and provable is to be found not in sight at large but in the sight of simple and minute detail. A man looking at a painting is not primarily trying to find a spot of red and have another man see it too. He is trying to see a whole and *not* reduce it to simplicities. Which is why the other man may disagree with him about the merit or significance of the work. It is not their business to reach agreement about it. But they will agree about the size of the canvas in inches as they see the ruler laid alongside.

Here again the cultural consequences of our addiction to science are clear. It is no accident that some of our most popular magazines are called *Look, Pic, See,* and that nearly all of them print pictures. Life, in more senses than one, has become pictures. Our eyes are incessantly appealed to, overworked as never before. The chief quality now sought for in an object or a person is the new look, the slick finish, the high polish, the gleam, the glow and the glamour — all eyewash. We've become a civilization of viewers, and as I shall try to show later on, of *voyeurs.*

Meantime, we seem less and less able to understand what is merely written or said. It is too abstract and fugitive. We want graphs, tables, measurements. The housewife talks in per cents which are shown graphically in her newspaper under cost of living or fat off the hips. Pictorial statistics for her, visual aids for the school child, TV for the whole family. We are the pop-eyed people, and if we go on as we have it may someday not be enough to shout: "Look out! Here comes a car." Too many concepts. You will have to flash a prepared card showing a little man-unit being run over.

The believer in the universal use of scientific method is sometimes led to suppose that there can be no barrier separating the visible from the invisible. Because the physicist can compute the number and weight of molecules, he is said to measure the invisible. Out of invisible sounds he makes seeable shapes on a phonodeik, and so on. But in all these transformations he begins with a visible chunk of matter and ends with a visible sign that the hidden steps in between are correct. This leaves untouched something that our modern existence tends more and more to forget, even to deny — invisible realities of a nonmaterial sort. They need not be defined just in these words. It is enough to point to them by an example chosen at random: the love of a parent for a child, or any other kind of attachment, repulsion, fear, joy, faith, and intimation of truth. These are realities that are invisible, nonmaterial, and non-measurable.

It is irrelevant to suggest that the effects or concomitants of feelings are material and measurable, and that one could measure the fun of a party by measuring the noise, laughter, heightened color, and oxidation of the guests. Not only would the "score" be unsatisfactory but the means of obtaining it would dispel the very thing being measured. To say this is not to say that man is outside the realm of science, but that what he cares about most seems to be. Nor does laying stress on the difference between the tangible realities and the intangible mean that biology and physiology must shut up shop. But there are one or two points that our science-dazzled common mind would do well to hang on to regardless of the counterpropaganda. One is that "objective" and "subjective" are not elegant synonyms for "good" and "bad." In using them to praise or blame, scientists are sometimes a little inconsistent. They like to predict *Der Tag*, the day when all the data about man will be in their pocket and they can work us like a Bunsen burner, turning up or down the flame of our emotions. Yet when this possibility is challenged, they face about and discredit the experiences they cannot reach, calling your toothache "subjective" because nobody else can feel it. What interests them is the tooth and for that they earn our praise, but this interest of theirs — which is also their reason for being — arises from your pain, and nothing else.

About the results of science's efforts, ranging from ingenuity to genius, we are grateful, gaping, respectful even when we do not understand. We do not even question when the dicta of science contradict each other. Not long ago, between Saturday and Monday, the age of the universe doubled and its size was multiplied by eight. We took it all in stride, as we have done for a century past. It used to be "The world is running down, good people. Get your blankets, the night will be cold." (This was Old Huxley and his friends down to thirty-odd years ago.) After that, it became "Wake up, good people, matter is being created all the time. Off with that winter underwear, into your blue Jeans." (That was the party line after Einstein and the late Sir James.) "Light can rotate matter," says X. "No, it can't," says Y. "INVESTIGATION UPSETS ESTABLISHED THEORY," says the morning paper. We take it all like perfect gentlemen, and it is right that we should. But it is not right that the variations, doubts, and inconsistencies of any human enterprise should be glossed over so as to make it seem, if not superhuman, at least superior to other enterprises, such as art, ethics, history, or religion.

Nor is it proper that the speculators of the scientific game should end by considering trivial and negligible what science justly neglects — the subjective, or in other words, the whole inner life of man. To the panoramic eye of science, all our vague, vacillating, ephemeral sensations do not matter. Our pain, science does try to kill, for excellent practical reasons. But to the rest it says: "What of it? Poets and fiddlers may play tricks with our feelings and make us think we hold the secret of the universe in the palm of our hands. But that is an illusion. Let me remove but one gland, or cut the nerve leading to your solar plexus, and Beethoven will leave you cold. Anyhow, what does our consciousness of joy or despair lasting ten minutes or half a day signify in comparison with the process of evolution that took a bit of slime and formed through aeons the vast spectacle of animate nature? And what is even that, our miserable little planet, compared with the whirling, exploding suns and the nebulas receding to the bounds of space? And is it not true that this grand vision would never have been ours if it had not been for what you now attack as incomplete and insufficient — the solid edifice of exact, scientific propositions couched in mathematical form?"

This of course is something of a poetic frenzy in itself, and one which any modern man will esteem it a privilege to share. But it remains a fact that this magnificent revelation has meaning only for a sensitive, intelligent, perishable being such as man. As scientist, man looks at the show while pretending he is not there. It is as if he went to the theater and gave a report on the play, then declared that it was played to a totally empty house. For being "objective" means forgetting one's own presence and describing things as thus and so regardless of any observer. But at some time or other the scientist must get back into his skin, re-enter the stream of life, and admit that without a living audience there would be no spectacle — no *such* spectacle. Science therefore does not survey the whole of experience. It is only subjective experience that takes in the whole, of which science describes one limited province.

Now it is tempting to speculate whether the scientific outlook, like the error just analyzed, goes with a temperamental trait shared by many scientists. Perhaps they choose their profession because they shrink from looking into themselves. All civilized men bear neurotic scars, and scientists often seem afraid of human contacts, live feelings, and play of mind. The material they are used to is far from tractable, but at least it does not talk back or stir them up. They do the stirring. It is noticeable also that scientific workers keep harping on their care and precision, their amazing patience, which nobody thinks of denying. But other people use their minds too, in a no less patient pursuit of truth, and there is alarming naïveté in the claim to monopolize for one profession the common virtues of every good workman. Give a boy a B.S. degree and he can't tell you the time without praising his own exactitude.

The pretension has become a culture trait, so that now it sounds like a paradox to say that poetry is as exact, precise, rigorous, and painstaking as science. And without flying so high, it has to be pointed out that the law, for instance, is a sphere of precise thought which should make men of science think twice before pretending to be the only trustworthy thinkers. A little humility and gratitude would not be amiss. Our daily freedoms and opportunities have been won and are being upheld by a mass of legal research and reasoning as admirable as scientific work, just as our physical needs are fulfilled by business methods that are as ingenious as laboratory techniques.

It is true, as Dr. Johnson said, that business cannot be intellectually taxing or it could not be managed by those who go into it. But the same reasoning applies to scientific research. It was not always so, but in our century the great mass of scientists are very ordinary minds. This is an obvious statistical probability; it is in fact the beauty of the scientific method that it does not take a very high order of talent to apply it. From which it follows that we should be free to consider scientists as good, bad, and indifferent, just as we do artists, lawyers, baseball players or anybody else. "Man of Science" denotes a profession, not a claim to fame. A chemist at Dupont's can hit upon something very useful and still be just a patient tinker. Patience is a drug on the market.

The guild can be excused for not making distinctions, for not having as yet a clear sense of its own position in the world. Half a century ago scientists were still fighting for full recognition and support, not having yet conquered the universities and big business. But they should begin to recognize what other learned men know, namely that a profession has tenure only during good behavior. The people have got rid of their learned men before and can always do so again. This, if nothing else, should be an inducement to familiarizing oneself with the world as it is — not necessarily through the formal study of political and social theory, but through participation and, in the light of cultural realities, self-examination. The modern world takes at face value the gift that science is supposed to have made, "a harmonious edifice of tested truth." But in the last quarter-century this edifice has got entirely out of hand. There are so many isolated, unconnected little piles of fact that an investigator could spend his lifetime just finding out what has been done. Research and publication keep proliferating ahead of any possibility of indexing and cataloguing. This being true in most of the sciences, a spring-cleaning seems called for. What hope for the great synthetic mind, the Newtonian genius, when he finds the harmonious edifice hidden by a mushroom growth of lean-tos and outhouses? And the first step, I submit once more, is a change of heart and mind in the direction of greater self-knowledge. It is in the best interests of science that scientists stop thinking and speaking of themselves in the antediluvian terms of the last-century crusaders against religion. Science attracts most of our best boys in the colleges, and they learn there with the finest equipment the latest scientific doctrine, but they do so in a moral atmosphere that has long been obsolete. It is as if you clapped on their young chins a false white beard patterned after Darwin's.

To say this is not to underestimate our debt to science, nor to feel like James Russell Lowell when he said "I fear science as a savage fears writing." We may fear men but we must not personify objects. Not even the split atom should dismay us, since it stands in no different relation to mankind than fire, the flint hatchet, or gunpowder. To the extent that science is a collective cultural product, the bomb is our collective responsibility. But we may ask of those in charge of science that it meet the two basic requirements of business and artistic justification: Does it profit us? Yes. Does it yield esthetic satisfaction? Yes. When in any feature or tendency it departs from these guidelines to rational action, it must, like any other undertaking, be brought to book.

My observations and reflections on this great subject — halting and imperfect as they are — have come while listening to scientific friends and especially to a brilliant nephew, a mathematical physicist whose devotion to pure research is a moral teaching in itself. Besides, I freely admit that I too respond, like every child of the century, to the formal tone of science, its cool deliberation, its evident consecutiveness and great rationality, not devoid of happy surprises, as when the roundabout process turns out to be the straightest shortcut. My nephew is working on the Theory of Snarls, and his passionate intellectual curiosity is for the solution itself, not its possible applications. His aim is to devise a formula expressing the degree of intricacy of any given snarl — in string, hair, any substance, though he has elected Fiberglas. Since snarls do not happen by chance, they have measurable causes and a magnitude. Each hopeless knot is strictly determined, and if a factoring system can be found it will be possible to detect Inoperable Snarls. You will then know when to reach for the scissors. . . .

And I foresee the temptation to some other ingenious mind, a social scientist perhaps, to apply the formula to human affairs, which the odds are ten to one he will call Organic Snarls, and promise to undo if you will only sit still.

8. The Under-entertained

THE LAST PLACE, one would suppose, where man wants applied science and the way of the machine is recreation. Yet we find it there, proud of itself, and since we do not actively resist, improving its techniques. The very word technique, which is now used to dignify every human act but dying, is a record of our submission to system. Resistance is so little thought of that it no longer disables a technique to give away its secret. Listen to Mr. Billy Rose, the impresario, explaining how he planned to attract the masses to his nightclubs, how in fact he revolutionized the business:

1) "Red is the most successful and exciting color, so paint the joint red." 2) "Crowd them together — they'll communicate the excitement through their elbows." 3) "Keep the prices reasonable, the liquor good, and the food edible." 4) "Make the acts loud enough to outshout the customers and short enough to give them a chance to drink up." (*Time*, June 2, 1947.) We ask in vain what is being re-created here. Protoplasm is being processed in the name of entertainment.

All forms of mass entertainment develop a whole mythology of techniques, by the application of which each kind clicks. Slick's the word and what is slick will click. To use the language of men, this means the unexpected never happens. Slickness is the acme of routine, the technique of a squirrel in a cage, a technique of nothing at all. The idea (and the knack) is to make everything look alike, while claiming for it novelty, surprise, and strangeness. All the edges of singularity have to be trimmed off, for fear the object or idea might not fit. Fit what? The technique. At the broadcasting studio —

... unheeding the sneer
On the face of the engineer —

hard-working talent dwells on the fine points: not to muff, cut what might offend, count the laughs, sing in tune of hair oil, and finish the program "on the nose": twenty-nine minutes and forty-five seconds flat.

Open the newspaper, sob story or society column, and from day to day it's as nearly the same as genius can make it. News is news only when you've heard it before. The dateline changes and the names, but the contents are a load of interchangeable parts. Life is like that? So they say, and if we trust the camera eye, we may come to believe it. The caption leaves us no choice:

Glamorous Georgina, a piquant brunette, takes time off to smile invitingly at unflagging suitor. Friendly Dentist Carmichael is wildly enthusiastic, for come-on is unprecedented. He takes it literally, though end result cannot be foreseen. He is hearty, jovial type who moves swiftly to a showdown. His affairs, however, may get badly snarled, for Georgina is mass of contradictions, and he is conscious of calculated risk. She says they have many things in common and often reach startling agreement. Planning honeymoon in Southern wonderland, his good looks are devastating. Her favorite pastimes are tennis and jilting.

What we ask for is simple enough, and because we get it now and then, we know it is not impossible to provide. We want involvement, not excitation; drama, danger even, not mechanical assault and battery. Hence sports and the new passion of the age for skiing. A broken leg is a trifle after all that unpolluted hazard, to say nothing of the preparations, the special train, the chance meetings and the still natural scene, then — speed, swoosh, and slalom. Can we even wonder at the excess we deplore in the dare-deviling of the hot-rods? The young concoct themselves a violent antidote to sameness and the prefabricated thrills of Hollywood gossip magazines.

.   .   .

Not that vicarious drama is to be despised. Love of the show is as old as man and starts afresh in every baby born. We had, we have, a wonderful medium for it — the movies. For twenty years, from about 1910 to the beginning of the talkies, it promised to outshine all previous ways of representing action. The one condition of success was that the new medium should remain itself and avoid competing with the legitimate stage, that is, leave voice and "indoor plots" alone. Sound effects and music were sufficient allies. But the second-generation leaders of the industry were too conceited to find out what the pioneers had done, too naïve to suspect that words might spell death to an art. Opinions will differ, but I confess I am shocked every time I enter the place of darkness and hear the hollow sho-shoshing that passes there for human speech. And what wordiness! We laugh at the old silent films and their elaborate captions. But each caption came only once, and toward the end of the silent era they were getting to be few and very short. The drama was on the screen. What we now get instead is the slowing-up of drama through the visual and verbal repetition of each passing point. To show a man momentarily angry, he has to smash a window and a plate and a mirror. Three incidents for every idea, with words on top of it to make it inescapable. The art is not for morons, as has been said, it makes them.

The proof that movies can be produced that are thoroughly popular and entertaining, completely movielike, and fine art at the same time, is found in the work of Mr. Charles Chaplin. Since Shaw's death he stands out as the greatest living dramatist, and perhaps the greatest literary artist as well. And it is appalling to think that if he had not had the means and many-sided genius to be his own backer, producer, and director, we would not have a single one of his great post-first-war creations. He would have been diluted and misdirected and vocalized out of existence — as happened to that other comic genius, René Clair, when he went to Hollywood. The counterproof of this, as you might say, is the career of Walt Disney — immortal for his black-and-white animated cartoons and lamentable in his vulgar fairy tales and fantasies in color.

What the movies offered was an image of our characteristic modern and American life, reshaped so as to relieve and refresh us. We could see speed, space, contrast, collision, simultaneity and all other physical elements of our machine world under the eternal aspects of comedy and tragedy. We could take all of nature, in huge slices, as our backdrop. There was no need for French or English drawing-room drama — museum stuff that could not possibly give us the feeling of novelty about the familiar, the sense of proportion about our own existence. Our first comics, from Mack Sennett to Harold Lloyd, did this to perfection, and so did the early Westerns, before everything got (supposedly) sophisticated. By forgetting the motion in moving pictures, we became inured to these indoor affairs in which people are always going up and down stairs and opening and shutting doors to give the illusion that something is happening.

The vaunted foreigners are hardly better. They spoil their thrillers with pretentious "poetic" bits, or they wallow in grimy horrors and self-pity. The movies are and should remain a popular art. It can be as fine as any if it sticks to broad themes instead of going a-whoring after "great literature." I don't want to see the classics on the screen. I can read them at home. *Wuthering Heights* is not for filming — it needs the precise words the author used to create her characters and atmosphere. Leave Brontë alone, and Dickens too, and Shakespeare's tragedies above all.

To be sure, there are other kinds of classics that almost ask to be put in motion for the eye — *The Three Musketeers* for example, or Wagner's operas. Has it been successfully done? *The Three Musketeers*, never. Wagner just once, in the German film *Siegfried*. Again *The Connecticut Yankee in King Arthur's Court* was excellent with Harry Myers, but *The Jumping Frog* was a terrible hash, odiously misrepresented as being Twain's "favorite — only he could write it" whereas most of it was Hollywood padding. Three attempts have been made to give us *The Hound of the Baskervilles* — surely a "natural" for lovers of shivers — all three films stupidly bad. Directors' minds are too lofty for Conan Doyle, they don't see what he is after. And by dint of trying to squeeze intimate "acting" out of the tailors' dummies they employ, they lose the panoramic eye which is the true camera eye. It's lucky that Shaw was able to collaborate in filming his own *Caesar and Cleopatra* or we wouldn't have had any glimpse of Alexandria burning and rioting. What we need in popular art is zest and imagination, not just the pressing of a familiar nerve. This means new, grand, and above all unexpected sights and actions, geared to some plausible cause in the story, so that the effect reverberates in our minds a little. Sensationalism is constantly decried as if it disfigured every movie. It is actually one of the rarest, hardest things to achieve.

One cannot help wondering whether something is wrong when we hear that the American movie audience at its fullest is two-thirds composed of children under eighteen. Not all of us can stay eighteen through life. What goes on, then, in the docile minds and sedate hearts of the adults who do attend the movies regularly, their chief refreshment week by week?

By chance I once talked with a taxi driver on the subject. Or, rather, it was he who, like most New York cabbies, unburdened himself to his captive audience whether I liked it or not. He had picked me up outside the theater where I had been seeing the D'Oyly Carte company in *The Mikado*. We hadn't rounded the corner before he began:

"What's that, *The Mickadoo*, some vaudeville? I never hear it before but I see the pictures of them Jap tumblers."

I said it was a musical play.

"I don't like plays and I don't have no TV yet, so I go to the movies. I like 'em better than plays. My missus don't agree, but I say it's cheaper too."

I admitted that movies were cheaper.

"What I like about the movies is they're real. I mean you see the people and everything like it is. In the theater, now, it's cardboard, you understand, painted and all but you see the doors isn't solid but cloth. And they talk so fast and then forget and turn their backs on you. You have to put your mind on it. They always look too big too, not enough room to move around in, because it's only whatchamacall — scenery. But in the movies now, they build it all exact, like for you and me, a store front like this here, or the whole of Yurrup if they want to. They believe in it out there, Hollywood, I mean, and they get the most beautiful girls and men in the country. They can pay for it, you bet, they sort 'em out.

"There's a word means all this, I can't think of it but you know what I mean, lifel — no, that isn't it, because it's not make-believe but real through and through. The word's on the tip of my tongue. But anyway in them movies there's a lot of high-class apartments with chandeliers nobody'd see nowhere else — and the girls, I tell you, you couldn't fake those, you know, curves — except a few eyelashes now and then, but then they put 'em on right where I live in the Bronx, so they's just as real when they're false, y'understand, but I don't mean falsies — that's out!

"But I was telling you, there was a movie once, I forget the name of it, it don't matter but they give it a prize, I read in the papers, so we went, me and the missus. Anyhow there was this fellow, you didn't expect much, he was a small-town boy, kinda dumb but very likable, y'understand? A big husky guy, too, good-looking and a soft voice. But shy, y'understand. And he got into some mess, I forget what, but he had this girl he didn't know how to talk to, so one day he takes her home, it was raining — hard. So they walk very slowly, they're in love o'course, only he don't tell her, so she don't know, but just waits, very sweet-like, getting soaked o' course, you could see it shiny on her hat. Well, finally they get to her house, a high stoop it was and there he pulls out a paper and starts reading to her in that slow soft voice. A pome, yes! He'd written it! Not that you seen him do it but he reads it off his own handwriting, you can see. It's a good pome — my missus don't think so but it is. And you watch her, I mean the guy's girl and pretty soon you see a tear gl-glistens on her cheek. Or maybe it was rain.

We had an argument about it. But it was wonnerful — Realism, *that's* the word I was looking for!"

Recreation, refreshment, reverberation — I find I have used these words to try to say what it is we want when we knock off work. Reverberation is the opposite of flatness, of something that just is, and then is gone. My friend the taxi driver evidently experienced a slight reverberation from *Mr. Deeds Goes to Town*, but too much of what we do for fun passes into oblivion the minute after. We make the mistake of supposing that if something calls for effort it can't be enjoyment, and so we fall back on the ready-made. Yet there is no pleasure without effort, or at least attention; none, that is, which we can capitalize, carry away and find working some good upon us. From what we hear of our grandparents' time, the theater, the lyceum lecture, the county fair, just because they were rare events long-awaited, yielded a great return in satisfaction. Quality hardly mattered — the appetite, the talk before and after, made the experience full and memorable, made it an experience instead of a time-killer. With us it isn't surfeit alone but inexpectancy which makes entertainment so feeble. It's available in familiar capsules and we swallow it without tasting. We're overdosed and under-entertained.

I understand (because I feel it too) that in the twentieth-century people want to let go, be on the loose ("relax" is the word) and not sit husking corn to a serious discussion of Joseph Jefferson, who came last December in *Our American Cousin*. Some have taken to square dancing again, or to playing chamber music with other amateurs. In doing those things we do not have to like the people we are with, or talk to them intelligently. Fun that lets us daydream in company and not care much about any result — that is what we seem to want. We are all so tired after the last century's orgy of work and since the release from certain Victorian taboos, that there is a violent drive towards irresponsibility. The stiffer the discipline of practical life, the more we need repeated whiffs of nonsense to the nostrils, like smelling salts in a close room. It is no accident that industrial Britain in the last century produced Edward Lear and Lewis Carroll, and that we have made them into great men.

And yet our bad habits trip us up. We wreck our intentions by turning games into drills and sciences. The vogue of quiz programs is a horrifying example of mass pedantry and a perfect instance of what does not reverberate. Nothing flatter than a fact, a lonely, unbefriended fact, rising out of a warehouse mind. The transformation of British whist and good old "five hundred" into bridge is another case in point. Sailing, too, we have spoiled. Once a modest and refreshing sport — on a windy day you can be refreshed to the skin — it calls for the right kind of effort and it reverberates from all the facets of Nature. And it used to be relatively inexpensive. But solemnity in the form of racing got into it, hull designs became more and more "efficient," and now it is impossible to find a good, cheap, seaworthy, one-man sloop or cat. If, on the other hand, you own a boat capable of racing and do not race it, you are a slacker, a scab, a perishing amateur.

Fortunately, thanks to our national cult of the pioneer life and our intelligent uses of state reservations, the woods, the streams, and the mountains are still at our command, free or nearly free, wherever we may live. The paraphernalia for getting the most out of them is also at hand in almost ludicrous profusion — a different rod for every individual fish, sleeping bags in which Rip Van Winkle would never wake. But here again we skirt danger by developing the professional touch. The literature of field sports is a mass of expert technicalities held together with a sticky kind of nature loving. There is a book club devoted exclusively to publications on the manifold branches of this science, and some of its connoisseurs have learned from it how to be and not to be at the same time: they can apparently revel in the emotions of tropical fishing by simply taking out the right subscriptions. At that point, I admit I am no longer sure what true reverberation is. The barracuda certainly reverberates in my ears when I go and visit a particular stay-at-home friend.

Then let us get out of the city. But suppose I have no country house or farm and I do not want to visit friends. Such is the lot of thousands. Well, there is the summer hotel located, precisely, in those mountains, on that lake, by those streams that we have access to. Here surely is America at play, vacationing, seeing the world. It is inspiring and sad, worthy of respect for its friendliness and decorum, but somehow not quite the true haven of rest.

There is the scenery, grandiose or consoling, young as the first day. The expression "as old as the hills" is absurd here — what date has our landscape if people are not there to date it with their clothes? Why, the hotel is visibly much older than the hills — a long three-story wooden structure painted a dirty gray, with rocking chairs on the side porch, and the mail desk almost as you enter. The rooms are clean and spacious and there is a coil of rope under the window by way of fire escape. A sprinkler system was installed ten years ago, but in drought summers it has to be disconnected. The food is plain, solid, and edible, though it doesn't make you kiss your finger tips. The residents are very much like the food, very proper and solid and fundamentally good. They come for two–three weeks or two–three months and most of them come year after year. That is how the routine got clamped down on the place and why it begins molding the newcomer as soon as he has unpacked.

The middle-aged men go off after breakfast and after lunch to the golf club ten miles away or to the fishing pools all over. The women are left to knit, gossip, or write letters in the morning and play bridge in the afternoon. Men and women together play bridge in the evening. That is the woof. The warp consists in the "attractions" of the place, the expeditions. There are five climbs and six walks, but it is virtually impossible (i.e. antisocial) to go on them alone. Arranging the party is obviously the main source of everybody's pleasure. There is a protocol of Chinese intricacy about it. Seniority and specialization decide who chooses the route, the sandwiches, and the order of march. Inevitably somebody makes a *faux pas* and feelings are hurt. At which point, a short stout woman with scant hair the color of shrimps makes it her business to keep the incident alive for the rest of the summer. She is the same who, in the interests of all, communicates in confidence her doubts as to the real occupation of Mr. A and the real age of Mrs. B.

Yet it would be wrong to suppose anyone guilty of intentional meanness. In the face of an accident you would see all these people touchingly affectionate and tactful — as happened the summer a young couple lost their four-year-old boy by drowning. It is plain living, not social graces, that these people have an instinct for; their love of nature bears witness to it. The bird watchers, who are unionized and sternly led, avoid all human broils. They get up at dawn and tread secret paths. (One keeps overhearing the name "Wildwood.") And at some point in the season come "The Alpine Pedestrians," a famous group who travel by car and rail to certain chosen spots which they proceed to conquer, for the record. Their after-dinner report on the number of summer cardinals this year as compared with last obtains the hushed attention that nothing else deserves — not even the discovery of deer tracks leading straight to the kitchen door. On being asked, the misnamed Pedestrians will agree that there are no longer any genuine walks in this country. The highways or the woodpaths — that is the choice, and the aim of the group accordingly is "to explore," in the words of one of them, "every avenue to worthwhile flora and ferna."

To betray a mild indifference to any of these energetic aims is of course to court open reproof. What! No bridge, no golf, no fish, no binocular birding? The feeling for community action is very strong. As you walk into the parlor you will hear one earnest white-haired woman challenge another to take up Canasta — and soon — "or what will you do, dear, when your husband slips away from you?" A taste for solitary strolling seems odd. Perhaps you're unhappy and ought to be "taken out of yourself." From sheer sense of duty some good soul will make a point of drawing you in, and then you must respond — co-operate.

The only group entitled to their separate pursuits are the young.

Hotel society leaves them alone, confident that they are swimming, playing tennis, or courting. In fact there aren't very many young people at hotels, except on the kitchen staff — college boys and girls earning money by waiting on table. They feel and act as your equals if not your superiors, and if they like you, they will rope you into their undertakings, middle-aged though you are. By the end of the first dance of the season, they'll call you by your first name and at Christmas send you a greeting card. It is all very sweet, but as you thread your way through the mixture of codes and cultures, you may be pardoned for wondering where the refreshing influences came in, except through the eyes.

People who care less for gentility manage things better. They don't bother to leave the arid city but spend their surplus there on pastimes they can enjoy without feeling cramped. They follow boxing and wrestling, burlesque and vaudeville (when available), professional football and hockey. Above all, they thrill in unison with their fellow man the country over by watching baseball. The gods decree a heavyweight match only once in a while and a national election only every four years, but there is a World Series with every revolution of the earth around the sun. And in between, what varied pleasure long drawn out!

Whoever wants to know the heart and mind of America had better learn baseball, the rules and realities of the game — and do it by watching first some high school or small-town teams. The big league games are too fast for the beginner and the newspapers don't help. To read them with profit you have to know a language that comes easy only after philosophy has taught you to judge practice. Here is scholarship that takes effort on the part of the outsider, but it is so bred into the native that it never becomes a dreary round of technicalities. The wonderful purging of the passions that we all experienced in the fall of '51, the despair groaned out over the fate of the Dodgers, from whom the league pennant was snatched at the last minute, give us some idea of what Greek tragedy was like. Baseball *is* Greek in being national, heroic, and broken up in the rivalries of city-states. How sad that Europe knows nothing like it! Its Olympics generate anger, not unity, and its interstate politics follow no rules that a people can grasp. At least Americans understand baseball, the true realm of clear ideas.

That baseball fitly expresses the powers of the nation's mind and body is a merit separate from the glory of being the most active, agile, varied, articulate, and brainy of all group games. It is of and for our century. Tennis belongs to the individualistic past — a hero, or at most a pair of friends or lovers, against the world. The idea of baseball is a team, an outfit, a section, a gang, a union, a cell, a commando squad — in short, a twentieth-century setup of opposite numbers.

Baseball takes its mystic nine and scatters them wide. A kind of individualism thereby returns, but it is limited — eternal vigilance is the price of victory. Just because they're far apart, the outfield can't dream or play she-loves-me-not with daisies. The infield is like a steel net held in the hands of the catcher. He is the psychologist and historian for the staff — or else his signals will give the opposition hits. The value of his headpiece is shown by the ironmongery worn to protect it. The pitcher, on the other hand, is the wayward man of genius, whom others will direct. They will expect nothing from him but virtuosity. He is surrounded no doubt by mere talent, unless one excepts that transplanted acrobat, the shortstop. What a brilliant invention is his role despite its exposure to ludicrous lapses! One man to each base, and then the free lance, the trouble shooter, the movable feast for the eyes, whose motion animates the whole foreground.

The rules keep pace with this imaginative creation so rich in allusions to real life. How excellent, for instance, that a foul tip muffed by the catcher gives the batter another chance. It is the recognition of Chance that knows no argument. But on the other hand, how wise and just that the third strike must not be dropped. This points to the fact that near the end of any struggle life asks for more than is needful in order to clinch success. A victory has to be won, not snatched. We find also our American innocence in calling "World Series" the annual games between the winners in each big league. The world doesn't know or care and couldn't compete if it wanted to, but since it's us children having fun, why, the world is our stage. I said baseball was Greek. Is there not a poetic symbol in the new meaning — our meaning — of "Ruth hits Homer"?

Once the crack of the bat has sent the ball skimmiting left of second between the infielder's legs, six men converge or distend their defense to keep the runner from advancing along the prescribed path. The ball is not the center of interest as in those vulgar predatory games like football, basketball, and polo. Man running is the force to be contained. His getting to first or second base starts a capitalization dreadful to think of: every hit pushes him on. Bases full and a homer make four runs, while the defenders, helpless without the magic power of the ball lying over the fence, cry out their anguish and dig up the sod with their spikes.

But fate is controlled by the rules. Opportunity swings from one side to the other because innings alternate quickly, keep up spirit in the players, interest in the beholders. So does the profusion of different acts to be performed — pitching, throwing, catching, batting, running, stealing, sliding, signaling. Blows are similarly varied. Flies, Texas Leaguers, grounders, baseline fouls — praise God the human neck is a universal joint! And there is no set pace. Under the hot sun, the minutes creep as a deliberate pitcher tries his feints and curves for three strikes called, or conversely walks a threatening batter. But the batter is not invariably a tailor's dummy. In a hundredth of a second there may be a hissing rocket down right field, a cloud of dust over first base — the bleachers all a-yell — a double play, and the other side up to bat.

Accuracy and speed, the practiced eye and hefty arm, the mind to take in and readjust to the unexpected, the possession of more than one talent and the willingness to work in harness without special orders — these are the American virtues that shine in baseball.

There has never been a good player who was dumb. Beef and bulk and mere endurance count for little, judgment and daring for much. Baseball is among group games played with a ball what fencing is to games of combat. But being spread out, baseball has something sociable and friendly about it that I especially love. It is graphic and choreographic. The ball is not shuttling in a confined space, as in tennis. Nor does baseball go to the other extreme of solitary whanging and counting stopped on the brink of pointlessness, like golf. Baseball is a kind of collective chess with arms and legs in full play under sunlight.

How adaptable, too! Three kids in a back yard are enough to create the same quality of drama. All of us in our tennis days have pounded balls with a racket against a wall, for practice. But that is nothing compared with batting in an empty lot, or catching at twilight, with a fella who'll let you use his mitt when your palms get too raw. Every part of baseball equipment is inherently attractive and of a most enchanting functionalism. A man cannot have too much leather about him; and a catcher's mitt is just the right amount for one hand. It's too bad the chest protector and shinpads are so hot and at a distance so like corrugated cardboard. Otherwise, the team is elegance itself in its striped knee breeches and loose shirts, colored stockings and peaked caps. Except for brief moments of sliding, you can see them all in one eyeful, unlike the muddy hecatombs of football. To watch a football game is to be in prolonged neurotic doubt as to what you're seeing. It's more like an emergency happening at a distance than a game. I don't wonder the spectators take to drink. Who has ever seen a baseball fan drinking within the meaning of the act? He wants all his senses sharp and clear, his eyesight above all. He gulps down soda pop, which is a harmless way of replenishing his energy by the ingestion of sugar diluted in water and colored pink.

Happy the man in the bleachers. He is enjoying the spectacle that the gods on Olympus contrived only with difficulty when they sent Helen to Troy and picked their teams. And the gods missed the fun of doing this by catching a bat near the narrow end and measuring hand over hand for first pick. In Troy, New York, the game scheduled for 2 P.M. will break no bones, yet it will be a real fight between Southpaw Dick and Red Larsen. For those whom civilized play doesn't fully satisfy, there will be provided a scapegoat in a blue suit — the umpire, yell-proof and even-handed as justice, which he demonstrates with outstretched arms when calling "Safe!"

And the next day in the paper: learned comment, statistical summaries, and the verbal imagery of meta-euphoric experts. In the face of so much joy, one can only ask, Were you there when Dog-face Joe parked the pellet beyond the pale?

An American had been saying this, or some of it, once, to a British friend, on whose responsive face he saw signs of distress that made him stop. The American respected his friend's judgment and mistrusted his own headlong flights.

"Baseball," said the Englishman, "is an excellent game, no doubt. I can hear that smack of 'the pellet' in my palm, and almost feel it too. But aren't you a little unfair in taking all the credit for the game and calling it American? Shouldn't you mention the fact that baseball comes straight out of cricket, which is a wholly English game?"

"I'd mention it," replied the American after a moment of deliberation, "if it weren't for one thing — the fatal flaw in cricket, which, to my mind, puts it right out of consideration."

"What is that?"

"Simply the fact that no one understands it, I mean knows what it is."

"You mean no one in the United States?"

"No, no. I mean no one at all, anywhere. Just between you and me, I don't think cricket has ever been played."

"What *are* you talking about?"

"It's my belief that at some time in the past an Englishman may have had the idea of a game to be played with bats and balls. He started to explain it — as many Englishmen have done to their American friends — but he couldn't go on. It was too complicated. What saved him and his idea was that he was talking to fellow Englishmen. They hate theory anyway, so they went ahead and got bats and balls — of sorts — and to oblige their friend, they stood around with them, running here and there very quietly from time to time, making believe they were playing the game. That's how the tradition started."

"What tradition? I'm lost!"

"The tradition that cricket is the national game and that every Englishman loves it. In a sense he does love it. 'Playing the game' means he wouldn't do a thing to dispel the general impression that there *is* such a thing — it's an exact parallel to what they call the British Constitution."

"You're pulling my leg. There *is* such a game."

"I assure you there isn't. You'll admit, surely, a thing that everybody knows, namely, that Englishmen don't know when they're beaten? Well, that follows logically from the fact that Englishmen don't know when they're playing. Name me another game than cricket which you don't know you're playing when you are?"

"You're juggling with words!"

"And you're blinding yourself to the evidence. Is it likely that people capable of inventing a game would make it consist of such objects as sticky wickets, creases, fast bowlers, overs, and centuries? One of their terms gives the show away: every so often they have a *Test Match* — it's to find out whether the game is possible or not."

"What do you suppose happens then?"

"After a few days on the field, the excitement dies down. The issue remains in doubt. Meantime — and this is conclusive — every British subject has a perfect right to say to any other: 'This isn't cricket.' How do you reconcile that with a set of rules for an actual game?"

"B-b-but, you can't be serious. I can make allowances for the fact that you've never seen a cricket match but you must have read about the game in *Punch*. If you can't follow the sense of it, there must be some reliable source — "

"Would the *Encyclopaedia Britannica* do?"

"Certainly."

"Well then. Get hold of the last British or fourteenth edition and look up cricket. What do you find? The history of the local clubs. Names of great figures. Older and modern style — style, mind you! Not a single word about the rules or who does what. No diagram, even — in an encyclopedia too. But no wonder — it's as I told you. The best you can hope for is that by watching our G.I.'s play baseball, some of your brighter fellows will find a way to make cricket come out. Compared to a real game it's in the chrysalis state."

If I like the ballet quality and speed of baseball, I should also like the circus. Am I not an American, whose early memories of the oncoming of summer include the arrival of Ringling Brothers to town? The trouble is — and this differs from ordinary likes and dislikes — I have never become reconciled to the circus. It spells to me the dark side of life. Whereas baseball shows me man moving freely and adroitly, the circus shows me man enslaved — like the other animals. I see freaks, real or contrived. I gape at the clown's contortions; I laugh hysterically at his perpetual catastrophes. But I don't really know why I must laugh at his disfigurement. Isn't it also my own? Am I to be put on good terms with myself by pretending that his antics have sopped up all the misfortune, clumsiness, and disproportion there is? No: on all this I agree completely with Huckleberry Finn who said: "It warn't funny to me, though."

Besides, the smell of bread earned under duress clings to every element of the circus. I love trapeze work and feats of horsemanship, but under the tent they fill me with despair. I want to cry when I hear "Alley oop!" and see the tinselly tights and the challenging smiles. The master of ceremonies seems to enjoy himself, but I have a nervous feeling he's going to be arrested as a bogus duke. And isn't it here, in the barker's lies, that advertising fraud and false promises have their ancestral source? The pickpockets inside merely carry out the theme.

I also feel it in my bones that the animals come straight from the Coliseum at Rome — who would have thought of them as a show except by the old association of wild beasts with Christians? But now the poor brutes haven't the consolation of eating us. I am no great lover of animals, but I don't want elephants to travel in box cars on torrid days, and I cheer for the one who broke away the other summer and lay down for twenty minutes in a busy square. Nothing could budge him, and I wish his name had been Gulliver, to re-enact the proof of his contempt for us Lilliputians. So don't take me to the circus: I'm liable to do myself in with an overdose of Cracker Jack. . . .

Long, long ago, in the days before talkies and TV, there flourished a noble refinement on all the decent pleasures of the circus — I mean vaudeville. I see, by the way, that it is dying out in England too, and that Shakespeare's native town has appropriated two hundred pounds a week to finance its coming back in competition with the bard's Memorial Theatre. A woman councillor of the town explained why: "A lot of people simply get tired of living with Shakespeare's spirit day and night." Shakespeare himself found it hard to bear, judging from his gloomy passages. In work as in play, the human spirit asks for variety, and variety is the essence of vaudeville. It too can be full of reverberations. I shall never forget three beautiful damsels in green evening dresses who played the trombone in parts, with perfect intonation and musicianship. Singers, magicians, acrobats, mind readers, sword swallowers, tap dancers, and comedians in the great tradition thrived on the applause of really devoted audiences. There were dog acts — but only one to a show, for those who have to say the word "cute" a certain number of times a week. An habitué would go back especially for

Thurston, Houdini, Mulholland, or in a strange town take a chance
on a program that could not be all bad. As the man in front of me
said to his companion, "When you can get all of this for two bits,
why go to a theater and be in agony?"

The successor to vaudeville, I am informed by my lawyer friends,
is burlesque. They must mean successor to the audience, which has
been deprived of variety shows and is unwilling to spend five dollars on elaborate drivel like . . . choose your own example of an
overpriced and overpraised musical. I have nothing against drivel —
only against elaborateness and expense — and I always believe what
my legal advisers say. So they are probably right about burlesque
because they seem to be particularly fond of it. I confess I think
it dreary, on three counts: it is repetitious, it is weak in all-around
talent, and it relies on the appeal, either senile or infantile, of the
strip-tease system. Though the name suggests medieval agriculture,
the act is said to be America's only original contribution to the
theater. Too bad for America, and especially (as I think) for Americans. It is no moral disapproval I am expressing, but regret that
so many of my fellow citizens' search for voluptuous sensation
translates itself simply into eyestrain. Apparently they do not mind
the shrill or whisky voices and the "scratch" orchestra, but I do,
and to suffer through the eardrums as well as to be bored is not
my idea of entertainment.

The apologists of burlesque will say I miss the point. They maintain that in a world of rigid conventions and depersonalized contacts, it's soothing and sound to be reminded of the fundamental
realities of life. These are presumably expressed in the verbal exchanges and eloquent gestures that pass between the sailor and the
girls in the chorus line — all on the one subject to which every
phrase in the language refers if you're minded to have it so. This
is "realism" in another sense than my taxi driver's. On top of this
solid foundation, I am told, burlesque supplies "art" — the various
tricks and styles (with technical names) by which a good-looking
girl takes off her clothes. It's a democratic way, supposedly, to give

the common man the illusion of being personally favored by a beautiful woman — the redistribution of pulchritude. And it is plausibly argued that the cabaret shows of every price and social pretension thrive on the same simple commodity.

The rejoinder would be that burlesque specializes a little too obviously, and that the confusion of art, democracy, love, beauty, and theater is a bit hard to swallow. It is very likely that no woman is ever as beautiful as an *actress*, even when the woman and the actress are the same person. So burlesque intensifies one of the real dangers of all theatrical shows — viewer's pleasure. And that, in turn, seems to me the very opposite of reality and the fundamentals that my legal friends think they find. In fact, I would guess that the taste for burlesque reflects a general neurosis, a special affliction of modern life having to do with sex and sight, to which I'll return.

Remains the demand of the under-entertained for personality and mind. A pathetic demand struggling against the tendency of mass media toward techniques and substitutes. The great personalities of the stage — where are they? Stars are made to specifications in Hollywood, with different hair, teeth, nose, and name — the true plastic art of the twentieth century. Whether "vibrant, magnetic" personality results — or survives — is another question.

As for mind, it is much sought in that old and favorite pastime of Americans — the lecture. Since true platform magnetism is rare — even politicians are not the spellbinders they used to be — we have to accept, here too, the conventional substitutes: the man who was there when it happened, the housewife who swam the Channel, the visiting fireman or acquitted murderess. We are the greatest lecture-gobblers in the world, and this without harm, because we have intuitively found out that a large dose is better than a small one. Always attend a series of lectures. One neutralizes the other and all are eliminated together. The only care to be observed is to alternate between acid and alkaline subjects — world affairs (very acid), art and literature (practically pure bicarb).

But the supply always threatens to run short. How can it keep pace when nearly every organized group regardless of purpose, every school board and museum and club, decides that in addition to publishing a bulletin it must hold lectures? The reason is, there must be something to show for the $6.50 annual dues. I have before me a solicitation to join which says: "Magazine and lectures for life — One hundred dollars." For life, mind you — a sentence I for one would want commuted to capital punishment.

If Americans get thoroughly lectured, it is because so many of us write books. This is no paradox. The physician who from a sense of public duty writes *The Doctor Looks You Over* and sees it turn into a best seller, finds that he is swamped with invitations to lecture. People want to see what he looks like, how he talks, and whether his opinions are the same as those of the author of the book. Drama critics, novelists, political writers, and latterly poets are in great demand to feed a curiosity that is by no means contemptible and far from uninformed. It is encouraging, for behind it, surely, is the laudable desire to persuade ourselves that the books being talked of, the ideas in the air, have come out of human heads, preferably distinct and attractive ones, and not some machine made up of sad lads with a technique.

9. Are You a Globe Sister?

IT IS A LIFELONG BURDEN once you start, like getting into the clutches of a blackmailer. But nowadays it seems the inevitable lot of a great many people in this country — business and professional men and women — provided they have an assured position and a kindly temper. The name I give this time-consuming (often time-wasting) occupation has of course no currency outside my own thoughts; or rather, it has a local currency, which is this: one of our prosperous Eastern newspapers has a department to which anyone can write who wants advice, not merely on love — the whole gamut. He or she is assigned a "sister" who will comfort and succor and advise, without duties or obligations, of course. The newspaper acts as go-between in a relation increasingly characteristic of our time. How its clients thrive, I do not know — and I hardly care; my own sisterly hands are full and I can only take a little time off from my global duties to say something of what they involve, what they come from and lead to.

The root of the business is plain enough. It springs from our democratic attitude toward our neighbor. Being another human being, he needs no special claim, though he may need a letter — a dozen letters — of introduction. If he thinks I can help, why, his need establishes my duty right then and there. The reason I come to shoulder these and the ensuing responsibilities is also clear. I meet, besides the students explicitly entrusted to me, hundreds of other people whose earlier life or occupation has not the remotest connection with mine. They drift out of some inexhaustible reservoir, and here they are, here I am, listening to them. Ordinary civility is to them sufficient encouragement. It gives me no pleasure to hear of their affairs or to play the counsellor, the conversational Globe Sister.

In the beginning I wondered why so many otherwise intelligent, educated people required my indefinite and unpaid services. Why did they think my aid decisive in their own plans? They seemed to have survived independently enough for thirty, forty, fifty years and now suddenly I was that hypothetical creature, the indispensable man. What I gradually learned from experience was that all but a few of the people were addicts — Advisees Anonymous — who had already exhausted dozens of friendly counsellors about earlier projects. For they belong to the projector type that understands only the first phase of any enterprise — projecting.

Why they fail to carry out is partly their fault, partly that of society as we find it in contemporary America; or to speak more exactly, the failure comes from the invisible conflict between two sets of ideas and feelings that do not mesh. Our social organisms are complex and subtle; they call for qualities in the individual that cannot be laid down in advance but have to be improvised at the right time — tact and aggressiveness, attention and indifference, sensitiveness and a thick skin — at various times all of these, but each at the right time and in the right dose.

In addition, one must have knowledge of practical arrangements to succeed: who has charge of what, and how things actually happen. As to this part of "the ropes," our multitudinous institutions and establishments are becoming ever more intricate, and it is no wonder that the high schools have begun to give courses in subjects we may laugh at — how to choose a dentist, where and how to shop on a given budget — courses that take the time formerly devoted to Shakespeare and the Constitution, but which are undeniably needed in some form at some point: living in our society is simply not something that comes by the light of nature; it is a technical subject, and the ever-enlarging number of techniques, whether real or empty, demands what the Navy quaintly calls "indoctrination."

Some of this is provided by the press – how to cook, shop, bring up your child, and strike a balanced diet. The newspaper (like much of our popular fiction) goes into the finer particulars of courting, interviewing employers, and reducing family dissension. But this leaves uncared for what might be called the art of conducting one's career, and that is the point where my colleagues in all professions as well as in the executive branch of business meet the great army of the rudderless.

One reason why these are disabled is that they possess ability along a single track. Whatever their project, they think of nothing else; but discovering little by little that this brings them nothing but discomfiture and disappointment, they look for the nearest support and to it they cling. That is why there is no relief, no holiday from the involvement of being a Globe Sister. Clinger and clung form an unbreakable union, closer to the once-for-all theory of marriage than any marriage ever was. For what the clinger wants is at one and the same time security and a scapegoat, a secret and a grievance, a father and an enemy. This may suggest something abnormal that a psychiatrist should look into, but the trouble I speak of is too usual, too normal to attract the notice of science or make the victim submit to treatment. The situation is, statistically, a familiar one. In good times, our country has two million unemployed, a large part of them unemployable. Now among the sixty million holding down jobs, a larger number than we think are equally unemployable, virtually useless. They are the people who make all the mistakes and get the whole office embroiled. They do not stay long in one place – "not the job I really want." They go from firm to firm, keeping thousands of us busy interviewing them and filing their credentials.

That is one set of potential barnacles. Another is the annual crop of youngsters. They are a touching lot, well-meaning and incredibly ignorant of the nature of institutional life. Not that they are ill-trained or empty-headed or lacking in self-confidence. They have done things and know it; they have developed a knack in some direction — outdoor camping or building radios or driving a truck. But they have also acquired or made up breathtaking ideas about the world. Hearing over the years that youth has its rights, they put you at your ease and give you the coolest exhibitions of individual-collective bargaining you ever saw. The undersized youth of seventeen who might run errands asks what his pension rights will be. When does he expect to retire? "As of the year 2000."

Silly and bumptious as it is, this attitude is on the whole preferable to that which prevailed forty years ago. My friend Giuseppe has told me several times (and no wonder it still galls him) that when he started out, the youngest in a big barbershop in Bridgeport, his hours were seven in the morning to ten at night five days a week. On Saturdays, seven to midnight — except that midnight only meant the doors were locked. There would still be a dozen customers inside waiting to be shaved, and he would get home about 2 A.M. Since he would sleep most of Sunday, his priest scolded him for not going to mass, and when the boy said he was just too tired all the time, he got the reply: "Five hours' sleep is enough for any workingman."

Yes, we have come a long way in a short time, but as regards work we are as yet in a betwixt-and-between state of mind. Business is still business, but outside unionized mass employment we are no longer sure what to do and say as employer and employee. Which calls the tune? Who is indebted to whom? The old harsh rules are gone, and because they were harsh any new ones are frowned on as likely to be "rigid." At the same time our personnel testing is itself rigid, and crude with all the crude trimmings of fake science. Meantime the working population grows in number. The American wants to work, regardless of sex or social position or need. The young pour out of high school and college, eager for a place. The older people live on and on and resent premature shelving, while everybody's claims on life grow stronger and more complex.

The result is that the notions of what is possible or probable tend to get lost in a haze of hope and energy. Once a month at least I have a call from some personable young woman, recommended by someone I know as socially and morally above reproach. All she wants is to be my "girl Friday" at a hundred and twenty-five dollars a week. The phrase is expressive and quite innocent — she imagines herself the ideal assistant to a busy man, and banks on the chance of marrying one of his unattached colleagues. Meanwhile she might take courses and work for an M.A. leading to government work. Far, far from her mind any thought of drudgery. But after all — no, she's "never tried office work," and she's "not *too* fast" at typing and shorthand, and she confesses to an "emotional block" when it comes to filing — "the alphabet, as a child . . . you know how it is." But she simply *loves* books and everything to do with them — the alphabet excepted.

This fantasy is easy to deal with because the applicant is not friendless or in desperate need. But any more pressing case, where real talent or friendship or simply the Good Samaritan impulse is concerned, leads directly to the fathering and sistering I describe and deplore. There are, for example, the refugees of all vintages, nationalities, and professions, who are unquestionably entitled to special care — but how much, if they are ever to become self-sufficient? And on what terms of give-and-take if they are not to develop exaggerated ideas of their worth?

Then there are the women of middle age or nearly, who for one reason or another want to work. They are widowed or divorced or they married young and their children are off their hands. What can they do? Where did they go to college? No degree? Then the first step to a good job is to get one. Four years of night courses somewhere with undergraduates, learning (among other things) the binomial theorem and the pronunciation of Chaucer's English. It doesn't strike one as very sensible, yet one hesitates to discourage the willing or to denounce the academic rules. The personnel managers do insist on formal certificates even when they are offered the equivalent in education and experience. So our ambitious (or restless) lady goes to school: MOTHER OF THREE SEEKS HER A.B.

In the public mind, that huge distorting mirror, all the pieces of hundreds of individual stories like these combine in a fantastic picture. The abilities and experience called for, the personal interest taken or not taken, what Maisie thought because her uncle said, and then what *really* happened — come together and create, even in the well-adjusted native American, something like the refugee feeling. There simply has to be a mysterious secret to getting on — or why don't I get on? You mustn't go to that Business School, go to this. Then you have to take the most awful tests (that is all too true) but don't let 'em throw you. It's the bunk — just know the ropes (first *contactate* someone on the inside) and of course, you've got to have pull. You see the right guy and you throw him the right line, then you're all set. You get the job and it turns out exactly as you've always wanted — you're now like the people whose pull you used. You work, of course, nobody expects a sinecure, but you work like your idea of an Old Master in his atelier — creeyatively. All day long it is *exciting;* every evening as you think it over, you find it *rewarding.*

For the disabled talents I spoke of earlier, reality takes quite a while disposing of that dream; and when it does, globe-sistering begins. The person first approached with a letter of recommendation, and who out of kindness or duty gave advice, is revisited. If he listens with an unreproving eye, he gets the whole story. This intimacy turns him into a sponsor; the bewildered job-seeker becomes a protégé. There is a hint of reproach in telling the sponsor that his first suggestions did not produce the desired result; there is a touch of apology and placating of the protégé in the sponsor's willingness to try again. If he is wise, he will probe into the circumstances of the first failure and urge a change of attitude. This is heard but not heeded. The second and third tries are as useless as the first. At that point the sponsor gives up polite understatement and puts the blame where it belongs. He elaborates and gives instances. It is comical when the office boy calculates his pension, but it is no joke when the mature applicant summons the world to use his talents. He must be more attentive and adaptable, show his usefulness. And this, dear Globe Sisters all, is the critical moment when the relation may happily for you be terminated. The protégé turns on you for giving him shameful worldly advice, for trying to make him into a bootlicker, a yes-man, a prostitute. His ultimatum is: "If this is the way to succeed in this poisonous world, well then, may I be forever a failure!" This victory over crass commercialism, as one can tell from facial expression, is more satisfying than any actual success.

Get up at this point, and if you can put on an air of wounded dignity, saying in a muted cello voice that obviously no further good would be served by prolonging the interview, you're safe. But it so happens that you are not a stuffed shirt and you cannot say it. Whereupon, accordingly and deservedly, you have octopus number ten (or twenty-five) around your neck for life. Your conscience bothers you both ways. There is just enough truth in the image of our business world as a mass of rules, ropes, and pulls to confirm the outsider's angry suspicion; and there is just enough truth in his desire to be honest and pure to make all your explanations sound fraudulent and so nullify the good of your advice. Sooner or later every globe sister has to take the veil.

Perhaps I may be allowed to recount an actual case, that of Dmitri Stroghine, a Russian refugee from the first emigration of 1918. When I first met him in the forties, he seemed a thoroughly acclimated American. He was an engineer who had escaped with just enough to live on. Now that prices were rising with the war boom he had the legitimate ambition of adding to his income by joining a manufacturing firm in his own field. I don't remember who sent him to me, but it was because I knew George and others in the radio business. Stroghine spoke English fluently if not well, and he began by praising Lincoln-Vocal to the skies. I pointed out that I knew the man at the head but next to nothing about the works. He then switched to praising himself and finally left some papers he had written but not published. I showed them to the head of research department, a very quiet, excessively judicious fellow, who said they were full of brilliant notions mingled with heavy irony and irrelevant skirmishing. Still he'd be glad to meet Stroghine.

I never found out exactly what happened but they didn't hit it off. Knowing him as I do now, I guess Stroghine did not hesitate to tell the research man how to reorganize his department. Dmitri would feel surprised that this should not endear him to his prospective employer — especially if the other said nothing in reply. On another occasion, I tried to explain our American courtesies — in vain: "Thann I say he is not scientist or true Amerrrican. Scientists we take the truth wherever we find her, and Amerr-ricans we form a Team. Because he has a job and I have not yet, am I a fool? In five minutes I could see he should — "

Useless as it was, I kept at it for some four years, coaching, making phone calls, writing endless letters of introduction, trying to get those articles published. Any kind of conformity — such as reducing a paper to less than the length of a whole issue of *Electronics* — would bring forth lectures on the turpitude of publishers and the jealousy of editors, which together were ruining American science at the expense of "the man of knowledge." He undoubtedly was a man of knowledge, and he could have been very valuable to the country, but no one ever found the secret of taming him.

In the end, I made up my mind that what he really wanted was to fail. He needed a grievance to nurse, in close connection with his hobby, and also a relation of child-and-colleague with someone, so as to feel that the hobby was serious. He was in fact older than I and traded on it to command my attention at all times. If I left town without notice or my secretary put him off, I got a suave rebuke. "Where can I reach you?" came at the close of every meeting. Like all the disoriented, he wanted to be listened to, play partners, bounce every fresh fancy or project off my skull and — as I found out — give himself airs in talking to others: "Sorry, I have appointment with a very high Director."

Poor Dmitri was incurable and I was lucky to escape without fracas. By chance, someone asked George whether he had somebody who could do a small job of assessing machinery. George told me that it fitted Stroghine's abilities and might lead to something more. Dmitri took the job and made the inventory. Next he withdrew from circulation and dropped me a couple of postcards saying how hectically he was working on his report and how instantly I must be at hand to look over the first draft. Then . . . nothing. More than two years have passed and no one has heard another word, though I know indirectly he's still alive. I've crossed off one octopus from the list, but there are times when like the hero in *The Toilers of the Sea* I still dream about those tentacles.

As long as I felt the weight of this particular incubus, I was inclined to see in him all the causes of his own failure, but with the passage of time I have come to see other true causes outside the man himself, though without changing my conclusion about his hopelessness. It is not for his sake that we might profitably change our employing habits, but for the sake of less hardened cases and especially for the sake of the young, whom we bewilder and turn into cynics.

For one thing, we do not show enough definiteness in word and act during the preliminaries of employment. Making people feel good then by the use of fair words is the quickest way to make them feel extremely bad and have them turn sour and vicious, regardless of outcome. We make this mistake, often, because so-called personnel work attracts men and women of the smooth-arrogant type, not managerial so much as imperialistic and full of pseudo-science: they have the blanks, the tests, the scores — no secret in man or the universe is hidden from them. And with all this, in proportion to all this, they lack judgment.

I do not speak of industrial employment, of which I know nothing, but in every other, white-collar kind, our present ways are characterized by two serious errors that recur in various forms throughout our devices for choosing people, whether the aim is to hire a comparison shopper for a department store or admit an applicant to college or medical school. The first error is to fish for lofty motives. This is worse than unwise, it is immoral. "Why do you want to work for us?" The young and inexperienced will say: "I heard the name and it sounded all right." Those who "know the ropes" say: "No firm has a better reputation in its chosen field." "Chosen field" is sure-fire. Very few come out with the truth: "I need money and want a job I can do" — the only decent answer to an indecent question.

In applications for medical or other schooling, the same kind of flattery is asked for and duly received. Some of my colleagues argue that you can tell character from such answers. That is absurd. It implies that each statement must be "interpreted" as being either sincere or hypocritical, so that the beginner who has had the bad luck to be tipped off in any way writes himself down as smooth or blunt when he is neither — being in fact only an anxious and confused neophyte. No need to coddle him, but why make his introduction to his job or career a request for perjury?

To a culture in which work is not disgrace but fulfillment, the most important business is that of employing as many people as possible in ways that satisfy their desire to be useful. In that business the recourse to lying — or perhaps one should say the abuse of lying — is very dangerous. It undermines the very thing that is being attempted, which is institutional harmony and unity. The young have been brought up, for the most part, on the merit system, which goes with truthful reports of success and failure. In dealing with the employable it is therefore better to say "No, we haven't a job. No, you would never do in that position. No, don't bother to come again." Those words can be said with kindness, coupled with a warning that half of what they will hear elsewhere is blarney.

One must add that this special branch of business lying is our second great error — the counterpart of the desire for paragons. Having abandoned the ways of Simon Legree and taken to "co-operation," we are as demanding in office mates as in marriage. And despite Form 51 and all the tests devised *in camera*, most employers hesitate to try people without experience. Everybody wants only first-rate people with new ideas and superhuman energy. In fact, paragons are less than adequate; they must also be seers, who will know even before stepping into the office where everything is and how our arrangements work — our arrangements are so impossible to explain! Failing paragons, we take high-class apple-polishers. Remember the survey in *Fortune* about the qualities required in rising young executives? Besides driving a make of car that was fashionable but not pretentious, success lay in the wives. They must look like models, be virtuous, full of small talk, and keenly interested in opera. . . . Discount relevancy hereafter, but — what has become of American practicality?

When it leaks out that such-and-such a post is vacant, those in charge of filling it begin to get letters from friends and strangers about bankers who are at liberty, clergymen without a cure, and disaffected chimneysweeps; their friends make a point at lunch or cocktails of pushing — "selling" — their candidates. This is fair enough, or better than fair. The country will remain what it purports to be, a land of opportunity, if it fills good jobs by actually searching for the best man instead of the nearest relative of the top shareholder. But to read all the letters of recommendation one would think they were all about the same demigod — his looks, his mixability, his raconterie, his level head (level with what — the footstool?), his long experience, and finally his wife, "gracious and beloved of everyone who knows her."

I confess that when it is my turn to write letters of recommendation, what I know of current practice gives me pause. The only people left who tell the truth and are not shattered by it are the oldest generation of working people. A janitor will write about his grandson: "John's a good boy but not what you'd call wide awake yet," and never suppose this will do the boy harm: he trusts to the reader's reasonable knowledge of human life. But in writing to executives instead of to simple honest folk, one's impulse to describe things as they are lands one in paradox. A true description of a man, faults and all, will make him appear worthless by comparison: the truthful letter conveys an untruth.

And paradox carried too far in practice leads to insanity. One morning shortly before noon my sister called me. Her voice was strangled and shaking. "I had to talk to you: I'm so mad I don't know what to do. Dick's out of town and I'm afraid if I don't let off steam I'll be horrid and cross to the children all through lunch."

"Yes, dear, what is it?"

"You remember you said Margie Dow could use your name and get an interview for a job in that demonstration — you know, the exhibit. Yes, well, she filled out the thingamajig — all very pleasant and nice — and she was supposed to go back this morning . . . I'm sorry, I didn't even ask you if you're busy or have someone with you?"

"Nobody. Go ahead; what did they do to little Margie?"

"She came home in tears, poor thing, and then rang me — "

"Yes, but what is it? Did somebody wink at her? Is she going to sue?"

"Don't be silly. She's very mature though she's never worked before. Well, she got there and saw the same woman who had interviewed her. She told Margie very effusively that they were impressed with her qualifications. That seemed a little odd, and Margie also noticed two other women with her in this inner office, but she paid no attention, of course. Then in the middle of something Margie said the woman behind the desk yawned and leaned back in her chair, staring at her with an entirely blank expression. Margie's not one to run on, so she stopped and waited a few seconds to see if the other would — would come to. When she didn't, Margie got up, she was quite flustered by now, and stammered a bit and started to walk out.

"But the woman snapped her chair forward, slapped her hand down on the desk and shouted 'Sit down!' Poor Margie was hypnotized. Then the woman began to abuse her in a cold deadly voice. 'You think because you know somebody you can come around here and get a job just on your looks . . .' And more on that order for a couple of minutes. Margie was gaping but the other woman didn't give her a chance. 'Cheer up, girlie,' she said suddenly, 'and talk to me some more.' Margie thought the woman had gone out of her mind and she'd better not provoke her, but the woman just fiddled at her desk, making little meaningless remarks, and looking at Margie with a sort of leering 'I know all about you' expression. By then it was Margie who was mad. She'd caught on because of the two women. They were taking notes. But before she could open her mouth the Lady Inquisitor got up and shook hands very politely and said they would let her know *how she'd done*."

I was curious enough to follow up the incident, which was not difficult since I knew the director of the museum and he proved as taken aback as I. His place is so large and diversified that he had no idea what they were doing in the Science and Industry division. A phone call, and I was shaking hands with the head of that branch, who understood that I was interested in Personnel Methods. He said he would take me to Miss Carson and let her tell me about it. The Science branch had special funds, he said, with which they were able to experiment. He did not elaborate.

Soon I was face-to-face with a stunning double-glazed and triple-baked article, sporting a streak of hair bleached white, and who walked like a Dresden figurine on a clockwork conversation piece. But the china effect was deceptive. She seemed guaranteed not to crack and the blue eye was not paint but sadism. Her affability was great. In answer to my general question she said she always gave a battery of tests — not a couple or several, but a battery. Miss Carson never used any other expression. She had been wound up that way. I then asked about the particular test that had started my inquiry.

"Why, I thought everybody knew about the Hackle-Riser Personality Test! It's been used in leading department stores, hospitals, showrooms and public relations agencies. A point-six correlation, I think. Being scientifically trained myself, I naturally follow all the latest tools. When I knew we'd need these people for the Exhibit, I got Dr. Hackle to send me two of his best note-takers. They have to be trained, you know, and learn to be inconspicuous to preserve the control conditions."

"Would I be allowed to see those notes and how you score?"

She went to a filing cabinet, brought back an armful of folders, and pushed her chair around so as to sit practically in my lap. I had spotted her before as the vestal-in-your-bed type of business girl and I put a little cool air between us. She smiled. "You see," she said, "we reproduce the actual conditions of contact. . . ."

"I see."

"There are four of them — Indifference, Hostility, Needling, and Excess Lubrication. . . .

"What I do at the beginning. . . I'm *too* pleasant, which means nothing at all. For a desirable contact between operator and customer, something closer and more real is needed, what we call Operative Grip. I'm sorry to say it, but the young lady you sent us the other day will never develop operative grip. She has many charming qualities, but no technique and apparently no notion of her dearth. She will never become a Resource Person. But I was telling you about our procedure. The test-application of each contact condition lasts four minutes. My assistants have stop watches and they compute the readjustment performance of the prospective Operator, noting down what he or she says (the Content-theme) as well as the Quality-quantum of saying it. At the end they put down a tentative score, but of course I go over each one. I have the objective score chart prepared by Dr. Riser from ten thousand actual answers, checked against the operators' later careers, measured in working-week percentage of sales, and corrected for the national average in co-operation with — "

She stopped, suspecting that from here on every detail was an anticlimax. She was anything but stupid, or she would not have had the job of — I read it on the card she gave me — Personnel Psychology Cogitationist.

What we hire and fire on the strength of this paper work is the nonexistent robot of our evil dreams. Meanwhile the paper work and the verbalism — Technique and Excessive Lubrication — foment the anarchical emotions. There is a touch of Stroghine in every man alive, and he was right to say, on seeing Form 51: "I am engineer, not genealogist-cum-prisoner at the bar." We shall never get good work, peace within the shop and within each breast, by combining the rack and thumbscrew with the application of external salve. When with the aid of some kind of Cogitationist the Navy discovered the presence of Floating Animosity in the ranks, all attempts to cure it by peptalks and synthetic bonhomie failed and deserved to fail. To cure a grievance something must change — physical facts if possible; if not, then states of mind, actual ones, and on both sides. There is such a thing as being lazy in our thoughts, and the more tests we use the less exercise our judgment gets. We babble about not making subjective estimates but our opinions of people are as hard as rock. We will do anything rather than revise them or act responsibly on them. We seize the excuse of every Stroghine to account for our failures with those who only resemble him superficially. In the spate of words that accompanies our institutional acts we forget the great African tale about the Timburu frogs. All you have to do to keep them quiet is to shout: "Silence, frogs!" Only, you must address them in their own language.

10. "Say, Bud!" ... "Hiya, Baby!"

THE THING ABOUT THE U.S. "which nobody can deny" is not that we are jolly good fellows. Half the world hates us, at sight or on principle. But nobody can deny that we have the best table manners of any people. The abolition of the toothpick, the injunction against using the napkin as buckler or towel, the rediscovery of the right side of the fork (while the English continue to pile up the curved side of theirs with mouthfuls of balanced diet) are worthy of all praise.

We go too far, quite often, we fall into the genteel and curl the little finger, or subdue chewing to lip motions that make a woman look as if she were expecting a kiss. With care and a fork, surely, one should be able to imitate the French mopping-up operations and not let good sauce or gravy go to waste. But the American principle is sound: not to make others disgusted at the sight of their fellow man. It is all the more important in a democracy where one has to endure close and continual contact with everybody else. The marvel of our collective training may be seen in any restaurant or dining car. Regardless of differences of income, speech, and occupation, those one looks at are eating in a civilized manner. The exception is so rare as to be memorable.

But the table is only one of the places of public resort, and talk forms a larger part of our impact on one another than eating in common. Of our spoken manners, the European would say that we have none. By his standards, we are rude or uncouth when we are not downright impudent. Americans who have lived even a short time abroad notice this on their return — as did the young lady who wrote to the papers of her experience at the airport. She somehow got separated from her husband and, looking bewildered, was asked by an attendant what the matter was. She said "I've lost my husband." To which his rejoinder was: "Don't worry, baby, we'll get you another." And he probably took her by the elbow to show her the right way.

Lord Chesterfield would have gone about it differently, no doubt, but it is a mistake to consider the American rude or uncouth. He is casual, free-and-easy, intimate. He is using to the limit his new-found privilege — tremendous when you come to think about it — of addressing anybody at will, without bowing and scraping or having to fear the consequences of forwardness. The worst that can happen to him is what we call the brush-off, some equally intimate formula for saying "Run along, I'm busy."

None of this has elegance; casualness can get tiresome, but the observer has no right to compare it with drawing-room *politesse*. It must be compared with the average of underling behavior abroad, which may be very high indeed and then again very low — as in the brutal snarl of the European petty official or the obsequious shopkeeper cringe. Whatever we may think, the one thing sure is that casual American manners, in spite of their seeming rudely personal, are quite *im*personal. "They're nothing to do with you" — as the guy himself would say. And the headlines of his paper prove him right. When Governor Stevenson's chances for the nomination began to improve, the tabloid scarehead bore the simple words: "STEVIE'S ROLLING."

If the situation were no more complicated than this, we could lean back and let time take care to rub down the edges and do the burnishing. The forces working toward a general raising of our common behavior are enormous. The airport attendant's son will go to college and have some of the surface crudity removed. The daughter meanwhile reads magazines and newspapers in which the propaganda for etiquette is as incessant as it is solemn. Her wedding, we may be sure, will be true to Emily Post or not take place at all. Through the women's social ambition for their offspring, the men acquire somewhat gentler manners and by the next generation a new crop of well-reared youth has to be credited to our institutions — to the very freedom which in its first outbursts we may deplore.

But a complication does enter in and qualifies this natural evolution. I have in mind the relations of the better-mannered to the rest and to one another. We have to recognize that there still is in the United States some difference of upbringing as between the workingman and the "genteel," even though that gap has been leaped by many an executive who started in the ranks. The desire to ignore the gap expresses itself in the refusal to talk about manners at all. It is considered undemocratic, snobbish, lacking in manliness, to notice their existence. We deny or disbelieve that manners are "little morals." And yet the most genuinely American in this respect will choose a college for their sons or a club for themselves on grounds of congeniality and tone that are, in the last analysis, taste in manners. In their own actions, moreover, these Americans instinctively apply the double standard, though it does not *feel* double in the daily routine. As he goes up to his office, the businessman will talk to any of the men who run his tier of elevators without any sense of constraint on either side. But he calls them Joe or Pete whereas they say Mr. Jones. Where then is the equality? In this, that Mr. Jones wouldn't dream of speaking to them as I heard an elderly Senator do down South: "Boy, I'm in a hurry, take me up!" A kind of familiarity, joking and kidding, are mutually accepted, and special favors are asked for as man to man, not as master to servant.

Out in the street, though, the social contract breaks down. The cabdriver and his fare don't know each other, and as often as not the driver feels that he must reaffirm Liberty, Equality, and Fraternity the moment a stranger enters his territory. He calls me Big Boy, asks personal questions, turns the radio on for the track results, and blows cigar smoke into my compartment, all with the best humor and fullest indifference to my comfort. If I have a headache and want silence or if I want to tell him the quickest route at that particular time of day, I have to use diplomacy so as not to offend and alienate him. To get my money's worth I must wheedle my own employee. The cash nexus has something to do with this: I mustn't think that because I pay him I can order him about. He's a free man, doing me a favor, really, and the tip I am supposed to give him, whether or not I feel satisfied, is but a meaningless ritual. Hence it will happen (not strangely but logically) that the taxi man I meet repeatedly will become less aggressive, more deferent, as we get to know each other better.

Cabdrivers here serve as a mere example. They are not a marked species and I was careful to say that "as often as not" their behavior is such. In the same way shopgirls will assert their independence by going on with private conversation while you wait patiently. You had better be patient. Throughout the day you will run into a dozen similar types who seem to resent your inquiry, your grammar, your manners. If, as with the cabbie, the strangeness wears off because the same doorman, the same waiter, the same boy from the dry cleaners has managed to identify you, then, ninety-nine times out of a hundred, a beautiful friendship begins. You're pals. They'll do anything for you; they pull the word "Sir" out of their unconscious where it has been repressed for so long, and you've regained your lost equality.

This characteristic phenomenon (don't say it's human — anything people do is human) is a clue to what goes on in the higher echelons. It's quite simple: all the echelons want love — why not make it the chorus of a popular song? It rings sad and true. We may think of ourselves as higher-ups, but we make one another as nervous as cats and want to be reassured: "I won't bite or scratch, please don't you either." What the old aristocrats believed about the discomforts of democracy was a shrewd guess. The competition of each with all, they said, will make people touchy, envious, ill at ease. There will be no protection to one's self-love such as comes from a fixed rank or status. In a hierarchy your rank may not be high but it is yours for keeps; it gives you that clear look and firm tread, for no one can belittle you or step on your toes with impunity.

This is doubtless an embellished view of rank, and it leaves out of account our American kindliness born of prosperity and much moving about. But the lack of some protection for self-love does leave us open to bruising, or we wouldn't put so much cotton-wool in our manners. Is it a coincidence that the compulsory lovey-dovey style began about twenty years ago, shortly after the Great Crash? Certainly the first Washington joke under Roosevelt was about his greeting a visitor: "Sorry, John, but I didn't catch your last name." The new brotherhood of man born of calamity and teamwork in reconstruction is with us yet. One of the knottiest questions in any business relation is just when to begin calling your correspondent Charlie. Too soon, you're rushing the deal; too late he thinks you don't really like him. Why should he care? That is easy to guess. If you were already on familiar terms, he would attach no significance to any little thing that was said or done between you. That great word "informal," which we work to death, means the sigh of relief that comes when the bars are down and the vests unbuttoned. But until then the conventions are as real as in the court of Louis XIV.

Consider the conference manners in a group where not everybody is Charlie yet. You can't hear the facts for the purring. Nobody dares say: "This is my view." They all say: "I'm only thinking out loud of course — " a form of indecent exposure that nobody minds because it proves defenselessness. To contradict the previous speaker argues premeditation, so you begin: "I agree in general with everything you say, but don't you think that — " It shows mutual respect, it is logrolling on the intellectual plane. I have actually heard: "Give me your thinking, and then I'll give you mine" — another lilt for a popular song. And I am wrong, on reflection, in ascribing this cakewalk to the New Deal. Part of it is an old American tradition that Benjamin Franklin describes as his own technique for getting things done: put your idea in such a way that others will think it originated with them. That's the way to subdue the ego and redistribute the wealth of ideas in one operation.

To be sure, the law of diminishing returns will ruin the game in time. I once attended as a guest an informal session of a very popular course in How to Get Ahead (for women it's the Charm School), and heard some recent graduates tell the wonders of the system. One pimply youth declared that whereas before he had suffered from an "inferior complex," now he thought nothing of addressing this large and distinguished audience — why? Because he was a success. He had made himself into a good mixer to whom everybody was "really wonderful." He could now develop a liking not only for people he liked but for people he didn't like. The whole world liked him in return and that was success. His family believed in him from the start, which helped him to maintain an "I'll show you" attitude. Toward the rest of the world he was invariably lighthearted, cheerful, and free. Add to this a good memory for names and faces — so that you can say right off: "You're Frank Sims in cosmetics," or "How's that growling appendix of yours?" — and life holds no terrors.

Most of us shudder at the thought of those hearty handshakes and are speechless at the naïveté that cannot see the worthlessness of cordiality by formula. But the march of psychology is like everything else among us, varied in pace, though not unpredictable. The Hackle-Riser school of thought has by now caught up with the folly and indignity of Excessive Lubrication. One more effort, one more scraping down and coat of varnish on the next generation, and our revolting young sycophant will be like the suave salesman who entered my office, whipped out a card, extended a hand, and said: "I want you to meet me."

Taking the broad view, what is going on in American manners is our characteristic process of education. We start with raw materials and the first licks must be adapted to the simple thoughts of large numbers. We begin "democratic" then turn "scientific," which means becoming shamelessly self-conscious and mechanical. Grad-

ually the grossness purges itself. We must not forget that what we
have undertaken, no other society has tried: we do not suppress half
of mankind to refine part of the other half. We let it spread out in
the daylight to do the best it can. So one may question whether it is
fair to complain at once of popular crudity and of popular efforts
to correct it.

And after all, who are we higher-ups to sneer at the pimply youth
turned good mixer, when all around us we see leaders of industry,
finance, and the professions turning into patterns of public relations?
Not all succumb but all are vulnerable because our world is composed
entirely of the likes of us, equals. By consent, our lives are more and
more in one another's hands, we do not feel strong or independent
even when we have the means or power, and we must compensate
besides for the anonymity of statistical living. On top of these emotional reasons come the practical ones based on our political and
economic structure. We have to sell and we have to get votes. If the
presidential candidates must kiss babies, the salesmen must try to like
their customers, and the big shots must endear themselves to one another by diminutives. To cry out with delight, "Why, Morgan!" is
still too formal: Morg's the word.

But what should be the goal, the ideal, by which to try and shape
improved American manners? The principle that we must not give
others cause for disgust or contempt is important but negative. What
can we aim at beyond avoiding offense? The answer, I think, lies in
one word: conversation. I once told a friend who, I know, loves good
conversation how surprised I was that he could stand the company
of a man I met at his house and found totally uninteresting. Ted explained that they had been to the same Western college, though several years apart, and were active alumni. "And so," said Ted, "when
we're alone, we talk Wabash." The phrase has stayed with us as a
means of describing conversation that is null and void, a reckless
squandering of words. Among the uneducated it is truly wonderful
how many times an idea is repeated before it is let go. It is as if each

party were not quite sure the language would carry across — a sad thought for democrats. In more fluent circles, the bane is not repetition but interruption. The eyes wander while the lips go on — interruption from within.

I like to watch her. She is handsome and intelligent like so many ladies of Dallas, and evidently proud of her careful suburbanity. Excellent drinks have been served. The talk has come to life in one corner, and naturally those engaged in it have momentarily stopped reaching for things, so she looks around for a dish of peanuts, a box of cigarettes, and, having heard that it is rude to break in, she signals in pantomime to the person whose eye she has at last caught. People turn and stop one by one; the damage is done. You cannot reweave a fabric that has frayed to bits. She does this again and again — to her family, her children, to the guests she has herself adroitly launched into debate. "See here," one wants to say, "hospitality is not all food and drink. On the contrary, we want to forget our appetites a little and refresh ourselves with new faces by an exchange of what dwells behind the face. Let us be and let us talk." O. Henry did warn us that "in Texas discourse is seldom continuous," but I am disappointed just the same, and to that extent my hostess has failed.

Is it because our manners are inept that many people prefer an evening of bridge or playing chamber music? Either takes as much practice as conversation, if not more, but at the end they feel less jarred, the time seems better spent, no words have passed except functional ones. It would be sad to think that ordinary democratic society was being reduced to communion without words. The trouble is not all on the surface. Those who are bored by triviality are too easily put off by other subjects, and especially by the clash of tastes and opinions. The old habits need a shaking out. From mutual tolerance here in America, we began by excluding the expression of religious views, then of political opinions, finally of all controversial utterance whatever. In many a circle that has intellectual pretensions you hardly dare talk freely about an actress or a movie for fear that your remarks will hit the favorite of someone present. Possessiveness and self-love can hardly go farther. The net effect is to make every-body talk Wabash, which is like the abdominal complaint known as Variable Dullness. The livelier minds conclude that anything is better than conversation. An unhappy friend of mine used to anesthetize himself with drink. His well-wishers pleaded, "But you're so much more agreeable when you're sober!" To which he would reply, "Maybe, but other people are so much more boring."

Work itself suffers from our systematic blandness. It was a recent Secretary of Defense who said that what this country needed was Tertiary Flap. This he defined as the hammering out of differences sharply expressed. It is normal and healthy, he adds, and helps to get things done. It obviously does not speak well for our poise and con-fidence in one another if the assumption is that the slightest breath of criticism must destroy the thing criticized. That assumption is so revoltingly stupid that I make a point of never using a certain phrase in common use, just because it implies that criticism is neces-sarily hostile and mean. I found it hard at first to break the habit because it is so widely shared. But now I don't preface a personal re-mark by saying: "I'm very fond of Tom, *but* . . ."

Thinking in this vein opens a wide field of observation. One be-gins to notice how often others say: *"Frankly,* I prefer Lucky Strikes." Frankly! Good God! It also turns out that what they have been telling you is their *personal* opinion. When they apply to you on some point, they excuse themselves with the formula, "I'm asking just for information." So! He won't make use of it, won't use it against me. To ask for use would be impertinent, cavalier, but if it's just for information, I can afford to tell him. It makes one pine for Lydia, the Lady of the Aroostook in William Dean Howells, who isn't any less delightful because we're told: "Lydia wants to know."

In this reproving mood, I confess I also begin to look askance at all the laughing and grinning that is *de rigueur.* I am all for finding comedy wherever life will let us. I think Shakespeare was right to scatter humorous scenes in tragedies — the same idea would improve most of our Broadway comedies. But I don't see why every committee meeting has to open with strenuous ha-ha's about nothing at all. Everybody brings his cackle under pressure and has to let it out before work can start. Is it meant to show that he's not taken in by what he's doing, that he's above it? Or alternatively is it a confession that he's an ass and knows it, but — saving grace! — he has a sense of humor?

Modern man's humor is a secretion he thinks would be dangerous to hold in. This is why, no doubt, it has become impossible, at the end of a quiet evening party, to say "Thank you" like a rational creature — just as it was impossible to say just "Good evening" on arrival. What takes place instead is a whinnying of mares and friendly snarling of stallions. When alone at home you see the image of it in the magazines. This led an inspired critic of our manners, Mr. Charles Morton, to summon advertisers who use pictures to "wipe off that grin." After a definitive study of the facts, he reports: "Three women, at a combination stove-sink-refrigerator: they've all got the giggles. Man in a new summer suit: he is much amused. Three people fondling cigarette lighters: something is convulsing them. Woman about to put an enormous dessert in a refrigerator already chockfull: the very idea has brought to her to the point of hysterics." With such training in deterging folly, Mr. Morton should go on to tackle public figures and newspaper photographers. In any situation except kissing their wives, our leaders invariably show their full set of teeth. Two of them shaking hands have of course more to laugh at, but even so . . . Meanwhile the voice of the people has embodied the affectation in a decisive phrase — a sentence, rather, from which there is no appeal:

"He hasnasensayoomer."

Manners as anxious and also as yielding as ours are a disadvantage not only to those who like to keep their activities separate and either really work, or play, or talk. They also put everyone at the mercy of the uninhibited. In public places, it becomes less and less possible to recover one's privileges when infringed. The sign may plainly say

No SMOKING and one may be suffering from a cold or an allergy, but the boorish will light up. One stands the discomfort rather than make a fuss. If two couples meet unexpectedly on the train, their loud joy at the surprise, and all the news since they last met, have to be heard by many who would prefer to read. The captive audience is shackled by its own excessive gentility — as was shown in the case of the radio commercials in the Washington buses. We are law-abiding to a point just this side of martyrdom.

But if life is to remain tolerable in the promiscuous modern world, a sharper line will have to be drawn between positive and negative rights to comfort in public utilities. It may be a comfort to the sailor across the aisle to be strumming on his banjo. But the negative comfort of the rest of the car should make him desist. Coming back to your hotel at 2 A.M. with colleagues you've met at the convention, you may find it natural to pursue the discussion down the deserted halls; but the sleep of your neighbors — so negative it seems quite useless — should make you shut up. We are so numerous, so tightly packed, our devices are so powerful and so inspiring to childish imaginations, that we must vigilantly protect ourselves and the un-represented public too. It was only a few months ago that a railroad proposed to floodlight from the trains the thickly peopled regions through which they passed.

And speaking of the childish, it is important not to let misplaced kindness to the young encourage them to forget themselves and go berserk in public. I have seen a whole subway car of adults terrorized by eight or ten schoolboys who wanted a roughhouse on the way home — satchels flying in people's faces, feet trampled on, and never a sign that the little barbarians were not alone in the place or that their behavior was not to be expected. Who can wonder then at the vandalism which the keepers of our national shrines and parks report annually? Six million dollars' worth of damage to public property, some of it irreparable, most of it the result of indulging whims at others' expense.

The proof that a democracy is not by nature irresponsible but knows how to raise itself to civilized behavior can be found every summer at Jones Beach near New York. The city's thousands are there in close proximity and utopian perfection. There are no messes, no flying papers or cigarette butts, nothing but reasons to admire the collective self-discipline. When one thinks of the manners of the populace a hundred years ago, this seems like the wholesale conversion of sinners. To go to a theater then was to risk having clothes torn or spat upon, to see the show interrupted by yells and missiles, and to court insult and violence at the slightest mishap.

On the strength of our progress I do not even despair of seeing some of my friends as civilized at home as they are at the theater. I do not mean that they are domestic rowdies, but that their carelessness often comes to the same thing. They will, for instance, allow their dog to do nearly everything except eat the guests. Yet if one arrived at the party in blue jeans, with a cake of soap and a towel, they would feel hurt. Offenses through the dog would make a long chapter, beginning with the inhospitable yapping that greets the sound of the doorbell. Small children, too, are positive comforts to the owner that should yield within reason to the negative pleasure of the guests. And finally, the word might go around that a large cocktail party is not just an opportunity for abandoned acts — holes burned in rugs and table tops, cigarettes crushed out in *canapés* or floating in drinks, sticky hands wiped on upholstery, half-eaten olives cached atop your books. But perhaps all this is a weak modern expression of the need for saturnalia — another subject altogether.

The more one thinks about manners the more one recognizes that the very idea is full of contradictions. One wants people to be tactful, but knows that to exercise tact is fatiguing and destroys sociability. No tact, then, formal manners which are like signals telling everybody how matters stand. But how rigid and silly and pompous! Let's be natural. Yes, but in the best of us nature is self-centered and easily detestable by all. One hates to hear even oneself going on, how much more that unquenchable bore Bumpus. And Mrs. O'Grundy who calls herself Organdy now her husband's dead, what an insufferable social climber! . . .

Here let me pause and digress, to make the dear lady amends and lay a votive offering at the feet of snobbery. Thou maligned virtue! Or if that is too strong, let me say Worthy Effort Misunderstood — and sometimes misapplied. How wrong of Longfellow to call *Excelsior* a "strange device." Climbing is the basic device — look at Evolution, one laborious social climb over the bodies of unfashionable dodos and dinosaurs. The ape in us is primordial and we should cheer when he apes something better. To emigrate and become an American is to climb. To follow etiquette and eat peas only off your own knife is sheer affectation — at first. To value education and buy books one does not quite understand — what is this but another climb upward?

Our favorite reading in modern times, the novel, is a school of snobbery. All the characters we are not meant to imitate are ticked off by the author's snobbish instincts: "His hair was parted in the middle and thickly plastered with oil." "Elsie bobbed her head and said 'Pleased to meetcha.' " Shame on you, novelists! Your character traits are nothing but hasty generalizations, like race prejudice. But glory to you also for leading us on toward that perfect delicacy of manners which you alone possess. It is thanks to you perhaps that our Western world is now outwardly one class in clothes, manners, and common thoughts — one world, if we do not dig too deep. It is to your fussing about trivial detail, perhaps, that we enjoy another unique American spectacle: the workman respectful of his hands and wearing gloves at his work — gloves, which were once the appanage of the princes of the Church, then of the noble lords, whom next the bourgois aped, until now they have found their true place with their utility. Gentlemen of labor, let nothing you dismay. And you who are not to the manner born, snob on, snob on — good always comes of it.

If the objector points to Hollywood as the revolting apotheosis of snobbery, he can be told that Hollywood is only the court of

Louis XIV over again. The bootlicking, the brief authority and the plunges from the heights, the desire to be seen and seen with, the refusal of grade A to talk to grade B, the prostitution of every kind, interspersed unquestionably with talent, integrity, and lofty contempt — those are the people and the manners of Versailles. We can esteem ourselves lucky if California drains off from our midst the unrepresentative snobs *à outrance.*

Who then is representative? Since I have involved the novelists, I give you Mr. Rex Stout's Archie Goodwin. In his thirties, a drinker of milk who packs a gun and takes shorthand, full of brains but not willing to let them show in public, he is the idealization of American manners. Compare his relation to his employer Nero Wolfe with Dr. Watson's to Sherlock Holmes. Archie is impudent and will be annoying if it relieves his feelings. At the end of thirty years, Watson was on less familiar terms with his friend and equal Holmes than Archie can be with a new client after ten minutes. Archie's vocabulary is also more extensive gutterwards, which makes him and not Nero Wolfe the memorable speaker. Holmes would not have stood it. Wolfe has to stand it. And he reaps ample benefits. Archie is loyal, infinitely more helpful because more emancipated than Watson, and just as devoted when circumstances require.

The one thing Archie does not tolerate and uses every ingenuity to puncture is affectation. No bad thing to tilt at, though to suspect affectation can itself become a pose. But such is the mood of Archie's generation, the median American style in manners. They are manners for universal, that is, democratic use. Why change when going from the family circle to the world of strangers? There are no strangers any more. True, the freight of feeling carried by these manners is slight. Feeling is nobody's business but your own — which includes your feeling about yourself. And this, favorable or not, it is your duty to suppress. You can make up for impersonality by giving casualness a twist others may recognize. Thus do we sort one another out for friendship, or more, or less, from among our common kind.

PART THREE
Autumn, or Carping

11. Assets to Conceal

FOR A LONG TIME I hunted for a good definition of an intellectual. I wanted something simple and inclusive, not just an indirect way of bestowing my approval. But the more I tried to be fair, the more the exceptions and qualifications swamped the idea beneath them. Then one day while strap-hanging and scanning my homeward bound fellow workers, it came over me in a flash: an intellectual is a man who carries a briefcase.

This, I hope to show, is not a joke or an evasion. If anything marks off the intellectual from the so-called man in the street it is that the latter tends to take things at face value — as he sees them or as he reads about them in the papers. Those who argue with him are queer, and when they try to prove him wrong there is abstract legerdemain about it. The intellectual, on the other hand, may be just as stubborn or prejudiced, perhaps even less intelligent, but he is aware of the world of opinions, of -isms, schools of thought, sides to questions, movements of ideas. He reads journals, books, special reports, memoranda for private circulation; he probably writes some himself. Obviously he carries a briefcase.

If you scan again the bearing of the definition, you recognize that in this country the intellectual group is a faithful counterpart of our miscellaneous social system. There is no fixed intellectual class any more than there is a fixed social class. Consult a "quality" magazine such as the *Atlantic*, which is addressed to "the educated reader." Who writes for it? Over twelve months taken at random, we find articles by: a surgeon, an army officer, a housewife, an industrialist, an astronomer, a playwright, a screen writer, a museum director, an architect, a rabbi, a schoolgirl, a judge, a naturalist, a literary agent, a civil servant, the editor of a farm newspaper, a golf champion, an actress, an administrator of scientific research, a criminologist, an Irish peer, a rear admiral, and a sailor in the merchant marine.

This wide scattering does not mean that we fail to make distinctions. We make choices in the light of our opportunities and miscellaneous purposes. A friend of mine, a financier, was sent as a young man to spend a year in a Yugoslav banking firm. Ever since, he has been interested in the Slavic languages, culture, and religion. He has endowed at one of our universities a chair of Slavic studies and until the last war he usually had in tow some scholar or artist from those regions. Unquestionably my friend is an intellectual — to that extent. His awareness of culture at large is slight, and on all subjects but his own he is diffident, so the professional intellectual would put him down as stupid. He would be wrong. In our intellectual class there are thousands, millions like my friend, men of one subject.

We can, if we like, explain this by our age of specialization, but the phrase restates the fact, inaccurately. Bankers do not decide on a congenial subject and then stick to it. They find themselves involved, and it is their one subject because it is their first. Travel and world business — mobility and publicity — lift up every day more and more people out of the inarticulate mass and turn them into unassuming but unmistakable intellectuals. Not specialization but self-consciousness and print are the forces at work. Any American whose mind is caught by a problem finds ready to hand all the means of study which formerly would have taken a lifetime to collect. For we carry out in things of the mind our tendency to socialize everything, to make it useful, available, widespread, that others may enlighten still others ad infinitum. We may say, then, that half the world carries a briefcase, or if we prefer, that ours is the most extensively intellectual age the world has ever seen.

I shall be told that if this is so my definition is misleading. These paper carriers aren't real intellectuals. They are dabblers and amateurs. The real ones would be what, then, professionals? We have a good many of those, too, but are they any less narrow than my banker friend? Judging by their productions, only a shade less so. The critics of literature do not usually write about concerts; the writers on social problems seldom bring in examples from the picture galleries. Within each field there are coteries that remain mutually incommunicado. Theirs is an intense specialization, arising from the same general cause — the abundant intellectual output of our times, which makes it hard to follow more than one line.

As for dabbling, it is rarely true of the modern amateur. The banker in question, whose avocation began thirty years ago, was during the late war one of three or four men in the country who could advise the government on the "Balkan mind." Whichever way we turn, we face the fact that if a man carries a briefcase, the odds are high that he is a scholar. And if we accept this as the new intellectualism — the result of conditions peculiar to industrial democracy — it is clear that once again the United States is at the top of the heap. From the progressive schoolboy doing a "research project" to the Ground Safety Officer of an air base who has to post accurate warnings about sunstroke and heat exhaustion, we intellectuals — and you can put us at possibly one man in three — are incessantly boning up on something, "getting the facts," writing them down, and breaking out in print. Parnassus stretches from coast to coast, and like the angel in Shaw's *Simpleton of the Unexpected Isles,* the nine muses each carry a white zipper case.

Yet the European visitor (and many of his American friends) will tell you that underneath the paper work the United States is strongly anti-intellectual. It is true we are distrustful of ideas in politics, and I have said how wise I thought this was. Skepticism and suspicion in that part of our life have certainly rubbed off onto other subjects, and we may be paying for our political flexibility by a general unresponsiveness to thought as such. In addition, the ways of science shackle our minds. By habit we resist the lure of speculation and seek facts. Our schools teach facts rather than principles, and the popular use of "theory" to mean what is very fine, no doubt, but will not work, expresses the same prejudice. On top of this, those who manage our so-called mass media are persuaded that by excluding "highbrow stuff" they are catering for the public taste.

Now it is possible that these slow-working parts of our culture form a piece of machinery we dare not be without, a governor on our engine, which might race to perdition if we harnessed our colossal energies, or even a portion of them, to ideas. Where would we land, who would do our work, what would happen to our peace of mind if we were all sensitive to the latest idea, vision, speculation? What would result if many more of us set up shop in the business of marketing ideas? Our European critic should for a moment look homeward. His continent may be said to be perishing from ideas, ideas which won't let its component parts unite either their minds or their coalpits. Our native temperance about doctrines, moreover, is a strong point against our inconsistent intellectuals who already complain of confusion and "loss of values." They mean nonagreement on abstract subjects. If our whole people took to ideas, there would necessarily be ten times the confusion, and the objectors would need ten times as much strength of mind — or else police power with which to put the heretics down.

Let us, in this light, moderate our blame of America's indifference to ideas. But let us also distinguish the inertia that stabilizes from the stupid envy or political malice that flares up as animus against intellect. For this there can be no excuse. It is indefensible, ignoble, and dangerous. But to be effective our attack must stop being frothy-mouthed denunciation in general; it must become a bill of particulars.

The worst thing the American intellectual has to contend with is the convention of false respect and real scorn with which his person and his ideas are received. The shuffling and shame on both sides when intellectual subjects come up is ludicrous and low: the ordinary educated businessman feels impelled to mutter: "I dunno nuthin' 'bout any of that 'ere," and the intellectual feels that he owes the other an apology for being alive and having a mind. If he has a title that "gives him away" in society, his kind friends will introduce him as "a nice fellow just the same" — guaranteed not to cerebrate in public.

There is a subtle misconception here of what society has a right to require. The intellectual might argue that his is a profession like any other. He handles ideas as others do cotton goods or disease. Justice Holmes's reference to "free trade in ideas" certainly implies that a democracy ought to respect the traders on that market. At the same time, it is a sound rule to exclude professional concerns from sociability. The edict against pedantry in the drawing room antedates democracy, and I have a strong suspicion that intellectuals have always been looked at askance — in other words, that anti-intellectualism is endemic in human society.

This makes it all the more imperative that the unwritten code should be closely interpreted and enforced. Let the citizen at home defend himself against lecturing or any other form of misplaced academicism, but let his intellectual guest also stand upon his rights. There is no reason for him to apologize or tolerate innuendo. He has even a duty to attack and show up the "plain man" as an unsuspected scholar, a crypto-intellectual. Scratch a suburbanite and nine times out of ten you find a pedant with a pet subject.

The principle holds a fortiori in public situations. No manifestation of deliberate anti-intellectualism should go unrebuked. The person who in 1943 wrote to a magazine: "The Liberal Arts — let 'em rot!" should have her letter printed (as it was), but with a quiet editorial comment about the liberal arts of reading and writing and the liberality of opinion which permitted her thus to contradict herself in public. She may be hopeless, but other readers of the correspondence column deserve a boost to their faith. Likewise censorship, book burnings, and the myriad insidious controls that may stifle ideas, are the particular concern of all intellectuals. They haven't a lobby, they *are* one from the very fact that they write and speak. No one person can fight every battle single-handed: it is folly to attempt it. But each one can watch the corner where he works, where his authority and his knowledge are greatest, and can see to it that the fresh air keeps blowing through.

Besides the public, there is the government to be tackled. It certainly discriminates against intellect in obvious and subtle ways, directly and indirectly. The most evident of the indirect ways is to be found in the changed attitude toward what a great nation's Post Office should be. When first invented, it was meant to help the circulation of ideas above all things. Now only a few indications of this purpose remain. But the gradual decay of Benjamin Franklin's great invention deserves detailed treatment by itself.

Direct discrimination occurs in the income tax and copyright laws. Some work is being done on improving the United States copyright, which for years has worked against the American writer in order to create a monopoly for American printers and book manufacturers. This has kept us out of the world copyright union and helped to make us seem barbarians in the eyes of foreign writers and publicists. Instead of changing the law at no great economic cost, we spend taxes on a dozen programs that attempt to prove in feebly boastful fashion that we are cultured people after all — or at last. The plain fact is that Congressmen, who certainly are men of words and even of ideas (28 million words were uttered by the Eighty-second Congress) know nothing and want to know nothing about American writers and artists. Intellect has by definition the fewest votes, so they do not count — except when suddenly it appears that a couple of oil paintings in modern style are going to overthrow the republic. With some honorable exceptions our legislators reflect a state of mind suitable to the United States of 1829 — and even then, Andrew Jackson was a truer intellectual than some of our headline getters from Capitol Hill. They should wake up to the fact that this country teems with talent in other fields than farming and business, and that the demand for it is growing all the time.

This does not mean that the Federal government should subsidize the arts or establish a Bureau to promote them. The proposal seems to me entirely at odds with our traditions of federalism and self-help.

And it would be harmful to the arts besides. The official mind has many virtues and uses, but administering culture is not one of them. We might not get Goerings who, as you may remember, was Minister of Aviation, Chief of Anti-aircraft Artillery, General of Fliers, Grand Master of the Hunt, Head Forester of Germany, President of the Reichstag, Chief of the Prussian Secret Police, and Director General of State Theaters and Operas; but I think we would get "fat" men in some form — probably at the top of their form.

No, American intellectuals and artists will have to do with the support of their local communities if not of the general public, and they will have no cause to complain provided they are treated on a par with businessmen when it comes to the income tax. No deliberate conspiracy exists against brain workers, but it is obvious from public and private reports that the tax inspectors squeeze pennies from professional men and let slide fortunes from those in business. Individual examples are out of place here, but the principles should be officially recognized (not merely here and there) that intellectual work entails expenses like business, different but just as fairly deductible. When a famous (and intelligent) actor-manager is challenged over an item of forty-four dollars for a costume in one of his productions (*New York Times*, September 19, 1952), one cannot help comparing this with the "normal" deductions granted to business firms for lavish trips and entertainment, for "losses" which have no equivalent in professional work, and for supplies whose nature is never questioned — not to speak of unused hotel suites on a permanent basis, advertising in the void, and other modes of lowering the surtax. Intellectual occupations may be less familiar to the inspectors than business, and herein lies the unfairness: they should be better informed.

Official discrimination in these and other ways may have something to do with the ambivalent emotions aroused by intellect at all times and places. Even when the needs of defense are directly concerned, the majority is jealous of the supposed privilege given to brains. Many people opposed the deferment of college students, and the government was inclined to respond. Again, during the war the Army threw five thousand highly trained minds into the Battle of the Bulge and the losses of talent were naturally enormous when compared with those sustained by less specialized groups. This may have been unavoidable but it would hardly be wise to make it a precedent. Skilled workers in factories are also privileged by deferment yet they seem to arouse no animus of the kind that made even college presidents turn tail and virtually pooh-pooh the value of brains. To all this there is but one remedy, which is: not to act like college presidents but resist, argue, counterattack — educate. It's un-American not to lobby for your rights.

It is true that lobbying requires a sense of solidarity, a virtue which intellectuals do not seem to overstock. They are likely to be hipped on some point of difference from their professional opponent and will cheerfully let him go under, thinking: "It's good riddance." In a highly organized society that is the quickest way of going under next. No doubt it is difficult to support X without appearing to further X's poisonous ideas. But there are degrees of difference, and if intellectuals cannot make and take distinctions, who can? The only answer that occurs to me is: abler intellectuals. If trained minds "react" like untrained, and professed artists in thought refuse to exercise judgment, one is bound to ask *Quis custodes ipsos custodiet* — who shall throw custards at the custodians?

It would be idle to pretend that a time of hurtling social change makes things easy for men of brains. They are moved and upset by forces that scarcely exist for others — such as ideas. But one sign of true devotion to ideas is the desire to keep them straight regardless of momentary discomfort or advantage. This ability in turn has been interpreted as implying a duty to engage in politics. *Noblesse oblige:* those who have knowledge and a conscience cannot stand aloof from the struggle, unless they are irresponsibles. This argument overlooks many things, the first being that politics is an art by itself, not necessarily mastered by a master of ideas. Politics means living from moment to moment and never losing ground, whereas ideas have largeness and fixity. The "line" may change in ideas but not abruptly and in shamed secrecy. The fact moreover that in America the intellectual group is miscellaneous and scattered blurs the identity of its members, in the public eye and in that of their colleagues. This makes a politics of ideas unworkable. Then, too, the absence of "grand old men" is a handicap. There is no one to rally and guide. With us the most solid writers have vogue and authority for a decade more or less; then, owing to slight shifts in taste which are grossly magnified by the advertising mill, they go into a half obscurity, to emerge only near death or after. It is a stupid waste of our spiritual resources, quite apart from its souring effect on the victim and its hampering of political leadership.

Finally, our intellectual rank-and-file are not prepared. Every year a new generation of youths — some of them "veteran youths" — are educated out of the common purse and join the ranks of the briefcase carriers. Many are fresh from the soil or the shop, and ideas to them are new and shiny tools of self-expression. The ideas of principle, for instance, or of compromise, of truth and relativism, of science and history, of justice, morality, and art, stir up their strongest emotions. They read a little, follow a leader of thought, they turn critic or sociologist or moral philosopher; there is always a still more naïve lot to listen to them. Then, using our amazing openheartedness and our numerous facilities, the more ambitious get published, and pretty soon — at twenty-five or thirty — there is another professional or semiprofessional on the market. He only needs a job and some leisure to become really educated and responsible.

He gets the job but does he get to work on himself? Not often enough. This is where the political atmosphere of the age spoils good material. Politics does two things: it hardens the mind before it is ripe and it disillusions the heart. Whereas the born intellectual has the flexibility and toughness of tempered steel, these miscast people are always torn apart by the discrepancy between the world as it is and their ideas of love and justice. They grow angry and cynical. By middle age they are what my puritanical friend Fred West used to denounce as swaydo-intellectuals, people who love ideas and live for them, but because they don't really know how to handle them, are made incurably unhappy.

This is sad enough. The effect on the community is even worse. These unfortunates make up in will what they lack in mind. They accelerate the "political" drive and force on others the habit of labeling ideas instead of weighing them. Any book, lecture, or article has to be classified as making for or against their -ism. No one can utter consecutive words without their being taken as "nothing but" some deadly heresy or other. In short we have here the ideal personnel for a totalitarian bureau of thought-control. The too frequently irresponsible attacks on writers, artists, and educational institutions in this country show not only that we have a plentiful supply of these swaydo-intellectuals, but also that our democratic habits are no guarantee against intellectual tyranny. Which is another reason for paying more regard and more precise attention to mental powers than our former casualness allowed for.

The typical flaw of weak minds — it's almost like a visible crack in a piece of pottery — is the habit of committing the fallacy known as the "undistributed middle." It runs like this: "All Communists are atheists. Mr. Jones is an atheist. Therefore he is a Communist." This is guilt by mere association — of ideas. To visualize the error, just draw a circle and mark it "Communist," then draw a bigger one around it and label it "Atheist." You see at once that all Communists are a part of all atheists, but that some atheists are not Communists. This fallacy, which is not peculiar to our country, is notoriously a danger to life and limb. It is the root idea of the purge, and it tends to prevail wherever "the people" are in power and feel responsible to culture, ideas, -ologies. The French Revolution gives massive examples of this abstractionism, which is far more murderous than the simple plan of destroying your actual enemies. Ideas are larger than politics, as I have said, and have a deadly fixity. Hence the present contagion. There are times when discouragement tempts one to let events take their course. We may not have learned to distribute our middles, but the atom bomb will take care of that. Perhaps it was providentially invented for the purpose. The survivors of the grand purge will very likely be more tender of logic, of ideas, and of one another.

The political ferment at work in half-educated minds may be the worst, but it is not the only force working against the American intellect. Those whose business it is to manage and circulate ideas and works of art also have a lot to answer for. They are supposed to be transmitters, high-fidelity instruments. But too often vulgar conceit turns them into bottlenecks. Some are disappointed intellectuals. They hadn't the energy or talent to run the race, or they wanted the higher incomes of editors, publishers, and managers. If they succeed in those roles they begin to think they are captains of industry, that they should control and streamline output because they have to feed and "protect" the public. They get "ideas" about what is and what isn't wanted. In talking to intellectuals, they put on the stern look of the big executive. Among real businessmen they assume the airs of a prosperous poet: in short they're swaydo-businessmen and real intellectuals should call their bluff.

Apart from silly affectation their folly takes three harmful forms: (1) pandering, (2) cowardice, (3) false shame. Pandering is giving the public not what it wants but what the lowest supplier in the trade is getting away with. A real businessman would know that it pays to improve quality and public taste. These men forget it. The day when publishers of twenty-five cent books decided to put a pornogram on every cover, regardless of subject, they spoiled their future business in serious literature. Now they're stuck. They might like to bring out, let us say, *The Story of the Flag*, but they can't very well show Betsy Ross spilling out of her nightgown. The public would balk, it has ever so much more taste and good sense than it gets credit for. Its chief fault is to be too patient with its providers.

Sin number two, cowardice, can be illustrated by one of my few ventures into the world of scientific letters. A well-known magazine of some pretensions asked me to review a book on the history of technology. I looked it over and reported that it was very technical indeed. Did they still want the review, though I would have to dwell on the conclusions and historical connections and neglect what lay outside my competence. Yes, yes. The subject was of tremendous importance to every American in our age of — of — technology. I did the best I could and the editor rang up to say how pleased he was. The whole staff, according to him, were reading me instead of going to lunch — "lovely material to cut from," as he put it ambiguously. I thanked him and waited for the proofs. They came with a note to please ring up the managing editor. "It's a fine piece, just dandy," said this experienced man. "There's only one thing: you remember where you speak, near the end, of Descartes' revolutionary application of algebra to geometry? Now that's a splendid point, splendid, but I don't think the name Descartes means a great deal to our readership. It's hard to pronounce for one thing, and — well, I was wondering, we were all wondering — couldn't you make it Newton?"

As for false shame, it is half-hearted badness — doing the thing because you almost believe in it and then apologizing or snickering it away. For example, in the trade of broadcasting the programs dealing with intellectual matters are always jokes: "Invitation to Learning" is known as "the Hour of Silence." Damn funny. "That'll put those windbags in their place — nobody listens to them, the poor fools." . . . The bigger fools being those who hire them and pour out expensive juice into the ether for nothing.

There is a noticeable connection between false shame and engaging in intellectual activities deliberately, in a group. Each one is willing to be a high-brow by himself but not in front of others. Visiting some friends out West, I was told by my hostess one Saturday afternoon that she would abandon me to her husband's sole care — "I'm going to something very, very silly: I belong to a sort of women's club that reads plays out loud. Doesn't it sound too awful? But it's amusing, you know. One of us chooses a play — usually a Broadway hit — buys the copies, gives out the parts. Sometimes it's dull; usually it's very good fun. Then we have tea and sit around and talk till it's time to go home."

Since it was fun I could see nothing the matter with it. I was curious to know how often they disagreed about the play.

"Oh, we never talk about the play! The one at whose house we meet that week sees to that. She has the tea and food all ready and shoos us out of her living room the moment we're through. Once or twice there were complaints that the reading took too long, or some of the lines weren't quite — you know. . . So the person in charge times it first and makes cuts if necessary. Oh no, we never discuss it. We'd be laughed at all over town."

"But when you and Max go to a show, you talk about it on the way home. I've heard you."

"That's different. Max and I aren't — I don't know how to put it. But at our Saturdays it wouldn't do."

I let it go at that and thought back to what Dr. Schlagobers told me about some of his frequent psychiatric cases involving an intellectual mother and a homosexual son. If the women are still on the defensive about ideas, then the boy who feels drawn to them finds very slight support indeed. Dad scorns his gifts or tastes, Mom thinks they're just cute. No one can say that this emotional isolation of the growing boy is the cause of sexual deviation — thousands of normal men are writers, painters, and musicians — but it is clear that the connection, whatever it is, has cultural significance. It comes out of our false shame and returns to plague us with irrelevant suffering and scandal.

Perhaps this aspect of the intellectuals' minority problem is undergoing a change right now. Nobody has called General Eisenhower a sissy because he paints. Thirty years ago he probably wouldn't have painted or wouldn't have got away with it. Thirty years ago, college boys didn't do much part-singing or violin-playing — sissy occupations both. Now music and painting are increasingly common pastimes for Americans who have artistic tastes but no pretensions to talent. It would be sensible, then, to change our "line" in accordance with the facts and instead of pooh-poohing take a grave interest in *any* manifestation of intellect. I may be suspected of loyalty to my shop when I say I'm attracted by the figure of the seven-year-old boy who was recently licensed in California as a radio operator in the "ham" class. The officials of the FCC were amazed at his ability to pass the regular adult test about "parasitic oscillation" and the rest of the jargon. They should learn that that's the way brains hit you — they show up early when they're first class and they stay with you. Gainsborough was a draftsman and Mozart a composer before adolescence. But in an environment that is not on the lookout for brains, in a family that feels they're unmanly or undemocratic, young talent goes to waste or has a hard time making the best of nature's gifts. It is not enough to recognize ability only in emergencies, as we did in the last war, when the most unexpected kinds of brains were suddenly found indispensable to the common defense: EXPERT ON SEASHELLS BIG HELP IN OKINAWA LEAP. Our hangover of underdog resentment against intellect is as harmful as Europe's bourgeois resistance to the arts: let us be of no class, old or new.

The great American paradox in these matters is that the country is mad about education. In any small town the building that takes your eye for size and looks is the public high school. Drive through any part of the country, and every fifty miles you go past a college. They are not all great centers of learning, but they are busy centers of teaching. Teachers college or junior college or business college or mechanical arts college, our faith in teaching equals only our faith in God and business. And one must confess it would be hard to find a nobler trinity. It is in fact permissible to say that ours is at least striving to become the mystic trinity that man aspires to — wisdom, right action, and justification.

At any rate we were the first people in the world to attempt the

heroic task of bringing the millions and their offspring out of ignorance and uncouthness. Everything bears witness to the fact that
we have succeeded to an unhoped-for degree in an incredibly short
time. Only half a century separates our truly free and public high
school from our almost free and public college under the various
G.I. bills. The Western countries that are only now beginning to
copy us in popular secondary education are going to find that it is
not the easy thing they bargain for. Their old superiority was
easily attained by ruthless selection — 5 to 10 per cent of the children, mostly from cultured homes, gave them little trouble.

With us, the outward result is our acceptance of education as
a panacea and a way of life. Every American you meet has been
exposed to teaching. On some it confers an early immunity, but
most of them sooner or later have a relapse and take a course. It is
a form of rededication we find very congenial. But we don't associate it especially with intellect or ideas, rather with work and technique. Care of Disabled Called Education, says the headline. And
every day at the bottom of the page come small items about "leisure courses" given by Art Workshops, the Planetarium, the libraries, universities, and museums. The newspaper itself is a five-cent
encyclopedia that goes daily into every home. Cures for body and
mind, solutions of etiquette or spelling problems, recipes for lining
your attic or your stomach — the items of knowledge far outnumber the news. The books that sell most steadily are the "How
to . . ." books: *Gift-Wrapping for All Occasions*. We invented
the correspondence schools, and with complete impartiality our
record companies will sell you discs to teach you colloquial Spanish or tap dancing.

"He had a course in it" is the first and also the last thing we want
to know. Like the Army and Navy, most firms have indoctrination or training courses for their employees. Some are elaborate,
others only a couple of days' drilling in set forms. When my late
friend George owned that chain of restaurants I spoke about he
took me to see how the beautiful hostesses in period gowns were

taught to make the entering guest feel in paradise. You arrive with your party and shed your wraps. A damsel in chief smiles and lifts a graceful arm with the right number of fingers outstretched — "Four?" You reply, "Yes," or more likely "Four." Then (and not sooner) she turns on her heel and addresses a second debutante: "Four!" You are then asked what kind of table you would like — if available — and are led to it. Then your guide finds your waitress and says to her very distinctly: "Four!" It takes about a week to master this ritual, thanks to which you know where you are — and you must admit it wouldn't come about simply by force of nature.

Some of this artificiality is bound to exist in all of our teaching. We cannot make people graceful or attentive, so we teach them how to go through motions suggesting grace and attentiveness. In other words our indulgence in courses for everything is something of a sop to ambition. And since we are well past the first stage of popular education, perhaps we ought to revise some of our methods and beliefs. We ought to be tooling up, as George would say, for a different kind of product. We have found out that some people think best with their hands, at the workbench or the designer's desk. This is true ability and not of a lesser kind. But for those having the power of abstract thought education should come to mean ideas, not rough-cast but rigorous and exact ideas, combined as carefully as if the handling of explosives were at stake. For we must never forget the danger of childlike or ignorant abstraction which threatens the incomplete mind.

I dwell on this danger in political life because it is immediate and never-ending, but there can be a corresponding blight of undigested abstractions in cultural life. Artists are especially subject to getting ideas in the bad sense. Shaw's account of the way Mrs. Patrick Campbell ruined her Lady Macbeth because somebody told her the part should be played "as if she were seen through a sheet of glass" is the typical instance. Sometimes a notion of the sort is only comical, as when the late Dr. Koussevitzky decided to give the subscribers of the Boston Symphony their money's worth in atmosphere by dressing up as Haydn to conduct one of his works. The delightful touch was that, in order to transport us back to that olden time, the maestro walked on with bent knees. The truth is that artists are very busy men and it is rather a new thing for them to possess general education, read books, and know one century from another. Some have yet to learn that playing with ideas takes as much practice as playing an instrument. You can't just strum your way through. And on the other side, connoisseurs have to be told that looking for technical points and being choosy is not synonymous with love of art. The hairline difference between having a trained mind and intellectualizing everything into a game is the last thing that can be taught. It can hardly be explained, and usually can't even be mentioned without offense.

During an earlier visit to my Western friends I had a demonstration of this unhappy truth. "I can hardly wait," said my hostess, "to have you meet Gus — Gus Heckerling. I've told you. He's our leading light. His whole family were artistic from way back, to the time when they left the old country. He's on the board of all our cultural activities. Takes a great deal of time, but of course when you're in natural gas you can take life pretty easy. He's immensely rich, and *generous* — I can't tell you! The point is, he really knows what's what, just like you. That's why I'm so eager to hear you two together. Max and I go to things just for fun — you know us, we like everything — concerts, ballet, the good plays from Broadway, anything. But we don't really know a thing about it. Gus, now, has been abroad I don't know how many times. He has interests in Germany, chemicals I think. And Germany to him means Salzburg. Mozart. I believe he dreams of Mozart! Oh, he'll give you a good time, I promise you. I told him all about you, and it's lucky he's in town or we couldn't have *really* entertained you — "

She stopped at my somewhat impatient gesture. I had said two or three times, and it was absolutely true, that I was having an excellent time. What wasn't true was that they "liked everything" and were dull companions. Peggy especially is full of adorable hates. But she and Max had a rooted belief that you had to know. *He* knew all about architecture, which was his trade, and though I didn't come out and say so, it was exactly his "knowledge," his ideas, that spoiled some of his buildings. So I waited for Heckerling with a rather lackluster eye. I hoped that Peggy had maligned him.

He came in, a plump, jovial man of fifty in a well-fitting dark-blue suit, and began by being loudly affectionate with the children, for whom he had presents. Then he was introduced to the ladies, and finally to me at the far end of the room. But before he held out his hand, he stopped dramatically, and said: "I'm afraid of you."

"There he goes," thought I. His voice was not unpleasant but it was tuned to board-meeting strength, so everybody turned around to see if he wasn't playing with some forgotten child. I smiled as convincingly as I could and let him tell how nervous he was to meet a New Yorker who must see everything and know everybody in the world of art. If he had known how rarely I saw any bright lights, he might have been disappointed and Peggy too. So I said nothing but a few conventional words. We drank a cocktail of his own invention, which he called a Salzburg (though I thought Cologne would have been more appropriate) and then went in to dinner.

We spoke in twos, this way and then that. But toward the end Peggy decided to draw out her lions and pumped me on Stravinsky's new ballet *Orpheus* at the Metropolitan. Had I seen a rehearsal or heard how it was going? It had not opened yet; I knew very little. So I let Peggy down after all. But Heckerling picked up the subject and made something of it. He doubted, for his part, that an American troupe would have the grace, the polish, the perfection of real ballet. Nothing surprising about it — the audiences did not know enough. (This was before the great popularity of ballet.) Still, if he heard good reports and this new work caught on, he'd let them have a week. But for a connoisseur . . . He finished with a gesture. Of course, he went on, loose technique wouldn't much matter in a rugged modern work. But to think of having to endure

the defilement of something classical and ravishing like *Swan Lake*
. . . Words failed him again.

The Heckerling touch cannot be too strongly fended off — not
for what there is in it of crudity, but for its false delicacy. The arts
are tough and the connoisseurs of art ought to be. You may swear
at a bad performance but it shouldn't destroy you any more than
the performance. Things have to be pretty bad in art to be entirely
worthless, and to get the best out of the worst is the sign of the
true connoisseur. The proof that the imitation esthete has no claim
to "taste" and no business influencing that of other, simpler people,
is that he is usually half a century behind the times in his choice of
favorites. He takes only the contemporary work that reminds him
of the past. With him, really, the arts fail. Their purpose is to exercise the mind like a muscle, so that you can move freely through
experience with the aid of both masterpieces and slight works.
Failing this, it is better to be a striving snob than a complacent
Pococurante, proud of his ideas. The type stands as a warning
against the country's ever going in for "cultural goals." It would
be profoundly undemocratic. Only a police state can seriously pronounce the word *Kunstpolitik.* A humane society must not sub-
ordinate social and political realities to anything whatsoever.

It is a different goal to infuse artistic elements into social, political,
and business life. And here again I cannot help thinking — at the
risk of being mistaken for a jingo — that the United States is a
pioneer. We often have a clumsy way of going about such matters,
but we correct our blunders as we go. The introduction of ballet into
musical comedy, which I just referred to, is but the latest example.
The radio, which twenty years ago was despaired of as a cultural
medium, is still not Plato's Academy, but it has brought us a large
repertory of classical music, together with the leading artists in the
flesh or on discs. This began in the very heart of the depression.
whereas in Britain, which has many advantages of talent and monopoly, the Third Programme dates from 1946.

Advertising is of course behind it and through it, sometimes offensively — but generously too. The ten chief media, which include *Life Magazine, This Week,* and the great networks, earn in round figures three hundred million dollars. Assign any reasonable proportion of this sum to the cost of producing the ads themselves and you still have left a huge amount, of which a very fair part is devoted to intellectual purposes. People of taste complain that the literary and scientific articles, the pictures, the biographies so published are not the best. Perhaps so. But when before our age has one seen a selection of difficult modern verse reprinted in a national magazine reaching twenty-five million — *Life's* way of marking T. S. Eliot's award of the Nobel Prize?

Again, NBC gave the whole country Toscanini, who for fifteen years of his earlier career had been in the pit of the Metropolitan, scarcely regarded as more than a run-of-the-mill conductor by those infallible judges in the dress circle. *Life* keeps doing a job of illustration and dissemination for the great collections of painting, the great buildings, the remote regions and religions of the world, that no university and no art patron or art dealer has attempted or could do. Even the cheaper magazines, which most readers of books damn without ever looking at them, do their part in spreading light. Right amid the cheesecake and the boxing stories one finds good reports on the foreign situation, the state of our prisons, or the removal of slums. Our leading politicians — Stevenson, Brien McMahon, Mrs. Roosevelt, Senator Lodge — do not disdain to write for these barbershop media and our leading intellects perhaps ought not to disdain to read them. It is the acme of inconsequence to want "the people" culturally brought up and want to keep culture locked up in nonpopular journals.

But does the popular mixture raise the common level or is it true that intellectually democracy levels down? The tests are not easy to apply nor do the results easily win acceptance from others. One can only point to the signs enumerated earlier: our increasing devotion to music and painting, our tremendous outlay of money for education, research, and publishing, our gains in substituting attractive sights for industrial ugliness (everywhere but in New York), our happy uses of good design in common utensils, and generally our addiction to conscious improvement.

So far as I know very little of this was visible at the end of the last century. If Henry Adams, wise, angry, and bitter, came back today, he might revise his judgment about the degradation that goes with democracy. Judging by style alone, he might even agree that *Gone With the Wind* was preferable to *Uncle Tom's Cabin* and that Erle Stanley Gardner marked a vast improvement in maturity and workmanship over the dime novel. It is proper to use these standards when we discuss democracy, just as it is necessary to supplement them by noting that, in the same period that saw Mr. Gardner "hailed as the greatest living American writer" (six million copies a year), another part of the population, polled by a library group, named Robert Frost, Theodore Dreiser, Sinclair Lewis, Thomas Wolfe, Eugene O'Neill, Ernest Hemingway, and Vernon Parrington as the great American moderns. Considering the noise and heat of the battle of ideas, this seems at both ends of the scale a pretty fair display of judgment. Try reading the popular literature of the Middle Ages and see how far you get.

Comparisons are odious, as we all admit when they go against us. It is better not to make them, and American intellectuals might set a good example by not initiating the game at their country's expense — or if not their country, then their age. How many we have heard these fifty years who confess to hating the present day! And how childish to hate in the lump, like any rabble rouser! Can it be that the hateful emotion is in part the consequence of an idea, a lumpish idea of a state where they would be treated like princes and where every few minutes the whole population would quit work to admire the products of the creative mind? No one denies that artists and intellectuals undergo hardships in our industrial world. They have a right to complain and to improve their lot like everybody else. But they must try to do this on the point. They have many disinterested supporters, and by and large they have already won recognition in tangible ways beyond any previous group of their peers. The United States is the place where hundreds of establishments do nothing else but give "millions for tribute" to art and artists.

In spite of this, disillusionment rules their minds. They become scoffers not skeptics — or else they would be more skeptical of their own imaginings. In their urge toward a better life they neither create nor criticize, but scuttle or desert. They forget that the true creator's role, even in its bitterest attack, is to make us understand or endure life better. Our intellectuals do neither when they entice us to more self-contempt, not suspecting how lucky they are that we are not in turn so demoralized by the emotion they stir up as to discharge it violently on their own persons. If the artist has nothing to give but only takes away, then he might as well be buried under the parody epitaph that was once applied to the half-fascist, half-Communist intellectual suffering from "alienation":

> I worshiped none, for fear of being an ass;
> Nietzsche I liked, but more than Nietzsche Sartre;
> I played both sides against the middle class:
> It shrinks, and I am heading for Montmartre.

It is in fact a mistake to speak of the artist's political fantasies as a work of the imagination. They spring rather from the kind of abstract, divorced idea I keep harping on. Other things being equal, a ton of ideas is barely worth an ounce of imagination — a *fluid* ounce: it has to be fluid or it is not imagination. Ideas see the light, no doubt, but like moths they will beat their tiny brains out on a pane of glass. Imagination oozes under the sash, wraps itself around the obstacle and is beyond it while you still hear the obstinate buzzing of Mothbrain's wings. Ideas are explicit and talkative, which is useful but limiting. You accomplish something and people with ideas come up to you, perturbed: "But you said . . ."

What is imagination? Who can say? When the first railroad was built from Manchester to Liverpool, it had to cross a swamp a good many miles wide. The backers of George Stephenson kept worrying about it and pestering him: "How are you going to do it?" He put them off but they wanted to know, and not "just for information." Finally he said: "I can't tell you how I'm going to do it. I don't know myself. All I'm sure of is that I'm going to." He imagined his way across the swamp. You cannot give a course in imagination or buy a notebook equipped with a filler of it. Imagination cannot be taught because as far as anyone can tell it consists of holding at least two and sometimes twenty ideas in mind at the same time, each modifying the others and usually contradicting them.

In teaching, you disassemble the whole and make the pupil take hold of one part firmly. That is the beginning of the subject. But such is the learning mind that it balks at whatever seems to destroy the thing it has previously acquired. The imaginative student is the one who after a couple of lessons jumps to a vision of the whole and checks it for himself by the test of reality. The point of this difference for the development of the American mind today is this: we use all our best talent, our strongest imaginations, in teaching others. We disseminate and distribute and encourage until the whole intellectual energy of the country is on the blackboard side of the desk, with a passive multitude on the other. Even our painters and musicians rack their wits to explain their drift. Up to a point that is kindly and modest of them. But it is a loss of virtue on their part and harmful to the public. The more they succeed the more we are kept a people of undergraduates — or from another angle, *over*graduates. Too many continue to think that a given picture is "the same idea" as Lesson 23. The picture is what you see, what it means, and something plus, and that plus you have to reach out and seize in one imaginative lunge. The arts build up the imagination only by forcing this acrobatics on us, and the value to the athletic mind and to the country he lives in is that he can apply his trained and muscular imagination to life.

Our people has a dim sense of all that when it acts suspicious toward book-larnin'. Our deep instincts for craftsmanship and organization show that a fine imaginative grasp of matter is latent in all of us. What we need to do is extend it through art to the intangible nonmaterial realities.

We Americans should capitalize our fund of imagination, not "socialize" it quite so recklessly. When we have a healthy surplus we can go back and help even out the distribution, just as now we go back and make up for the deficiencies of our primary education. We still have illiterates who are of no use to production or defense and who miss pleasure for themselves. But we have many more pedants who need to have their flabby or shriveled-up imaginations roused to activity, kept in trim, by a cultural recognition of what imagination is and where it can be found. There is hope when we read in the diary of a convict which the *New Yorker* published: "Evil-doing is but imagination in the wrong place."

12. Cast-iron Olives

AFTER HERBERT SPENCER died at the turn of the century, his *Autobiography* appeared in two volumes. Since at that time he was considered a great thinker, the story of his life received respectful attention. But some reviewers regretted that such a powerful mind bothered to notice and discuss trivial things like the design of milk pitchers. Poor bachelor Herbert had lived in boardinghouses all his life; he could hardly help developing an eye for the conveniences. And as a pioneer evolutionist it seemed to him that a good many gadgets were evolving backwards, from better to worse. The milk pitchers didn't pour half so well as they used to.

The modern American is, or ought to be, on Spencer's side about the importance of the objects that he handles every day. From Jefferson to Mark Twain gadgeteering was a national tradition. Today, as everybody knows, our foreign critics call this love of appliances materialistic, and in response many of us affect a tone of irony about gadgets, as if we lived always in realms above and dealt with trifles only during rare descents from sublime thoughts. The truth is that more and more of the important things in life turn on pinpoints. Our frustrations begin in trivialities — a telephone out of order, a car that will not start, a claim check whose number has been misread. The thing in cellophane that cannot be got at — plain to the sight but sealed like an egg — is the modern version of the torture of Tantalus. Catastrophes we will deal with like heroes, but the bottle top that defies us saps our morale, like the tiny arrows of the Lilliputians that maddened Gulliver and set his strength at naught.

In ordinary objects, moreover, the features that make it smooth-working or awkward, handsome or hateful, are so many signs either of Imagination or of its absence — our characteristic social and ethical imagination, springing from fellow feeling and deserving to rank as one of the humanities. To it also is due the progress that has been visible in machine-made things since the early days when nearly all industrial products were ugly and dangerous.

It being the proper concern of a civilized mind to surround itself with agreeable artifacts, we should become adept at choosing the best on the market. We make much of the spoons and baskets of primitive peoples and tend to disparise ours on principle; we should rather try to influence the shape of our objects by setting up as relentless critics of machines, implements, and gadgets. It is already considered proper to be a judge of textiles and furniture, why not of smaller and larger products? We do not hesitate to complain of bad service from our suppliers, and this often leads to improvement: why suppose that their goods are unimprovable? No piece of handiwork should violate the esthetic and practical conditions that justify its existence.

To become such a hanging judge would be one way to remedy some of the evils of statistical living. The fine critical minds that waste their cutting edge on the mush of new novels in Sunday book reviews ought to give us essays on the real creations of our time, denouncing the flimsy, the mulish, or the malign in everything from toys to lamps; praising what is solid and satisfactory. If critics of the social scene trouble to let us know when newspapers scramble type or authors repeat themselves (see *The New Yorker*), they or their colleagues can inform us of scrambled intentions and repeated mistakes in objects of commerce. So many of the things we have to buy leave, I won't say much — they leave everything to be designed.

To the best of my knowledge, only Mr. Bruce Bliven ever wrote such articles — many years ago, for the *New Republic*. But he has not kept up his eloquent crusade as a gadgeteer. The consumers' research groups, of which I shall say more in a later chapter, confined themselves quite properly to mechanical design and strength;

they rarely considered the intimate convenience of the hand and never spoke of looks. A better model to follow for a consumer's review of the kind I have in mind would be the American Automobile Association, one of our most remarkable institutions, now half a century old. It is a clearinghouse for every kind of criticism about cars and roads, and its publications are surely as important and useful as the *Philosophical Transactions* or the *Crushed Rock Journal*. We need half a dozen such periodicals, with exuberant critics and spacious correspondence columns, to keep us informed and give us a leverage, a purchase, against the gadgetry of modern life. The manufacturers themselves could read and repent with profit. Lately, railroads have been asking commuters to test the seats of new cars, and grocery chains have circularized housewives about the layout of new shopping centers. This is only the beginning of consumer democracy. Nothing is as yet half as good as it can be made, and nothing is sacrosanct — especially when it appears that retrogression threatens. What we need then is the abolitionist voice of the old Boston lady who said, "There is no doubt about it, the modern thunderstorm no longer clears the air."

For the editor of my *Gadget News and Gold-Brick Trumpeter* I should want a man who had grown up in a small American town, say a county seat in a farming state, where a busy and brisk modern general store had started in business around 1910. The critic's youthful mind should have been caught, irradiated, by the poetry of the unique American invention by which, in such a store, the customer's money is conveyed to the bookkeeping department up on the balcony. You remember how it looks: a triple-strung trolley in perpetual motion, with its aerial track connecting every counter to the throbbing financial heart upstairs. The girl crunches your dollar bill with the saleslip into a little box. She lets it grip the moving line and it is wafted away, above. The cashier makes change and returns your rattle of pennies in the same way, all to a soft vibrating hum which in its way is as good as bees in immemorial elms. A true-blue American boy would pay money just to see such a marvel in operation and he would sit watching it with the proper divided mind — one lobe admiring perfection, the other trying to improve on it.

Esthetically, the trolley is superior to the later pneumatic tube which spits out your change noisily in a cylindrical bullet. But the latter is faster — and therein we have the two elements in the tug-of-war of progress. It is like the so-called "tension" in a work of art between form and contents. The pull now of one, now of the other in the great art of gadgeteering is the story of change toward what we mean by modern. It means latest and fleetest. It can and should mean fittest as well. If we are asked what is the typical architecture of Greater New York, we say "modern" and mean it in that honorific sense; though by actual count there are more frame houses and brownstone fronts. The old Flatiron Building was a fright, but by now the skyscraper has both beauty and convenience. The automatic elevator alone is something to enjoy and admire. Today's problem in all departments of practical life is wrapped up in that story of change — to make the efficient agreeable and vice versa.

It would be wrong to imply that we are just beginning to do this, or that the consumer is the only one who cares. All one has to do is to look at articles manufactured or advertised in the nineteenth century to see what a long way we have come since the first abject products of the machine. No one tries to sell us men stiff collars made of white-enameled steel, guaranteed washable, or hideous ready-made suits cut on a Robinson Crusoe pattern. And although the kitchen will be the last backward area civilized by man, we have left far behind the ungainly cast-iron utensils that our great-grand-mothers had to struggle with.

We are in fact getting back to the outlook of the handicraft era, when things were made locally and to order, filling the single customer's wants — the size and shape of his hand no less than the known requirements of use. Only, we modern Americans are carrying consciousness of purpose and variety of resources to the full limit of our imagination. It is stimulated by the fact that we no longer have slaves and drudges to do our work. So we are driven to think of ease and artistic satisfaction as component parts of the humblest tools of life. Just be good enough to come down from these high thoughts for a moment and look at a sardine can. You know the pattern with the lotus-leaf outline along which the metal is supposed to tear. It is the chief archeological vestige we have of the last century. That explains why it tenaciously holds its contents close. Among men of experience, the word "key" in connection with it arouses only sardonic laughter. Now pick up a can of vacuum-sealed coffee and see the modern application of the same principle. It's like passing from King Arthur's Court to Connecticut.

And yet quite a few other things in our kitchens still look like proofs that the world came together by accident, not design. In the super-modern apartment house built three years ago where my sister lives, one finds things from which the mind revolts as defying possibility — for example, a prefabricated kitchen unit which has an absolutely level surface next to the sink. This means that if you put dishes to drain there you later find a pool of water beneath. The makers need a refresher course on the law of gravity. And it acts, this law, where no one wants it to: on the handle of the saucepan in which to boil an egg. Unless filled with water this inane though recent construction tips over and rolls about like a live thing on its streamlined bottom. This is indecent and inexcusable: things should obey, and a woman's kitchen should be as closely adapted to use as her man's office. This, when it comes, will be revolutionary, for the amount of American imagination that has gone into business gadgetry would suffice to write a hundred grand operas.

Everything downtown is made smooth, round, and light; easy to work, to locate, and to store. It brings a smile to the lips, it's so right. The smile often becomes a laugh at the thought of the testing and fiddling needed to turn out so much mechanical self-indulgence. I mean not only the typist's chair which holds her in a lover-like grip, but also the electric pencil sharpeners, staplers, and tape shooters, the many-colored filing cards and trays and cabinets; the machines that make a package or an invoice with a quiet clearing of their throats — why can't a mere woman have a stove with an oven she can regulate and look into without bending down, a light ironing board adjustable to her height, and a refrigerator built to reveal, not hide, its contents? Is it not obvious that the true principle for refrigerators is that of the lazy Susan — or revolving bookcase, rather? Then you would not need a periscope to find that bit of last week's ham at the back of the box, you would swing it around to the front, and perhaps as quickly swing it back.

Moving on to the bathroom, I draw attention to the much too recent fact that electric light switches can be absolutely silent. A burglar must have worked on this, but it is also a boon to those who come home late or like to pad about when others are asleep. But then I pick up my electric shaver and my pleasure in its performance is spoiled by disagreeable thoughts. Instead of an outside opening to the oil cup, with a flap to shut it off, there are four long screws to undo; the case has to be taken off and the works turned over — all to put in one drop of oil. Nor can the screws be put back and tightened without inverting the gadget and having the oil flow out again. Will not the gifted Colonel whose machine gives us inestimable relief from scraping read this and redesign his brainchild?

To take the reverse type of nuisance, why do useful things suddenly disappear? Twenty years ago the manufacturers of good men's shoes discovered that if the tongue was stitched at one point on one side, it wouldn't roll back when the foot was put in. Now every tongue wags loose. At that time also, thick fountain pens were available. They were more comfortable for large hands and held more ink. Now all models of every make try to look like cannulas for infants — ask your doctor what I mean. The one object that I happen to want thin is a comb — and not just to match my hair — but thin flat combs are no longer made — only a sort of garden rake. So Giuseppe sells me one of his professional combs on the old model.

I shan't continue: I'm nearly dressed and ready to go out. But I may add that I suspect pointless snobbery lies behind many of these seemingly deliberate inconveniences, including the supremacy of the thin pen. I wish instead the snobs would go after the really reprehensible ball-point affair, which makes an uneven scrawl out of the best handwriting and thereby imposes on the eyesight of the intending reader. There is plenty of work for gadgeteers who won't take disimprovements lying down. With a long pull and a strong pull all together, it might even be possible to restore the shrunken shirttail to its prewar length.

Everyone will have a different list and not all wishes can be accommodated. But there are also common wants that many feel without expressing them. Such are the wants connected with transportation and communication generally. We all have so much to go and do on this biggish island of ours that trains, cars, and airplanes are bound to occupy a large part of our thoughts.

Our railroads are unquestionably the most remarkable and reassuring carriers ever built. Trains are more numerous and frequent in England; they are smoother and quieter for the overnight traveler in Germany; they display more luxury in France and more insect life in Italy, but on all other counts we surpass everyone else — we had to. To us also goes the credit for making standard equipment out of the chief safety devices — the Westinghouse airbrake, the Miller platform, the automatic coupler and block-signal systems. Other minds may have conceived this or that improvement but we put it through on a continental scale. In his books on American railroading, Charles Francis Adams takes a characteristic sour pleasure in the idea which he demonstrates that, unlike other deaths, those resulting from railroad accidents contribute to progress. The companies went forward under the pressure of public outcry and expensive damage suits, and by 1925 the railroads were at their peak.

The traveler in the United States had then the fastest, safest, most comfortable transportation available on the globe. Our huge all-steel cars, drawn by Baldwin locomotives averaging sixty miles an

hour over long hauls such as New York to Chicago, were the envy
of the world. Inside, one had the feeling of moving steadily upon a
solid base, yet not too fast to see the countryside. One knew the
train crew were professional men, capable and attentive right down
to the Negro porter, who was ready to father the innocents of all
ages. All this for two and a half cents a mile plus Pullman fare. On
extra-fare trains the company paid you money back if you arrived
late at your destination.

Then came the competition of long-distance buses and planes, and
the railroads began to slip. Service has declined in quantity and
quality, and only a few improvements have taken place. The diesel
engine is one; the roomette and the new spacious air-conditioned
coaches are another. This includes a truly convenient baggage rack
— its history a symbol of human fecklessness as well as a proof that
we need criticism not only of art but of artifacts. The baggage rack
started a hundred years ago as a lethal net borrowed from the fishing
industry. For generations it stayed narrow and inaccessible; then it
grew ornate with defensive curves and projections which threatened
the rising passenger and baffled the weak and short ones; later on,
when it grew rigid, it tilted its contents on banked curves. Now at
last it is as it should be — high, wide, and handsome.

What is not as it should be in our railroads today is that those who
run them — both management and labor — are resisting rather than
furthering change. It was not long ago that some of the important
lines entered into an agreement *not* to install air-conditioning. Somebody broke the pact, or kept out of it, and forced the rest to keep
us cool. But to stay put, to restrict service and make no changes,
is the typical state of mind. When that remarkable businessman, Mr.
Robert R. Young, became President of the Chesapeake and Ohio
some six years ago he startled the public with his full-page ads saying:

A HOG CAN CROSS THE COUNTRY WITHOUT CHANGING TRAINS BUT
YOU CAN'T!

This brought about the present shunting arrangement at Chicago — a makeshift by which you keep your same compartment, though you change stations and waste five hours.

Mr. Young is full of other ideas which suggest that railroads could pull out of their low water financially and give their passengers new sensations of comfort and confidence. As Chairman of the Federation for Railway Progress he tells us what some of these could be. To begin with, he would abolish the primitive routine for making reservations — standing in line twice and waiting while the employee telephones and writes out a yard of ticket. A central bureau, payment on the train or on a monthly account, would save hours of irritation as well as prevent block reservations by clubs and corporations. Unfair to begin with, the practice makes for empty cars with people turned away for lack of space.

Then Mr. Young would re-design most of the familiar equipment. He would run lighter and lower-slung cars of equal strength and greater riding smoothness. It seems we traipse up and down those rugged car steps simply because the aboriginal freight platform of 1830 was four feet three above the rails. The new car, weighing and costing one third as much and wearing the roadbed less in proportion to the combined ratio of weight and motive power, has been built. But the old guard refuses to budge, on the ground that thousands of station platforms would have to be changed. Our depots are made of such durable and beautiful material it would be a pity to touch them — even though the cost of altering these historic monuments would be quickly recovered. Similar reasoning prevents the adoption of the new improved airbrake with one hundred and fifty fewer parts — safer because less likely to go out of order. Manufacturers won't touch it because the railroads haven't insisted on it and the business of replacing parts is profitable.

As for freight traffic, nothing much seems to have been done since Walter P. Murphy introduced the corrugated end for box cars. Rolling stock for freight still largely disdains ball bearings, which would reduce delays and accidents and raise the transportation speed from its present average of seven or eight miles an hour. In addition to modernized freight cars, Mr. Young proposes truck trailers that could be used on rails as well as on highways so as to reduce the cost and dangers of long-distance trucking.

Simply as a contribution to national defense, all these practicable measures of reform should be carried out. Everybody would be the gainer, and in every capacity — as investor, as citizen under arms, and as peacetime traveler. The only feature of a truly modern railroad that I should like to see Mr. Young add to his catalogue of innovations is the use of tickets and regular sittings for dining car meals — anything to eliminate the barbaric waiting-in-line we now endure everywhere but on the California Zephyr. Then perhaps we would feel that the high price we pay for haulage, Pullman, and taxes was justified. If besides there were a well-organized official porter and taxi service at every main station, we might even imagine we were back in 1925 when American railroading led the world.

In those days the United States also had the best postal service. No longer. It is discouraging, at a time when people talk glibly of decadence, to think of our Post Office — the breakdown of communications is so obviously a sign of falling apart. The U. S. Mail holds a special place in our life and our minds: for it is one of our earliest national institutions, the creation of Benjamin Franklin, who clearly attached to it great cultural and political importance. When he founded a magazine, he called it the *Saturday Evening* Post. Poor Richard knew that there is no community life in a republic without quick and accurate communication of news and views, no business life without reliable mails. What is the situation today? The mails are expensive, slow, and uncertain. Postal workers are demoralized. In large cities more and more people say to each other: "I'll bring it around myself — the mail isn't safe." Or: "I'll send it to you by messenger, otherwise you won't get it till God knows when."

The government's notion that the Post Office Department should be self-supporting is entirely right if this can be achieved by businesslike means. Those in charge must reduce costs and increase efficiency — not merely raise rates and reduce service. But our postmasters suffer from *encephalitis lethargica* and their sleepy example narcotizes the whole organization from top to bottom. From the political grumbling that has lately been heard, the methods of the Department seem to be years behind the times, the good men (as usual) bound hand and foot by red tape. This is the time for the public to start brandishing scissors.

A full bill of particulars would make incredible reading. The facts suggest Darkest Africa or the impenetrable regions of Brazil, not the United States in 1953. "Service" now is one mail delivery a day to private houses, two (but not always) to business houses. The branch offices keep a forty-hour week — closed on Saturdays. Special Delivery survives only in name. It often comes *after* the regular mail from the same point and time of mailing, and it costs the price of two bus rides. As I write, I remember that a week ago I received a registered letter containing a document of considerable value. The sender spent 63 cents to insure its safety. Yet it was left by the carrier on an open shelf for second-class mail. No one signed for it. In talking to the carrier about this, I learned that his oversight — for which he was apologetic — was the result of too many things to do, both at his station and on his rounds. He and his colleagues are as disgusted as the public.

This explains why it is useless to write in complaints of specific errors or to try and trace lost articles. Weeks later an inspector comes around who practically says that in the circumstances you are a fool to expect serious attention. Bit by bit we discover how far disintegration has gone. Here in New York directory service has been discontinued. This means that a slight mistake in address — an "East" for a "West" — dooms the letter to perdition. Forwarding service goes on, but the overdriven clerks do it badly, without noticing terminal dates. In the stations themselves, every window has long slow-moving lines, because most of the equipment dates back to the First World War — just like the clumsy street boxes — and organization is unknown. For example, a whole line of people who want to mail at most a couple of parcels each will have to wait behind a shopboy who has to insure thirty or forty packages.

As for the classification of matter, it seems absurd that typescript should be considered first-class mail, though the sender is willing to mail it open; while in the present disorder, first-class mail is often handled like ordinary ads. Business firms have been forced in self-defense to stamp FIRST CLASS on all their 3-cent letters to have them go at the rate they paid for. Even so, sealed mail will travel at a colonial pace from New York to such a remote seat of learning as Princeton, New Jersey, and it often takes nine days to cross the vast sea between Manhattan and Staten Island.

Air mail is about the only service which is rapid and fairly priced — rapid, that is, while it is aboard the plane. The airlines get a good subsidy out of this, as does the merchant marine for overseas mail. Since first and last we spend a good deal for things that do not pay their way — agriculture being one of them; since it is social wisdom to subsidize soil conservation, forestry, and national parks, and to make the Bureau of Weights and Measures a service station for manufacturers, it would seem logical and just as beneficial to subsidize a modern Post Office. Appropriate the money and clear out the scum; abolish Letter-Writing Week and make it Careful Delivery Year. Do this and show by lowered rates and increased service how a great country speeds the winged word. We the people will even stand a while longer those ugly commemorative stamps that have no right side up, if you sons of P. O. Patronage take proper care of what we glue them on.

Although the first recorded automobile accident took place in New York on May 30, 1896, for all practical purposes we can say that the automobile is the same age as the century. In the autumn of 1900, according to his diary, the English poet Wilfred Scawen Blunt went out for the first time in a car and "attained a speed of fifteen miles an hour. Certainly an exhilarating experience!" A few years later, in a popular novel, one could read the following dialogue:

> " — or shall we take my motor car?"
> "No, no, it attracts too much attention!"

We have come a long way in less than a lifetime. It is not attention we attract, but parking tickets, and our speed, though less exhilarating, has transformed much more than just transportation. It is the internal combustion engine more than anything else that has made us a huge community of peoples and a giant economy of goods. In our individual lives a car is no longer a luxury and certainly not, as in Europe, a sort of foppish adjunct to egotism. It is a necessity. Motor travel, if we include the bus lines, is accessible to almost everyone, and at one time or another most Americans of either sex have driven a car, usually their own. Paying the purchase price is made as easy as driving the machine: any fool can do that, as every highway testifies.

And so we pay another price, killing more of our people on the roads than in foreign wars. For adapting our nerves and our equipment to the strain of speed has been painfully slow: the brake light in the rear took thirty years to become standard. It took fifty-six between the first recorded accident in New York and the opening of the first completely modern highway, the New Jersey Turnpike. Now that we have it we can look back on our amazing wayward course. At one point on the pike, near the Lincoln Tunnel, a driver has a panoramic sight of the entire industrial revolution: trains under him, airplanes above, Fitch and Fulton's steamers on the Hudson, and the labyrinth of roads which he is threading.

But by and large it is obvious we still think of ourselves as stationary — or at most as horsemen out for a trot: look at our ordinary road signs, their placement, confusion, poor lettering, directionless arrows, and abrupt inconsecutiveness. The cultural lag here is thirty to forty years; our model through-ways for motoring are only samples stuck here and there amid old-fashioned roads or enlarged but undesigned highways.

The same lopsided growth is noticeable in other agents of our conquest of time and space: buses and planes, despite the risks involved in speed and combustion aboard, are still prisons for the passengers in case of accident. We have yet to design and install the standard window that pushes out with one simple motion, and which gives an exit large enough for an adult. As things are, we ride and fly in sealed boxes just like those in a department store's pneumatic tube. The railroads were at that stage about 1840, when passengers were locked in from outside and burned helplessly under the tunnels when sparks set the coaches on fire. Only it didn't take more than half a dozen such accidents to modify those incinerators. With us, there is something altogether too happy-go-lucky about air travel, and we are idiots to tolerate it. The simple fact we can note in the news of almost every disaster, that the names of one or more passengers are incomplete or unknown to the company, is an indictment of method.

This carelessness is also a cultural characteristic. We're a little afraid to fuss in front of others when they seem to think that "everything will be all right." Who wants to be an old maid? Nobody. But some of us, regardless of sex, wouldn't mind the chance to get older instead of swelling the totals of travel casualties. If so, one of the things we might do is ask where that emergency brake is gone that we used to have on our cars. In those simple-minded days, if your friend fell across the wheel in a dead faint while driving, we could yank the emergency and not have to use a ditch or a pole as buffer stop. Now in many cars the brake has crept around to the driver's left side, his weak hand, and it takes a great heave to make it catch. It can even catch and not hold. One man was killed last August — crushed against a tree — while he went around the front of his car to open the door for his passengers. To be sure, with no mechanical handbrake, the discovery that your hydraulic brake won't work is twice as thrilling. The simple mishaps that can let the hydraulic fluid pour out suggest that car designers re-invent the handbrake and put in a gauge on the dashboard for the fluid supply.

All of which confirms the need for all who pay good money in good faith to carp and criticize whenever they find cause. Our admirable, inexpensive, mass-produced, democratic *objets d'industries* are still far from perfect. The corporal who painted lemons on his car and toured through Washington was arrested under a statute forbidding any decoration of a vehicle so as to cast derision or ridicule upon its make. But he won his case and the Commissioners of the District of Columbia repealed the law. Bravo for the corporal, the Patrick Henry of our day! His is the spirit of '76. His example tempts me to go on and paint in words the modern car's unfortunate looks — bloated like a bad case of glandular disturbance, and in the slightest scrape turning out even worse than it's painted. . . . But I have said enough. A better man found the perfect words, though he was not thinking of a car: "How the vision both of its form and its color came to afflict a single mind, as Heaven has not yet smitten it, let no man judge."

13. Greatest City in the World

NEW YORK IS A SKY LINE, the most stupendous, unbelievable man-made spectacle since the hanging gardens of Babylon. Significantly, you have to be outside the city — on a bridge or on the Jersey Turnpike — to enjoy it.

Manhattan, except for its harbor the least likely site for a modern metropolis, is an island tucked away on the map like an appendage on an anatomical chart. A hilly tract of mud, ledge, and fill, thirteen miles long and two miles wide, it is said to have been bought from the Indians for twenty-four dollars and a bottle of whisky. Only now, after three centuries' experience, can one begin to appreciate the Indians' long view; for until about fifty years ago, it was possible to think there was something cozy and quaint about New York straggling upward from the Battery. Central Park was way uptown, goats grazed on Morningside Heights, and a native poet, Joseph Rodman Drake, could exclaim:

My own romantic Bronx!

without being suspected of writing a caption for a *New Yorker* drawing.

All that was before we built a sky line; so that our greatness and our misery, as often happens, came simultaneously. Having become a city of cliff-and-canyon dwellers, our standards are set for us by our necessities. And when we compare what we are with what we endure, we can only groan and vent our disgust on our neighbor — as we do. Here is the greatest concentration of power in the world, the most feverish collection of brains, the deepest moneybags, the mightiest shipping, the most intricate communications center, the vastest publishing industry, the largest cluster of hospitals and richest array of physicians, the widest network of schools, museums, and universities, the most energetic population. Talents are innumerable and endlessly ramified, as are the opportunities for their use. Where but in New York would someone advertise himself as "Expert in pharmaceutical Latin" and hope to receive encouragement? Where else does every star want to shine, at least for one golden season? New York is the Mecca of everyone in the world who has an independent will and a conception of the century he lives in. New York is the gateway to the forty-eight freedoms — which may not be enough, but which are unquestionably better than the seven devils left behind.

New York means all this and earns its greatness, but by a paradox of equal magnitude, it fails in all the practical modernity it supposedly stands for. As a city to live in, New York is a squatter's camp.

For seven million people to pump themselves every day in and out of this great heart, and for some to dwell there in reasonable comfort, three things would be needed: transportation, sanitation, and policing. New York's public transport system has to be borne to be believed. To begin with, it is not a system. The city, half a dozen private companies, and one union play and quarrel over the management of a score of lines above and below ground. Some of these lines cross and connect, others merely cross. Transfers are haphazard, some are to be paid for, others not. Fares vary and so do the ways of paying them — silver into a counting machine, pennies into the driver's hand or on a tray.

Unlike every other city in the world, New York cannot afford to give its visitors a free map showing the routes and hours of service of the various lines, for it would show the chaos which is the sole working principle of the vehicular mess. It would show the abjectitude of the Forty-Second Street shuttle — three minutes' transportation sandwiched in ten of boardwalk trudge — the strangers following green and red lights stuck in the ceiling, jostled by the rushing crowd while they decipher a confusion of small signs posted in every direction. A map would show on two neighboring avenues, Lexington and Fifth, two different bus lines both numbered 4, the buses themselves being indistinguishable in color and shape. Elsewhere you find red buses, but don't imagine they all belong to one company. The route descriptions on the front are there to mock the passengers. On Fifth Avenue, the circular route number 6 is easily confused with the north-and-south lines, and everywhere the figures and words grow smaller and less legible with every new style of bus. In the subway stations, there is no such thing as a map of the whole city and the given route, with a marker for the spot where one stands. Even the latest city-built subways give only fitful directions to their complex meanderings, and the personnel throughout makes it a point of honor to answer inquiries in Gaelic or not at all.

No provision of any kind, either, for the convenience of surface passengers on rainy days or at busy intersections under the obsolete elevated structure. Waiting for a bus anywhere along Third Avenue is dangerous, and one person a day is injured at the Forty-Second Street stop. (*New York Times* of August 5, 1952.) The old streetcar rails there have not been taken up, which adds to drivers' sporting risk when they are wet. Bus stops may be on either side of a cross street and they change without notice, as do the intervals between. Crosstown routes are in perpetual flux. It does not seem to have occurred to anyone that diagonal runs might save time and money if they were adapted to the actual and easily ascertainable needs of daily users.

Except at rush hours — and this is partly a result of the city's shape — you will probably have to wait what is for a metropolis a disgracefully long time — twelve to fifteen minutes. Traffic is the excuse for delay. Actually, when your bus does come, it is ambling along with a tail of two or three others. They look like dinosaurs afraid to go singly. The first will be full of frantic people who have been gathering at every stop for the last quarter-hour. The trailers behind are nearly empty and *their* passengers are frantic because they had allowed twenty minutes for a ride which at this suddenly deliberate pace will take forty. The mind of man can fashion a directed missile that will hit the enemy in the left eye but cannot make a schedule for New York buses.

With time on his hands, the passenger — say on Fifth Avenue — begins to wonder why the Coach Company that keeps him waiting still has the privilege of charging more than other lines. Formerly it offered a topside view of the city — "Open Air to Everywhere" was the motto — it allowed smoking upstairs, did not take standees, and two men ran a civilized conveyance. Where is the superior service now? The same crowded, inconvenient one-tier bus, and motormen who are not one bit more disagreeable than their colleagues east and west. What is clear is that all drivers hate the public and rejoice in their discomfiture and delay. This is the only uniform condition throughout the city.

The trouble began with the inhuman one-man operation. Nobody should be surprised that under it the otherwise normal and decent Americans who drive buses become manic or sullen, refusing to answer questions or seizing open road space to dash and brake suddenly. The treatment of the men matches that of the passengers: why talk of human dignity in the face of the rubbing and drubbing and swaying and pulling of viscera miscalled transportation? No one in the history of mankind has begun the day's work by such an ordeal as a New York bus or subway ride.

It is pitiable to have to analyze and become articulate about things that taken one at a time would be trifles. But New York life is the piling up of a crushing load of trifles. If only for the future diggers of our midden-heaps, the facts must be set down. None of the vehicles in use is very old, yet none seems to have been designed for human beings. The entrance is too narrow and the coin receptacles, all different, are all a hazard. On Fifth Avenue, old and young are expected to balance on a careering vehicle while trying to insert a dime in a slot just wide enough to admit it. On other lines, most lately, the six-hole cup into which one could really put the coin without its becoming a game of skill is being replaced with a hooded rectangular slit which approximates the Fifth Avenue one in difficulty. Who is the sadist behind it all?

Inside the bus everything is arranged so that you cannot see the street signs. A few lampposts on Fifth carry a bracelet with a tiny number at eye level. There is but one emergency door, on one side and blocked by a seat: it would be useless in a turnover and is insufficient in any case. Of the stop signal, I can hardly trust myself to speak. It is so rigged up that a pull on the rope anywhere along two thirds of its length has no effect on the bell. The bell often has no effect on the driver, and the connecting spring often has no effect whatever, broken as it is by the desperate tugs of countless prisoners bent on escape. As for the automatic exit doors, the variety of their working is a menace. An innocent woman or child stands on the top step, level with the floor of the bus, and so prevents its going. The driver shouts abuse. In the next bus, one has to leap down to the bottom step if one wants out, or again incur the motorman's wrath. Meanwhile a certificate above your head implores you to love him for not having hit other buses — not even those of rival companies. Going about New York, in short, you are hard at work keeping your balance, temper, and a whole skin.

If these are not quite the drops of water that wear away stone, they are certainly the rubs and pinpricks that make so many New Yorkers irritable and rude. What is astonishing is that some few have the heart to reason themselves out of their fretted state and act civilized. For their daily grinding down by public transportation is only one of their legitimate complaints.

Their city is filthy. Everybody has read about the horrors of medieval town life — garbage and slops in the streets, and a separate stench for every locality. That is a gross libel on medieval towns, but it is New York to a *t*, with industrial smut added to man and nature's. The streets are lined with cans of ashes and refuse that get picked up after much of their contents have been scattered. The removal trucks are huge, slow-moving, earsplitting contraptions which block traffic. At times, especially in winter snow and ice — which the city has never learned to deal with — the trucks skip part of their routes. This is true not solely in the slums — inexcusable as that would be — but everywhere. Surely not in the fine residential districts? I know of none such. There are islands of good brick and mortar among jerry-built slums, a patchwork of styles, incomes, and cultures. The famed East Side is simply a *campo santo* for dog droppings. On lovely, damp spring days, the air is charged with an ineffable smell.

Fortunately, there being two noble rivers, one on either side of the island, great winds blow in every direction. But the litter and silt of the streets swirl into eyes, mouth, and nostrils. New Yorkers are always full of grit. Baskets for waste paper at some of the street corners (there still aren't enough) are ingeniously made of wide-mesh wire so that the contents can blow where they list. On very hot days, when the women are out on the streets in their slips and nightgowns (trimmed up a bit to look like summer dresses) and when the poor men are packed so close together in the offices that they haven't room to wear their coats, a few antiquated water trucks try to lay the burning dust with water, having first scattered most of it upwards with a cylindrical brush: it wouldn't do to deprive the citizens of their re-enforced atmosphere. For that reason, too, landlords and factory owners are waging a holy war to preserve the right of polluting the air with soot and smoke. Twenty-eight tons of greasy matter are deposited annually over all our dwelling places, where it eats away fabrics and furniture. Everyone gets his share, though there is a fanatic, a Rear Admiral named William S. Maxwell, who is vainly trying to stop this blessing from falling upon the just and the unjust alike.

But enforcement of any kind in New York is almost the last article of Utopia. There is an ordinance against noise, and a society to reward noise-abaters, but noise increases. Trucks and fire engines are equipped with piercing staccato whistles, and every ten minutes indoor conversation has to stop while the race screams down the avenue. Late at night, private cars toot horns to gain entrance to their garage — no one could enforce the use of a sidewalk device that would ring inside the garage as the car wheels pressed it. And almost any day of the week wedding parties have license to blow horns steadily as they endanger life on their way to collision on the highroads. Besides these trifles, three uncontrollable airports send out low-flying planes in droves. Schools, hospitals, and Stadium concerts must endure it, the sign QUIET on their streets being chiefly a reminder to those inside. The city itself is the worst offender with its Elevated clanking through the night, its cobblestoned avenues and its endless unco-ordinated ripping up of streets. In so much noise, noise disappears. New Yorkers gradually lose the power to listen while retaining their sense of hearing. One of these hardy creatures was once found napping in a phone booth.

These are the amenities. Remain the last necessities. First, protection of life. The metropolitan police are a picked and trained body of courageous men, deservedly known — in spite of graft and corruption — as New York's Finest. But they're sometimes so fine you can't see them at all. There aren't enough for the lawlessness that haunts the streets. Go into the parks at night and you will have your teeth knocked in and your valuables taken. In the daytime anywhere bag snatching is a common risk, and children coming home from school are held up for their pennies, marbles, or belts by older gangs. The sense of being in a city, a *polis*, metro or not, is disappearing as the inhabitant fingers his service revolver and writes to the *Times* about the right to bear arms in self-defense.

One of the causes for this state of siege is of course the appalling condition of the public schools. The system employs thousands of hard-working, well-meaning people, and yet it is in most quarters impossible to send a child to public school if one wants it to be (1) educated, (2) safe from bodily harm, (3) reasonably sheltered from indecency of language and behavior. Teachers themselves have been attacked with knives, and their control of overcrowded classes full of rowdy, restless youths is made harder by the physical condition of the school buildings (ceilings fall and sanitation is scant) and the apparent lack of leadership above.

All this comes down, ultimately, to the maladministration of the city and the natural effect of patent cynicism on the young. The smart guys are in some sort of racket, in city government or on the dark streets — or so it must seem to simple minds.

What is depressing is not that with cramped quarters and a mixed and shifting population — all but a few New Yorkers are outsiders who commute, from Jersey or from Calcutta — there should be many opportunities for laziness and corruption. The maddening thing is that the spent millions yield so little. As I write, a few inspectors are exhuming sewer pipes to see if they've been properly sealed. This makes one sigh for the days of Boss Tweed when park railings cost a thousand dollars a foot, but were made to last a thousand years. You can still see them and even lean on them.

The solution of the one problem of traffic would make every Manhattanese loyal for life. He asks in vain: "Why are there not more parking lots, why do trucks obstruct the path to Pennsylvania Station all day long? Why are New York taxis the longest in the world and the most poorly distributed? Why did it take forty years to install on them a roof light showing when they're free — but so arranged that it is of no use in the daytime? Why have the newest buses on the 15 route been permitted to be of such length that they can't turn corners without a general retreat of cars to the left or right?"

It makes one want to organize a general exodus. To prevent this, the exits from the city are kept dismal, incomplete, and badly marked. The parkways surrounding New York are models of civil engineering, landscaping, and traffic science. But to reach them on the east, or the tunnels on the west, is like a game of chance played in the dark. Again, why is that Toonerville trolley run by steam, the Long Island Railroad, tolerated? Or the antiquated equipment for commuters on the New Haven and the open disregard of schedules on the West Shore branch of the Central?

Both riverbanks long ago turned into eyesores, of course, and their waters are hopelessly polluted. A man who wants to kill himself by jumping off Brooklyn Bridge risks almost certain death from typhoid. But why have neighboring beaches been allowed to become sewers, and the harbor as far as Sandy Hook permitted to greet shipping with floating garbage and dead ducks killed by detergents? The Statue of Liberty has her feet in a sludge bubble, alas, but why must we have at our transatlantic piers the foulest debarkation and customs procedure that can be found the world over? The foreigner's first view of New York soil — as distinct from sky line — is the square of wet or dry mud at the bottom of a baggage chute, among a moil of distraught passengers and predatory porters and cabbies. Welcome to the greatest city in the world!

New York City has one splendid Terminal, Grand Central, which is spacious, quiet, and well-appointed. All this soothing influence was going to be nullified by incessant broadcast commercials, when public protest, ably led by *The New Yorker*, forced the railroads to retreat. One case is enough to show what the public can do. The first thing it should do is try to civilize Pennsylvania Station, with its deafening, raucous announcers, its unreadable red-and-yellow track signs put up at the last minute, its multiple exits that make it impossible to meet a friend at the gate, and its anarchical scramble for cabs. Every New Yorker will think of plenty to be done. Our hospitals alone would profitably occupy a real organizer for years to bring them up to something like adequate room and first-class performance. Any one civic improvement would shine out like a pocket flash in the Tunnel of Love. But it's about time we had a gleam, for the seething emotions in that dark place are anything but love.

As if public discomfort were not enough, private life in New York has also sunk into a kind of servile hebetude. My sister, as I mentioned earlier, lives in one of the cliffs, a three-hundred-unit affair, with as many balconies as there are choice flats, so that from the outside the structure looks like a tallboy with all its drawers half-pulled. Having moved in with a score of others before construction was quite finished, her initiation was perfect: the workmen were still putting in fixtures (later found not to fit the Venetian blinds supplied) so the entire building was in the jurisdiction of the unions. In the midst of unloading the tenants' furniture, everything stopped: a tenant had brought in his lamp shades in his car and a woman had been seen scraping spots of paint off window glass with a razor blade. The delinquents were admonished and life resumed.

After labor's innings, management had theirs. Word went out that no one could install any private lock on his outside door. In the public interest, some forty bonded employees would have passkeys. For three weeks they kept barging in with the briefest knock of warning until angry protests compelled this gestapo to give notice before breaking into one's nap or dinner. Then news came that the master key had been stolen; all the locks would have to be changed. Meantime, watch your goods! When the new key came, it was charged for on the bill. Only a few sharp dealers crossed it off.

Came a rainy day and the prudent householder sported a doormat. By now the house was full and a printed order was issued: no doormats. They were deemed dangerous underfoot and spoiled the pleasant uniformity of the corridors. This notion has been carried even further at Chicago, where tenants must put up curtains of a certain color, for the sake of visual harmony. At my sister's, no work is allowed to be done in any apartment except by the placemen, and it is a circumstance to have, say, a picture delivered by the framer. Servants have to have a signed pass in order to leave at night with bundles; new visitors are virtually frisked. And every so often comes to the tenant sheltering under this paternal autocracy a directive from the central bureau. For his sake, at the cost of blood, sweat, and tears, something new has been installed; or more often, some convenience has been curtailed — side doors shut or upstairs mail delivery abolished.

I do not say this chrome-plated prison is typical. It is only the latest style of block life and its regimentation. This may not spread, but the tendency is all that way. In high-class public housing, for example, the rage for order is such that inspectors are sent round to see if tenants rushing off to business on some late morning haven't left a coffee cup and cereal bowl unwashed in the sink. Reprimand with warning follows. For a tear in your own carpet your lease may be broken. With each improvement in the new, the older houses become more preferable, especially the remodeled ones. To live in one is to stand halfway between the cliff- and the closet-dwellers and thus enjoy premises partly designed for occupancy. Elsewhere, apartments are built like Pullman cars on a long corridor, or scramble anyhow, from a kitchen as you enter, to a bathroom off the dinette.

Indeed, when you go to see friends in New York there is no telling from their address or style of life in what type of caravanserai you will find them. It adds zest to visiting. You may find a sort of Gothic fortress with portcullises and massive doors that most women can't push, especially when carrying parcels. But there you can be sure the management provides door and elevator men in force who must be tipped. There are so many and they change so often that one envies King Lear being cut down by his daughters to fifty retainers. At other places, there are no attendants at all, no one to take packages or messages, and mail delivery is precarious. New Yorkers expect no more than they get.

All these belong to the "better 'oles." New York's millions live in shacks piled on top of one another. Some are firetraps, some leak gas at every pore, all lack sufficient air and light. Again and again, the good buildings of a certain class get torn down while the cold-water flats go on forever. Only two basic requirements of civilized man are assured him on Manhattan: The Board of Health does manage in the end to enforce the rules of heat. In winter many are cold but few are frozen. And at all times and places, New Yorkers are automatically supplied with roaches and waterbugs, share and share alike. Just try to keep them out!

For what unimaginable good do we consent to live in these catacombs? For theater and opera and night clubs? Perhaps — though the legitimate theater has been choked to death by rent regulations and has become mass entertainment for tourists, rather than sophisticated pleasure for cosmopolitans. The great days of the Theatre Guild, Winthrop Ames, and Gilbert Miller; the early genius of Rodgers and Hart, and of the Garrick, Grand Street, and Provincetown troupes, are not likely to come back under present management. As for the Opera, its location, acoustics, and inherited ideas make it a place one visits from a sense of duty, an old ladies' home where one's presence may bring a little cheer to the ancients. Every effort to bring the opera uptown and make it esthetically and financially justifiable has failed. That leaves, for pure delight of the senses, only the busy hum of men and the thrills of jaywalking.

Eating? Good restaurants are few — or rather, their life is short. All are expensive and the service too often harried and indifferent. One must get to know Tony, that is, get him to know you; and even so his subordinates think you have the evil eye. Nervous eating makes for irritable colons and sagging paunches. The double-breasted suit was invented right here to conceal all such tremors from view. No, New York is no lotus-land. When everybody finds it harder day by day to conduct the simple business of living, paying his bills and keeping his trousers pressed, conviviality becomes a task. When you call up you say: "How is life with you?" And the answer goes: "A little mad, thank you." We all keep thinking of the poor gorilla who committed suicide three years ago in the Bronx Zoo — disillusioned with evolution. We would settle for Hell as our next stopping place: living conditions could be no worse there, and the climate would be better for our sinuses.

Still, can we not enjoy it as the spectacle of grandeur it undoubtedly is? Not from inside. New York has never risen to providing vistas. We are so starved for an actual sight of the majesty we sense around us that we're content to take the lower Palisades, or Astoria, or the roofs of Harlem as grandiose views, ruined though they are by the hand of man. If we wear side-blinders, the George Washington Bridge is a glorious vision. But none of these is New York proper, which remains strictly invisible, a concept. The makings of a noble sight existed on Park Avenue looking South. But the gilded erection at the end was put up by a reactionary who leafed through a book for his design, and the silhouette is disastrous. By some perverse and significant fate nearly all of New York's summits are failures, the Empire State and the Chrysler buildings especially. Rockefeller Center wisely refrained from campaniles, and so did the makers of that pure marvel, the Lever building. The rest are unimportant — yet together, what a sublime, unsurpassable sky line!

14. When the Doctor Is a Pill

ASK THE FIRST AMERICAN DOCTOR you meet and he will freely admit that the United States leads the world in medicine. We have the largest and most numerous hospitals, the greatest amount of machinery, the most schools, clinics, journals, research funds, and drug companies. With us medicine is queen of the professions, socially and intellectually. This is true nowhere else, and our doctors know and jealously guard their privilege. For the same reason that makes every reasonably well-to-do immigrant wish to have his son a doctor, the doctors think twice before lavishing expensive training on a person whose sole ambition may be social advancement. Besides, the doctor in practice requires great stamina and a heroic sense of duty. On call for good reasons or bad, he cannot claim any of the twenty-four hours as surely his. His own family sees him by appointment — and this is the only kind he dare break. A two weeks' vacation in August — perhaps — if no one in his ambit is getting ready to be born or to die.

One happy result of our collective pride and faith in doctors is that we consider health one of the natural rights and bolster it up preventively and institutionally. Visit the three or four floors occupied by the International Ladies Garment Workers' medical staff at 275 Seventh Avenue and you will see what is virtually a private hospital. It is typical. Most large concerns have them, though in keeping with American opti-euphemism they are called Health Centers. No wonder the undertakers are beginning to offer their services on the installment plan.

Since 1900 the death rate in this country has been cut nearly 50 per cent. Seventeen and two-tenths of a citizen died per thousand in 1900. Now nine and six-tenths do. Nearly half of our people reach the age of seventy-five, and nine out of ten babies live. In the first year of life, 968 out of a thousand survive instead of only 837. Taking the republic as a whole at this mid-century point, 80 per cent of the population can reasonably expect to reach the age of fifty. At first sight, the only thing wrong with this report is that those over fifty are not given a chance to reach it again. But if we allow for the fact that the South is still lacking doctors, nurses, and hospitals, it appears that the computed gains since 1900 do not represent what we have actually accomplished. If our best facilities were available throughout the land, we should be saving more infants and living even longer.

This is the kind of performance we especially shine in. From the heroic tale of Goethals and Walter Reed banishing yellow fever in Panama at the turn of the century to our later army doctors abolishing yaws at Okinawa in 1950, we love to clean up, to create mass health in place of rooted disease. A task of that sort can be organized. Once the mosquito or virus or diet deficiency has been tracked down and dealt with, the work is systematic, almost mechanical, and the statistics of Before and After reward our efforts. All honor, then, to those of our M.D.'s engaged here and abroad in cleaning-up operations.

But to be alive and breathing is not quite enough. Our other opportunities at home make us very demanding, and the fact that we are pulled and pushed and compressed by our systems of production and transport makes us very sensitive to mechanical treatment. We came alone into this world and expect to leave it the same way. When we are ill, we feel similarly alone in our misery; being sick is a highly individual affair, which makes us long for personal attention, not just "personalized" on the surface; and this is what our system overlooks, what too many of our doctors fail to understand.

They have been used since Hippocrates to forming a close corporation; mutual criticism is forbidden them by their so-called ethics; and they think that because they encompass our lives and are ready to work conscientiously at their job, they fully earn their prestige. They should perhaps reflect that they get it, in large part, from the distraught and the afflicted, who, once the danger is past, are eager to forget their misery. Gratitude may record the doctor's success and even his strenuous efforts, but seldom the quality of the treatment received.

Now no one but an ignorant savage is "down on doctors" or begrudges them their authority. Whoever has the good luck — as I have — of numbering doctors among his family and closest friends — will hesitate before offering any complaint to his own physician, much more to the profession as a whole. One understands that each good practitioner has probably more patients than he can handle. It is natural, efficient, normal to apply to them the methods of mass production. We understand the difficulty, and perhaps the state of mind. Medical techniques have the impersonality of science — tests, charts, averages. All this is right and proper, but one must ask how far the doctor's training as a healer is damaged by it. The patient survives, but why should he spend his worst moments in an atmosphere wholly mechanical and metallic?

If he goes to the hospital, he finds it has become a factory run by engineers. The word "care" has lost its humane meaning and acquired a statistical one which is not at all pleasant. It means that "the usual" was gone through in room 210 on the dot of 9:15. Say you have been in pain, unable to sleep. Finally you drop off. Ten minutes pass: you are brusquely waked up: the nurse is there to give you a sponge bath. It is routine. You are bright enough to see that if every patient chose his own time, the system would go to pieces. But the fact remains that you have been deprived of one of the rights of the sick. Hardly back from death's door, you have been forced to "co-operate" again. Your illness is not your own, it's a segment of community life. Very well, but if this is modern medical care, one somehow wants to spell it with a "k."

The hospital routine is so generally ruthless that a "study" has been made of it and published under the revolutionary title *Pa-*

tients are People. This is a beginning, though the study takes the cart-before-the-horse point of view that patients are bewildered by "being plunged suddenly into a world of illness." What is meant is that he is processed like a side of beef at the Armour plant. Hospitals exist, we used to think, in order to minister to the "world of illness" that the patient brings with him. As for the excuse offered in this same study that "the average hospital employee does not realize he is judged by the sick man in accordance with his humanitarian rather than his scientific impulse," that is pompous nonsense. Most nurses, internes, *and doctors* have about as much scientific impulse as Huckleberry Finn when he was extricating his Negro friend Jim — and it's quite enough for ordinary purposes. Nor does the patient ask for "humanitarian feeling" — just plain courtesy and considerateness.

The state of mind of patients is apparently such a mystery to many doctors that another study ascribed one fourth of all heart cases to the "acts and words" of the doctor. The report goes on to instruct the profession not about the physics of heart disease but about the lost art of medicine. The figure arrived at in this study seems high, but the recognition of "iatrogenic" (doctor-caused) disease is extremely valuable, especially when taken in conjunction with another report and warning delivered about the same time by a dean at the Western Reserve School of Medicine. This deals with the doctor's "frustration" in trying to treat incurable cases: "Since the average doctor is a human being, he naturally prefers to deal with problems he can solve successfully." Deprived of this source of satisfaction he "tends to withdraw from the situation or tries to find some scapegoat. This may turn out to be the patient."

In other words, Success is interpreted by doctors as complete cure (or death) — anyhow the crossing off of the name from the calling list. And this notion prevails because the comfort, good spirits, and other experiences of the still living patient are no longer felt to be part of the doctor's responsibility; they are no longer opportunities for achieving day-to-day "success."

Given this present machine-shop-view, one must not let gratitude for past benefits interfere with intellectual rigor. It is no argument to say: if you've been to a hospital and are here to tell the tale, you probably owe it to your doctors and nurses. True, but one may be grateful to them individually and go on to add that they themselves supply evidence that all is not quite as it should be. One of my doctors admits that he would hate to be a patient at his own hospital. The place, he says, is badly run, rent with feuds, and the patients are ill-fed and hardly used. Another tells me that he is appalled at the coarse grain and narrow training of his colleagues and the bad habits they impart: "So-and-so will take a group of third-year students on ward rounds, and in a loud voice tell them that here is an *incurable* case. In addition to being anxious, that patient is in constant pain, but as the doctor lectures he leans against the foot of the bed and rocks it with his large rump." Many will testify that the surgeon who took out appendix or gall bladder would regularly plump himself down on the foot of the bed, at the risk of causing — I won't say a recurrence or a pair of broken toes, but certainly discomfort.

The attitude that nothing is of importance short of death (which looks bad on the record) is exemplified by the Los Angeles physician who reported that Smog was no menace. "Of course," said he, "if it is bad enough to irritate the eyes, it must also cause temporary irritation to the nose, throat, and lungs." The fact that his colleagues in St. Louis noticed a decrease in nose-and-throat trouble after the elimination of smog was nothing to him: "there was no proof of permanent injury." Now that there is worse than smog in the air, namely radio-active particles which were not there before and which keep increasing after every discharge, we obviously can't count on our doctors to protect our well-being. Well-being, ill-being do not matter to them; they are only temporary. Now talk to me about a permanent injury, something I can sink my teeth into, and I'll do my best for you.

We survive, to be sure, the irritation, the doctor, the treatment, and the hospital, but is this what we pay for at such high rates, what we give gratitude for, prestige, warm admiration? Surgical and obstetrical patients are especially full of feeling. The ordinary sequelae of a major operation are a dozen of whisky to the operator. Even the harassed G.P. is showered with love-tokens. Whenever I see a handsome new object at my sister's house, I know it's a present to Dick from a wealthy virus pneumonia or a sentimental female sinus. I have even noticed that for some reason deserving of study, strep throats run to leather. But I wander: my point is that illness is getting to be more disagreeable even though more under control, and more expensive even though mass-treated.

Nearly twenty million patients were admitted last year to the nation's seven thousand hospitals. I hate to think of the amount of unnecessary discomfort, noise, heart-rending delay, unconscious brutality, and deliberate gambling with life and death all this represents, side by side with: high intelligence, brilliant professional performance, thoughtful attention, and unselfish devotion. Neither account cancels out the other. And speaking of accounts, it is important to add that the costs are rising out of sight. As more than one medical agency has reported, sickness has become a luxury to those who pay their way. If something is not done about both aspects of this problem, patients are going to reach the point where they will be glad, delighted, to turn in a few years of Life Expectancy for its cash value and freedom from the concomitants of cure.

It is generally wise to suspect comparisons between old ways and new. The memory plays tricks, and idealizing tends to fasten on one's early years. But I happen to have the means of verifying some of my impressions as regards doctoring. For one thing I have at various times lived abroad, where mechanization is much less advanced. For another, my own American doctor (outside the family) is nearly eighty and a remarkable combiner of new knowledge and conservative skill. He is the one who supplied the catch phrase for these remarks when early in our acquaintance he said in his flat

Yankee voice: "The doctor shouldn't be a pill." He does not like to give drugs or injections or even tests when in his judgment they are not absolutely required. He is therefore the antithesis of the ordinary practitioner. Twenty years ago, at a cocktail party, you could hear the popular young M.D. sing out: "So I put him to bed and filled him full of sulfadiazine." A few years later the line would be: "I've stuck 30,000 units of penicillin in his — h'm — thigh, and in a week he'll be fit as a fiddle." Nowadays he'll be telling you: "You just take these little aureomycin pills four or five times a day — so they add up to about 500 units — and you'll be all right."

In between, very likely, you ingest Vitamins A, B_1, C, G (or B_2), and D, washed down in nicotinamide; you add riboflavin and calcium pantothenate to forestall colds; you harden your teeth with fluorides and stiffen your bones with a mineral quota tablet — half a dozen metals that industry is bidding for, plus samples of the most interesting geological strata. But you're not all bone and sinew, you have glands, and to balance the secreting budget you shove hormones, insulin, or adrenalin here and there, hoping they will reach the spot. By bedtime you are a walking pharmacopeia and, with the yellow gold salted away besides, a Federal Reserve vault as well. The financial responsibility keeps you awake, naturally, so you put the whole menagerie to sleep with bromides and barbitals. The wonder is that the next morning you wake up.

In vain do a couple of doctors at Duke University demonstrate that vitamins "are of no value except in cases of actual need." In vain does a serious student of fluorides, backed by a great many dentists, warn against putting the dangerous stuff automatically into our drinking water. In vain do groups of clinicians tell their colleagues to go easy on the INH (anti-tuberculosis) compound, or chloromycetin (for typhoid and other bacterial infections). With the last, "severe blood abnormality has appeared. Even deaths have been reported." Nothing stops us. There's a triple-plated resistance to wisdom in these matters. Unless from childhood we have been

in the hands of a wise physician, a doctor born, we shall probably
be caught in the current of overmedication, to suffer and survive
statistically: "Whether chloramphenicol continues to remain as one
of the more useful antibiotics, or whether it will be relegated to a
place where its use will be confined to the treatment of patients
with typhoid or serious infections for which no other therapy is
available, remains to be seen." (*Journal of the American Medical
Association*, July 5, 1952.) This being interpreted means: "it's a
toss-up whether the drug or the patient *remains to be seen.*"

It would be wrong to throw all the blame on the doctors: the
public loves pills. When vitamins were discredited as daily food,
there were letters of protest to the press. Next, the drug industry
lives by pill making. It is not a large industry as industries go in
this country; still the public pays it a billion and a half a year. It
employs competent men in research and production and turns out
precisely what the medical profession thinks useful. But it also
showers physicians with unsolicited samples which the less informed
or less scrupulous feed to their patients, often without necessary
knowledge or precautions. All this is ethical by prevailing standards, but it is a question whether the standards match the needs of
twentieth-century life.

There is surely something wrong when the news is full of warnings by the profession, to itself and to the public, about the very
things the public goes to the profession for:

HORMONES TERMED EXPLOITED IN USE

CHLOROPHYLL POSSIBLY HARMS LIVER

DOCTOR WARNS CORTISONE CAN DO MORE HARM THAN AILMENT

STATE DRUG INQUIRY LEADS TO FIRST SUIT

This may look like the ordinary play of opinion such as obtains
about every other controversial subject, until it is seen that opinions on this particular subject lay claim to greater validity than
most. Medicine is supposedly an art resting on the sciences, but the
art of healing seems partly abandoned and the science of drugging

is the old empiric come back to try it on the dog. The ethics of proposing new drugs is apparently in its infancy, and the decision to scatter new pills across the land is — in whose hands? As for conscientious doctors who wish to discriminate and not merely hang back just on principle, they have to depend for information on journals that are heavily subsidized by the advertising of drug and instrument firms. This is not necessarily corrupt, but it certainly is not taking pains to be above suspicion. A politician comparably connected would have a hard time convincing us of his purity. The proof that the healer's situation is delicate is that medical ethics forbid a doctor to sell or market his own "cure." Why suppose that a group of outsiders will be less swayed by self-interest in pushing their wares? We the public are the ones who open wide and say "Ah," and the pushing is down our throats.

But the main trouble lies still deeper than all this. Modern medicine has made great strides with the aid of physical science. As a result the research M.D.'s usual view of the patient is that he is primarily a vessel for conducting chemical experiments — a not quite clean and not sufficiently transparent vessel, but the best to be had for the purpose. The research physician, having taken thought, tests it by trial and error. I am not saying this is wrong: there is no other way. But it would be good for all parties if the practitioner remembered what he was doing. He would be more tender of the vessel, to begin with; then he would be more ready to learn, not so much by counting as by observing the individuality of the person and the disease; finally he would retain a saving skepticism about his own devices, instead of being a faddist bent on a new trick or drug every five years.

Doctors used to have various ways of treating patients — from massage to baths to placebos, and other items in the materia medica of the period. Now it is almost all chemistry and physics — pills and surgery. The tolerated practitioners outside this, whether osteopaths or psychosomaticists, are looked on by the rest as interlopers if not quacks. But quacks are evenly distributed — it's a law of nature

— and talent does not wait upon degrees. The case of a Hartford physician who was universally admired, by patients, colleagues, and nurses, and who turned out to be self-taught and without diplomas is a speaking commentary the profession ought to take to heart. Disbarring this able man does not change the facts or "protect" the public: it merely enforces the closed shop.

It is not hard to follow the changes in medical fashion even if one is in good health and out of touch with doctors. The papers are full of trends and discoveries and the lingo changes accordingly. Besides which, if one works for any large institution, the medical report comes around once a year. By reading it one can see which way the wind is blowing. It was a few years ago that in one such report my eye was caught by the top item under

CLASSIFICATION OF CASES: DISEASES OF THE PSYCHOBIOLOGICAL UNIT — 11

This seemed an innovation. I wondered who had assembled and installed this new unit, this portable homunculus, especially since immediately underneath I found:

MENTAL DISORDERS — 1

And:

DISEASES OF THE BODY AS A WHOLE — 3

I inquired in the proper quarter, adding that the nomenclature reminded me of what a famous doctor said three hundred years ago: "I distrust the symmetry of those heads."

"This is quite different," said my informant with enthusiasm. "The psychobiological unit is nothing purely physical. It's that part of the organism which responds as a whole to mental stimuli in a physical way. You get functional disorders but not organic lesions. For example, you can have all the symptoms of stomach ulcers, but they're in your mind. What you need is psychotherapy — and then probably you get rid of the ulcer symptoms and develop an allergy instead. Psychosomatic medicine is a new branch but it's making rapid progress. Pretty soon every doctor will be convinced that every imaginary pain is real, even though it has no apparent cause, and will know what to do about it. The psychiatrists have been waiting for this to happen. They're ready for it."

It was reassuring to hear that imaginary pains were real and that ulcer-equivalents could be traded in for hay fever with, I suppose, imaginary sneezing. But the underpinnings of the hypothesis did not seem very solid. Not that I doubted the connection between the mind and the body — all the minds one comes across are bodies too. What was troubling was the distinction being made between the psychobiological unit and (so to speak) the arms and legs. It seemed to my ignorant eye that the doctors were trying to put Humpty Dumpty together again when it would have been simpler not to knock him off the wall in the first place.

Later indications seem to bear this out. Just recently British medicine has been rocked on its feet by the cure through hypnosis of a skin disease known as "fishskin." The editor of the *British Medical Journal* concludes that there is a "great need for further basic scientific work on the relation between the mind and the skin." So now my friend's "unit" is being covered with a bit of skin. How long will it take before we retrieve the rest of our equipment and doctors admit that the mind attends to the whole outfit? It takes mind to breathe and digest and grow fingernails, just as it takes mind to knit a broken bone and feel a pinprick. The hypnotists discovered eighty years ago that you can stick a man full of pins and he won't jump if his mind has been told to anesthetize the skin. And good doctors have known for centuries that a patient without the will to live can succumb to what are otherwise lesser ailments.

People are so perverse they will die of anything. For example the vaccines, whether against smallpox or rabies. It is true the stuff is highly toxic, being taken from sick cows or rabbits and merely frozen to lessen its virulence. But we are lucky not to contract general paralysis or a knockout case of the disease when we mix breeds inside our systems under the physician's unreflecting care. He is himself paralyzed by precedent, like ourselves, and he scarcely remembers that each of us is a separate problem for him to solve and solve again. This is why his repeated tests about the common cold — and in fact most of the work reported on in the professional journals — are inconclusive. Fifty people volunteer to get their feet wet, stand in drafts, or lie on the ground after perspiring, and behold they catch no colds. Therefore — therefore, nothing at all. A man in a test is not the same man as he himself is when tired, worried, and exposed to the weather at the end of a hard day. He will catch a cold then and *everything* will contribute to his getting it.

If you add to this human versatility the amazing variations in kinds and forms of disease — giving viruses and parasites the ability to resist our best (i.e. most poisonous) drugs, it is clear that our ignorance of what goes on in living beings is still fairly complete. The elements do not stay put; they are not even definable — as our new psychosomatic language shows: who will explain what is meant by "the mind" as opposed to "the body"? We are, if anything, body-minds. And who can fathom the meaning of an imaginary pain which is nevertheless felt; or in reverse, a real pain which is localized in a "perfectly healthy" organ? The wonder is that doctors can do so much for us in so weird a situation. When one feels especially imaginative and sympathetic, one resents almost as much as they the inconsiderateness of patients who up and die against the best advice, or who turn around and get well after being certified incurable. It does not seem fair. But would not everybody be happier if these uncertainties were more openly recognized?

Voltaire defined a doctor as a man who introduced substances he did not quite understand into bodies he understood even less. This was not meanly said: Voltaire was a lifelong sick man who loved his doctors and owed them eighty-four years of remarkable activity. But for his sake and theirs he reminded them from time to time that they were limited, not absolute, monarchs. Since then medicine has come up in the world. It being the gateway to many good things, young men beat their way to it. Not the money, but the kudos and the power of life and death is the lure, and for the best hearts and minds, the self-dedication. The temptation to act like Jehovah must be great, and is not always resisted, but that is a risk the public must run. It is inherent in the situation.

The sick person wants to believe the doctor omnipotent, and this very confidence helps. But was it not rather the old-fashioned physician who best knew how to enlist that aid? Modern specialization works in the opposite direction. Right now, one physician in three is a full-time specialist, and what he wants to know is "Have you got my disease?" You hope you have, so as to put an end to the shopping around and the interminable waiting and filling out of blanks. You undergo all the tests again at ten to fifteen dollars each — none of the earlier ones are acceptable to the new man — and he puts you through his routine, eager to *finalize the case.*

If your man likes to cut up, off you go, horizontal for weeks, vertical again provided they did not use too rich a mixture of anesthetics. You think of the public official whose letter of resignation to the President put your situation so forcibly — "the imperative need to undergo immediate, extensive, critical, surgical attention." And you remember the apt phrase in a book summarizing great forward steps: "With the first successful appendectomy in 1890, the abdominal cavity became the playground of the surgeon." A surgeon wrote this in all seriousness and self-satisfaction and his spirit lives on. Every convention discloses a busy group of specialists who discuss new and better ways of removing your liver without injuring your lights, and who deplore at the same time that half their cases are either inoperable or too far gone to yield anything but a technical victory to the operator. Lately one elderly man was completely remodeled inside at a cost of eight anesthesias, twenty-two hours total operating time, and a fee of $20,450. Is it possible — and I ask out of complete ignorance and humility, I ask "for information" — is it possible that if the patient had been under the lifelong care of one well-trained physician who knew his history, occupation, and mode of life, who stood in some permanent relation to him and was interested in his well-being, is it possible that this marathon with the scalpel could have been forestalled? In other words, is there such a thing as preventive medicine and can it be had equally well from a service station and a family physician?

So far as I can see, we have less contact with our doctors than with our lawyers and accountants, certainly less than a modern student has with his teachers. The only sign of greater intimacy is suggested by the decision of a midwestern hospital to televise its important operations — no doubt for student instruction. Why not extend this service to the public and let them get acquainted at one stroke with their friends and their doctors? Turn the knob and listen for the day's announcements on WYMD: "Mrs. Carl Deffendorfer writes in: 'It has made all the difference to me. I couldn't have believed it. My husband and I have had a happy marriage, with nine healthy children, but until I saw Carl have his gall bladder removed over your station last Saturday, I never knew what he was like inside.' "

Perhaps it is because the wise old practitioner with a beard and a bedside manner has died out that we have taken to mobbing the psychiatrists. At least they listen for their fee, which is high, and they are aware that the patient in front of them *is* (not *has*) a unit. In addition, they have acquired on principle the moral understanding and charitableness which the ordinary physician has lost. The latter does not see nearly so much of life as his old counterpart and he is much too often a moral prig. Whereas the psychiatrist has been taught that it is not his part to enforce the conventions but only to make them seem more bearable. Some psychiatrists are undoubtedly quacks or fools, but they are still under the inescapable influence of the great mind who established their discipline by combining close observation with the insight of genius: Freud's mind was equal to understanding other minds; he did not merely compound prescriptions of a mental sort; and whatever modern psychiatry accomplishes it owes to him, regardless of the modifications or corrections brought to his ideas.

But when full credit has been given these hard-working listeners and confessors, there remain a number of complaints to be made of their corporate acts and attitudes. Freud is said to have rushed out of his office one day, overcome by the baseness of the human motives he had to hear about. His modern descendants do not seem to take things so much to heart. They have given everything a name and pride themselves on the accomplishment. Public favor has gone to their heads, which may have been weak to start with, for many of them have joined the profession as a result of being cured by it.

That is not in itself a disadvantage, except to the extent that it may imply a poor start in logic, ethics, manners and the use of words. I judge not from couch, but from cocktail, experience. The number of snap judgments and flatulent pronouncements that I have heard at social gatherings from busy psychiatrists would fill several volumes of their own proceedings. They "interpret" every remark, trait, and opinion; they characterize public and private character on the flimsiest basis. They take words for deeds. If you say there is too much seeking for love in modern social relations, you are against the great principle of the universe and probably a miserly, self-regarding anal erotic. If you say the opposite, you're insecure . . . tuttuttuttah. If you like *Alice in Wonderland*, what a sadist you are, and a masochist as well. If you dislike the book, you are afraid of being both, showing how powerful and mixed are your aggressive drives in those same directions.

The truth or falsity of these instantaneous diagnoses has nothing to do with the case. They are improper, not as the psychiatrist will naïvely assume, because they deal with forbidden subjects; and not because they mark the victim down. They are improper first because the cocktail hour is not a clinic; and second because even a layman can see how superficial and therefore disreputable they are. The doctors here get all the honors — they wouldn't dream of giving you a diagnosis over a Martini. But both groups, I am afraid, have of late become garrulous and indiscreet. They illustrate their uninteresting points with intimate circumstances which it is nobody's business to know. One forgets the facts, fortunately, but one's privacy has been violated just as much as that of the easily identified patient referred to. I don't want to know his marital and medical concerns and he doesn't want them known. From a professional man we are both entitled to a little free ethics. The Hippocratic oath — whatever else it says — ought to have an additional clause: "And whenever I am tempted to show off, I will shut up."

Which raises the further interesting question, what happens to a psychiatrist's notes when he dies? They are presumably filed under the patient's name, and they contain a rich harvest of detail not only about the couchee but also about everybody under the sun who comes into the day- or night-dreams of either party to the treatment. Are some of these fanciful documents going to be found at large — in the hands of the doctor's relatives, among dealers in old paper and secondhand office furniture? Or in the safes of alert blackmailers and of novelists who have dried up? Perhaps in the archives of the Society? "Take, oh, take those slips away and bring back, bring back my complex to *me!*"

More serious still is the point of ethics involved in present practice when all the parties are alive. I mean the violent partisanship shown by some psychiatrists against other members of the patient's family. Engaged couples are separated, children told to live by themselves. A husband will be asked to visit his wife's analyst, after her case has begun to reveal its salient features, and submit to questioning. Some of this is reasonable enough. But more than one (namely, two — but two is quite enough) persons have spoken to me of being not only questioned but grilled and attacked as cruel, selfish, interfering, stingy — in short a brute who must do exactly as the analyst directed if he did not want to be responsible for his wife's distress — and delusions. One of my informants recovered enough from the shock to ask whether given these fiendish traits, he ought not to be treated too. And he had the satisfaction of seeing the analyst fall into the trap and reach for his calendar to set a regular appointment.

Quite apart from partiality or greed, there is in psychiatry the same danger for the practitioner as in physical medicine — the hardening and coarsening under the incessant spectacle of humanity's hidden sores. And this again points to the need for restoring humane relations between patient and doctor. The healer must somehow know the man otherwise than as a case, if only to be reminded of what life and its normal environment are like. Psychiatrists pay lip service to the idea of the whole man and recognize how difficult it is to know what is normal. But if, as many do, they see ten patients a day six days a week, by the end of a year they can have no notion whatever of average behavior in the outside world. This may be why they behave so badly when they come out for a sip of convivial alcohol. Maybe we should serve them turpentine on the rocks first, and if in their self-absorption they notice no difference, forgive them at once all their egotism and all their nonsense.

No matter who is right or what is right, any change is confronted by a tremendous practical difficulty — the pressure of millions of people on too few doctors. But there's hope when one reads that the Rehabilitation Therapists see the problem. Formerly, says one of them, "the most important person in a hospital was the superintendent. Now the most important person is the sickest patient." That is the echo, a century later, to the main article of the patient's creed as expressed by Dr. Oliver Wendell Holmes: "I would give more for a good nurse to take care of me while I was alive than for the best pathologist that ever lived to cut me up after I was dead."

To all that I have instanced, a student of human affairs might reply that we get the doctors we deserve. Like our rulers they have to be molded and resisted and criticized if we want to get the best out of them. No doubt sickness is a bad time to begin an argument, but the prospect of one should only make convalescence brighter: I admire the friend who, learning by chance that his wife had been examined for cancer and had received no report for two weeks, went straight to the doctor's office and delivered a philippic. He got a report and an apology on the instant.

In the long run, however, the laity can only rebel and protest; the profession itself must find the right means of carrying out the change, for criticism is necessarily destructive: it says No to an intolerable state of fact; it probably misstates the fact while correctly reporting its effect. Only from the fuller knowledge within can true reform come.

From outer ignorance — that I may practice what I preach — I would suggest the overhauling of the much-touted medical ethics. I have never known an instance of its application that did not cause embarrassment, trouble, and worry to the laity: doctors barely civil to each other in a life-and-death consultation; or making it impossible for the patient to know ahead of time what he may do; or worse still, ruling out what seem like free and harmless choices. Whether because of jurisdictional disputes or senatorial courtesies, the patient threads his way among formalities that have little to do with healing or ethics and a great deal, one fears, with trade.

Passing from form to substance, it would seem as if our national well-being could be enhanced by a better distribution of medical efforts. Cancer is a dreadful scourge, but it seems at the moment to be nearly monopolizing talent and resources. Is the reason for this wholly disinterested and practical? Why not balance the research with a systematic review of the effects of what we take into our bodies, together with a study of our actual habits? We might learn to forestall some of our ailments as well as some of the drags on our living powers, notably that of obesity, which is a national curse. Though we live longer we do not age gracefully. Modern occupations, which are sedentary, only partly account for this: we sit and thicken, true, but that is not all there is to it. Since all foods "fatten," we must for some reason other than greed overeat. The obsession of women after thirty, of men after forty, with diets, reducers, and other means of averting the apparently inevitable cannot be called either mistaken or healthy. It seems absurd to talk of our control of nature when all we can do is use rubber bands to keep our women's shapes within bounds.

Lastly, in addition to the re-education of doctors in the art of healing, I would humbly suggest that they be reminded from time to time — or better, remind themselves — of the limits of their powers, by contemplating a curious affliction that besets man and that they know little or nothing about. It has been known since earliest days; it is endemic in all countries without exception; when apparently cured, it usually recurs with redoubled strength, and when too long protracted it means the end. The English name for it is Sleep.

It would for many reasons be good to know more about it, since quite a few among us find it hard to master. The psychiatrists call sleep the realm of unreality, the place where we escape from all the physical constraints of which waking life is made. In sleep we float through solid doors and bask in illusion. If so, the question arises whether we have not, among the many artificial additions to our physical environment, created also such a realm of illusion that we hardly need that of sleep. Perhaps it is because we listen to nonsense in excess during the day that we have no fantasy left to sleep with. Our doctors help us here but little: WARNING SOUNDED AGAINST BROMIDES is sound advice, a thought for all users of the spoken word, but we should give a further thought to the possibility that not all bromides — and not all doctors — are pills. I propose no answer: I can only try next to describe the Great Illusion.

15. The Guff Stream

THE UNEASY SENSE we have of being surrounded by illusion is shown in the use and abuse we make of the word "realistic." We take it usually to mean "pretty bad," and in any set of alternatives it means "the worst." By the same token we are also convinced that our desires are always sanguine, our hopes rosy, our whole outlook and tendency, as we say, optimistic. The truth is that most of the time we do not know what we feel, much less what we ought to feel. Our powers of judgment, our accumulated experience are set at naught by the ever-changing novelty of our situation. The appeals to our senses, our fears, our vanity or self-respect or greed are too many, too various, too incessant for anyone to sift them successfully. We all try to "make sense" but the element we live in is nonsense — it is propaganda; it is advertising.

The first advertisement in America is said to have appeared in May 1704. It told the readers of the *Boston News-Letter* that "a very good fulling-mill" could be had for sale or rent in Oyster Bay, Long Island. The advertiser used the first and simplest words that seemed to state the case, and the space taken up was smaller than a visiting card. In fact, the owner of the newspaper would not accept any ad that was not "reasonable" or that would cost more than five shillings.

We have changed all that. Two hundred and fifty years after the *News-Letter*, advertising has turned from this penny-pinching, unimaginative use of paper and type into a vast institution whose many-sided pressure on our eyeballs and eardrums never lets up, whose ever-renewed inventions shape our fantasies of desire, and whose total effect is at once economic, cultural, and mystical.

Although it was the English who first used advertising formulas of the modern kind — to sell cocoa, originally — and although the French were not backward in adapting the system to intellectual products such as books, the great development of advertising techniques and processes is by common consent ascribed to the United States. To our best friends and critics every type of ballyhoo and raucous fraud is in fact equated with Americanism. Barnum is supposed to be our national hero. The fact that many Americans deplore and despise advertising does not lessen the world's conviction that if we were a civilized people we would not tolerate singing commercials or those thick wads of four-color illustrations, relieved by a trickle of consecutive print, that we call magazines.

The charge is such a commonplace that I have no doubt I forfeited the respect of some readers when on an earlier page I concurred in the tradesman's defense of selling — selling by all and any means. Perhaps these readers were puzzled later on to find me apparently condemning the same practices when I came to discuss the social force and authority of science. I hold by both attitudes at once and I mean this to suggest that the entire question of advertising, of propaganda, is a much more subtle and complicated affair than our routine disapproval would lead one to suppose.

We have, as in so many other things, made the issue large and obvious by sheer multiplication. But collective boasting, honorific name-giving, and deliberate myth-making are nothing new in the history of the race. The *Iliad* advertises the names of the prominent Greeks in the catalogue of ships; the Roman augurs were a college of public relations men (one of the gods, *Aius locutius*, was even then known as the announcing speaker), and if we want an example of the slogan driven in by tireless repetition, we have *Carthago delenda est.* As for grand promises which the makers had little reason to know the worth of, every religion has made them in the classic form: "God is on our side; follow this emblem and you can't go wrong."

Advertising, then, is only a part of the larger element in which man breathes and has his being — the element of guff. It is generated partly from within, partly from without. It corresponds to man's character and situation; and it constitutes in essence the fundamental problem of thought which the philosophers discuss under the heading of Appearance and Reality. Seen from another point of view, the question turns out to be also the central enigma of ethics — means and ends, the nature of compromise, the relation of the practical to the pure.

But one needn't go back to first principles in order to see that convention, nonsense, make-believe, myth, and *mystique* form an integral part of civilization as such. Hard as it may be to swallow, these are some of the "permanent values" that our publicists have been wailing about of late. Just imagine a world deprived of convention and in which they, the conventional moralists and deplorers, were taken at their true worth! Why, you couldn't get all the Commencement platforms staffed in any one month of June!

Modern make-believe, and particularly the American commercial kind, may well be worse than that of former ages; the American brand may be more sinister than the European; but these things cannot be decided out of hand: they must be seen in perspective and judged by comparisons.

To begin with, in an Advertising Olympics, the United States would have a hard time claiming the prize for crudity. Advertising among us declares itself openly and has a defined place. We can show nothing to match the modern Romans' use of their Forum and other ancient buildings as frameworks for electioneering posters and banners extolling Cinzano. In our papers and reviews, concealed puffing and *réclame* have gone out of use. The paid political advertisement is plainly marked, whether in reading matter or out of doors. Billboards have never threatened our monuments and are disappearing from our great highways.

We also observe some self-denial as to substance. All but the lowest kinds of periodicals automatically reject the sordid matter that ordinary European journals regularly publish. We have banned the "agony column," the promises of cure, and much of the apparatus of premiums and prizes. One cannot imagine over here a contest such as was run last spring by a leading "intellectual" paper in Paris, which set its readers discovering errors hidden in successive issues. The public went mad, stormed the public libraries where they mutilated books and periodicals to carry away proofs of their erudition, and generally behaved like undisciplined children.

As for the visual side of our American advertising, it surpasses all its competitors except an occasional French or Italian effort. This is of importance when one is considering cultural effects. It may be said that modern art has been made intelligible, and public taste in design raised to a high point, by the pictorial techniques and typographical skill of the best American advertisers. This has in turn influenced manufacturers and the machine-made object has gained its full worth and virtue in losing its "cheap and nasty" ugliness.

As regards language, it is plain to every close reader that side by side with florid nonsense, one finds in our ads some of the best, tersest prose now written. What is deplorable is that most of it perishes with the temporary object that called it forth, and that the compulsion to read so much posted fiction limits our attention to other kinds. A world in which the written word was confined to books and letters found it perhaps easier to take pleasure in literature and correspondence. We have taught everyone to read and write, but have abused the opportunity this gave us, until our organism, in self-protection, is torn in Hamlet-like soliloquy: to read or not to read.

To circumvent this ambivalence we are assailed through the ears, and in a manner which is our great weakness and true shame. It is no excuse to add that until foreign nations open their networks to sponsors, we cannot tell how low we have actually sunk. The fact remains that we are chiefly an eyestruck people, at once fooled by, and sensitive to the arts of design. This becomes cause and effect in our advertising and public-relations concern with externals, with surface, with gleam and polish; all of which shows again that the connection between advertising and science is not accidental, just as it explains why the radio substitutes for display advertising are so inane and repetitious. What comes through the ear makes a feeble impression. Singing an ad is but a desperate attempt to reach and hold the fugitive mind.

That the mind *must* be reached is no longer a question. Having changed the animal pace to the mechanical and thereby multiplied products and population, our entire life is geared to Time. Goods must move and be consumed at speed, for economic, social, and individual costs are tied together. Halt or delay means deprivation or frustration, just as conservatism in taste means a drag on technology. Advertising has educated us to a world in which novelty does occur and is the prerequisite to abundance. The difference between the advertisement in the *Boston News-Letter* of two hundred and fifty years ago and the ceaseless stream of ads today is the difference between scarcity and surplus.

All this again is meant as explanation, not justification. Though the need to sell is not to be argued, the means we employ have unlooked-for results that are detestable. It is as if we used a drug to aid economic digestion. We are addicts, and not wholly by choice. To the city dweller especially come days when he envies the deaf-and-blind. The forcing of the drug down our throats becomes emetic. The merest hint of the style and stance of selling makes our gorge rise, and we are appalled to find that this vulgar posture is not limited to objects of trade. A learned society soliciting subscriptions to its journal assails me with: "Let's become better acquainted. Your interests. . . ." When the *New Yorker* reprints the opening of such "letters we never finished reading," one easily supplies the reason for not finishing: the recipient is bending over a bowl. Yet there is no escape: pick up that same *New Yorker* and next to the protest is the thing protested against: picture of a man whose patch over one eye enhances the value of a shirt; woman posing the question "Would you streak your hair with platinum without consulting your husband?" and going on with annoying irrelevance to propose new shades of lipstick.

"But it doesn't fool anybody, so it's quite harmless." I am not sure, and my not being sure is a sign that the pretense is harmful: my doubt is my undoing. The world being a place of appearances and realities, life in it is one long and difficult diagnosis: which is which? Hence anything which relaxes the grip whereby we seize on the real is a menace. Homeward bound after a long day, when one is too weary to resist taking in the car cards, one has to repeat a *Non credo* to escape the contagion of folly and falsehood:

"I don't believe that soft shades of broadcloth worn with an exciting new tie will counteract my city pallor; I don't believe that Miss Iphigene Brown of 2421 Pampluna Avenue has written in of her own free will about the new detergent *Scrut;* I don't believe that I need a Super-Jumbo Paratomic Garment Bag; I don't believe that cornflakes and marshmallows baked together would make my wife a popular hostess; I don't believe the new Whatnot is a completely sensational car and that all I have to do is to drive one to prove the statement to myself; I don't believe that as an Old Master proudly signs his work, so does a manufacturer put his name on a tin can — I seem to remember that the first pair of pictures in this series, the Mona Lisa and the Rembrandt portrait, *were not signed. . . .*"

The encroachment, as all know, is not of the mind alone. There is not one of the five senses, not one of the instincts, not a function of the body, not an incident of family or individual life, not a corner of history or romance, not a moment of rapture or pain, not a fear or belief or hope about the here-now or the hereafter, that escapes the defiling touch of the advertiser's purposeful maundering and mendacity. Broader than any other genre of fiction, advertising mirrors the whole of life and distorts it.

Why then do we respond, why would we refuse to act as economic beings without it? If our whole physical and mental life has become the copywriters' plaything, it must be something in us that delivers it into their hands. Two hundred years ago, Dr. Johnson was already worried and wondering "whether advertisers do not play too wantonly with our passions." The only answer we can give is that every fraud implies in the victim a weak desire to be practiced upon. We do not have to take our examples from patent medicines. Every intellectual or artistic elite is taken in, wants to be taken in, by a certain number of charlatans and pseudo-masterpieces; it makes a beeline for attractive twaddle: that is a matter of record in cultural history. We can hardly blame the invalid or the housewife for wanting the magic pill or the dustless duster. If advertising myths dominate us today, it is as much because of a lack of competing myths as for any other cause. But seductive images, contrived illusions, we must have.

This, then, is the mystical role of the advertising art. The active ingredient in the art is defined in that same essay of Dr. Johnson's. "Promise," he says, "large promise, is the soul of an advertisement." Promise of safety, power, greatness, is what man has wanted from his kings and his priests, and this they have bestowed as much through ostentation — advertising — as by material means. The trappings symbolize the promise and secretly flatter the beholder. Appearance re-enforces reality, for what is showy *shows* in the sense of *proves*.

In church and state the English are still under this spell, and many Americans with them. They are ruled, as Walter Bagehot said, through the weakness of their imagination. What else is advertising but the secular, industrial, democratic translation of the same procedure? After the last coronation but one, a London paper printed a picture of the procession with the words: "The Queen raises an arm to show that she is human." The camera there had fought hard with the *mystique*. When we use the phrase window dressing, we may mean one of two things, but the literal and figurative meanings are close together and they equally emphasize the weakness of our imaginations. Why should a department store have to put on view elaborate theatrical scenes in order to sell women cotton dresses and men straw hats? Can't we tell that summer is coming? Apparently not. Our imaginations are weak, and few of us would go and buy our clothes off plain racks in the loft building where they are made. Some secret satisfaction and reassurance would be missing. Our mystical faith in clothes would suffer a setback.

Surely, then, when we say advertising we ought to mean a far wider range of deception, half-deception, and self-deception than is designed and paid for at standard rates. Every effort to establish social reality and prestige is part of this strange ritual which begins wherever you like, with the ancient Briton's painting his chest blue, or with the presence of the beautiful deceptionist in the outer office — with all façades whatever. The very word prestige means magic, the magic which in human society supplements force as the great motive power.

Democracy, we think, abolished all show and gorgeousness; and this is true as regards our rulers. But what we have done, in the United States especially, is to distribute the pomp and prestige. The greater our social equality, the greater our need for individual prestige and reliance on it. No other legitimate means exists to compel attention or favors. Hence there is logic in the advertiser's notion that this garment, that perfume, those accessories, will confer the desired power. Glamour means "spell" too, and as we use it the word is not wholly false. The fashionable woman will admit that she feels surer of herself, more *bewitching*, when well dressed. Poise goes with possessions, and the fact that display becomes ridiculous through excess only proves that up to a point, seeming is part of being.

Contrary to common belief, the farther we move away from material goods toward spiritual satisfactions, the more we require these qualities of surface; when we want perfection we want everything. So we say of an artist that his work lacks finish, of an actor that he is deficient in showmanship, of a political leader that he has every talent but no glamour. Substantial satisfaction is not enough for us. We want the singer's voice plus virtuosity or magnetism — the special pull, the added virtue beyond the reach of art. What more revealing of our *non*-materialism, of our freedom from gross sensuality, than our making the same kind of demand of the objects around us, our clothes and houses, not to speak of our dogs and our friends? And this being so, the attempt of advertising to endow commonplace articles with this magic is to be seen, at least for a brief moment, as the response to a pathetic desire for unattainable grace, for a touch of poetry that workaday life denies.

It is surely so in the adornment of women; they use a revealing phrase for the ineffectual object: "In spite of what the girl said, these earrings don't do a thing for me." What abysmal modesty in us all as we follow the myriad lures of color and shape, the suggestions of rarity and richness, the tokens of perfect design and adjustment, which at one extreme dignify the industrial article, and at the other explain what has been called (I regret to say) "provocative packaging."

No, we are not unwilling victims. We can measure our ready compliance on the one great yearly occasion when our unavowed mysticism about objects comes out in the open and indeed turns exhibitionistic. I refer to Christmas. No doubt the scheming of tradesmen fosters the universal madness, but as far back as the forgotten ages of human sacrifices for fertility rites it has been man's custom to greet the new season with self-indulgence in food, brotherly love, largesse, and noise. Nobody can exactly say what it means. The gifts may be made to propitiate the gods — or to defy them, since the riot of waste was after all the produce of the earth. Until quite recently all ceremonial occasions were similarly marked by conspicuous gluttony. One blushes, one almost faints, reading the menus of our ancestors' state dinners — or those of contemporary Russia. The modern Western world seems far less neurotic about the gullet, though it could probably better afford it.

Instead, at Christmas and other anniversaries, we gorge on leather goods and jewelry, elaborate toys and neckwear in orgiastic silks. We loot the stores and count the days and simulate frenzy until it is real. At Christmas, even the soberest philosopher turns into a wrapper-up of ill-considered trifles. He expects them in return, and feels a warm new sense of superiority to fate because of the smiling and the coming together of red and green, and the spilling cornucopia.

If advertising is responsible for any of this pleasant deception and self-deception, it is only as the ally of religion, which first invented mistletoe and, later on, good will to men. If advertising charges these charitable feelings with spiritual pride, it is only as the ally of science, which first conceived objective magic and then made it produce material plenty. And both these venerable institutions, of religion and science, also made the original promises of certainty and security, of knowledge and salvation.

Pride comes and goes. It may be doubted whether modern man as an individual is more subject to it than ancient man. The modern danger is rather that when institutionalized this vice begets the temptation to the quiet tyranny we call manipulation. The makers and users of advertising do not sneer and cry "Haha!" in the public's face — they would be more inclined to sneer at themselves. But being mortals they slip unknowingly from double thought to double talk to double deal — as the fable of Mrs. Albert Green is meant to show. It is called "The Survey," and the action is anywhere, any time.

Mrs. Albert Green is a smart little housewife aged thirty-four, pretty as a picture — to which she has in fact a startling resemblance. She is full of energy and, as you will see, of ideas. When the dollar bill that she had learned to rely on when she married began to shrink and shrink, she took the matter very seriously. She is the mother of two growing boys with enormous appetites and who keep protruding from their clothes. Albert, her husband, has simple tastes as befits a teller at the bank, but his raises in salary could not keep up with inflation. So she decided to become (in her own words) "really scientific." In the woman's magazine that she reads there appear frequent surveys of this and that, which always point the way to unerring solutions. She too would now conduct a survey in her own home to detect waste and put a stop to it.

She soon found out that the kitchen was no place to scrimp. Albert and the boys must stay healthy and contented. The laundry she did almost all herself and nothing would be gained by saving there: cleanliness is next to godliness. But at the end of three weeks (or as a good surveyor should say — at the end of a three-week period),

Mrs. Green discovered that the family made an extravagant use of what she, being quite a brought-up girl, called household paper. Could this be the fatal drain? What could it mean, and even more important, what was the normal American rate of consumption *per capita?* To set up control conditions was not feasible. She could only do field work herself. So she took to blundering into the bathroom when it was occupied and apologizing as she took a surveyor's look. The Greens were a loving family and it still did not occur to any of them to lock the door. Little did they know to what end her active brain was at work nor how soon they would reap the benefit.

What Betty Green found was that all her menfolk were incredibly prodigal where paper tissue was concerned. Albert wiped his razor blades and his glasses with it, cleaned the inside of the tub and the surface of the mirror, using handfuls at a time. Bobby and Tom not only overused it for its intended purpose but made of it streamers and spitballs and a hundred other things to play with during their bath. And Betty herself, as she had to admit, used it too often in cosmetic work.

Having drawn up a day-by-day chart, she estimated by how much she could cut down consumption. But she would have to launch a program of education. You cannot simply tell people to stop an ingrained habit, much less enforce stringent rules on fun-loving American boys. Should she have posters printed and hung up around the house? Maybe the minister, if primed, could slip in a useful word now and then in his sermon. But that wouldn't yield participation. It was difficult to know how to begin.

Then she remembered that her former boss at the bank (she had been a typist there when she met Albert) was a man of good counsel and was now the head of the City Chamber of Commerce. She went to this Mr. Lester Applegate and laid her problem before him. After a few moments' astonishment he declared himself vitally interested. He pulled a pad toward him, and filling in his own name under MEMORANDUM To: and FROM: he jotted down some notes, telling her to come back in a week.

When she returned after another seven days of recklessly mounting overhead, she was surprised to find not only Mr. Applegate but two other gentlemen. "Betty," said her former employer, "your problem's solved. Frank, you tell her." The nicer-looking of the two other men cleared his throat and said, "I'm Frank Ladd, Mrs. Green, and I represent the Better Spending Bureau set up by the United Retailers of this city. After talking over your case with my associates, we've decided to make you an offer."

"An offer?"

"Yes. Forty-five hundred a year on a six-months trial run, the contract to be signed after that for a three-year period. Allowance would be made for a secretary, of course, and expenses within reason. We sincerely hope you'll see your way clear to accept."

"To accept — but what? To do what?" Obviously Betty wasn't yet a full-fledged businesswoman.

"Don't you realize, Mrs. Green, that you've given birth to a great idea?"

Here Mr. Ladd became very earnest and started to use his fingers as markers in a series of points: "What you have done is create housekeeping science right in the American home. You've given women a new incentive in life — not merely to watch over expenses as they've always done, but to survey them, so as to be in a position to know whether their distribution of consumer goods within that expenditure is scientifically correct. Your revolutionary new principle — "

Though hitherto spellbound, Betty at this point could not help interrupting: "What principle do you mean?"

"Why, that food and clothes and soap and laundry and incidentals can in no way be cut down on by a self-respecting American family. In er — household paper, of course, the differential may be quite different, though even there the margin of safety has got to be watched."

"But what do you want me to do?"

"Tell the women of this community of your great discovery. Just give them the benefit of your experience, of your scientific approach. We've already reserved time on station WBUL and we're going to see whether we can't arrange a round-table program on TV — interviewing housewives, you know, finding out their needs and giving prizes for the most baffling problem of the week solved by you."

"B-b-but — "

"I know what you're going to say. You've never been on the radio. You're just a housewife. That's just the point. You'll be sincere, the real thing. Women will trust you. They'll come to you with their troubles because you're one of them and not a paid promoter selling them a bill of goods."

By this time Betty had caught on and was displaying again the poise and charm which had made her such an effective president of the senior class in high school. "I see," she said, and intuitively smiled the Better Business smile at the three executives. "And when do I begin?" she asked.

It was the third man, bald and awkward in the jaw, who took up her question. "Your program can't start, Mrs. Green, till you've established yourself with the community as an expert — you're not just one of them, talking without authority, but a specialist in domestic science. Since you've not taken courses in the subject, you must show your ability in practice. We suggest that you conduct a number of surveys. Questionnaires to elicit answers, data, and so on. We'll provide the lists of names, but you'll have to decide what to survey. You can call on us for help with the questions. The tabulated results will get space in the *Standard Star*. After three months your name should be a byword in Crassus County and then you'll be ready to personalize the whole thing with a half-hour morning program."

"We've thought of a title," added Frank Ladd, "which we hope you'll like: 'What Do I Survey Today?' And as a tag line to end each talk or interview, you could say, proudly, 'I am monarch of all I survey.' It's just a suggestion, of course. A woman of your proved ability needs no help from us."

.   .   .

Horrible. Disgusting. Asinine. But let him cast the first stone who has never been guilty of guff in any form, whether for himself or in a good cause; who has never weighed his acts in the light of "public relations"; has never assumed the duty of "educating the public to our needs," or done "missionary work" for a hospital, a school, a museum, or a charity; has never written a blurb or gilded a project; never drawn up a bulletin or padded an interim report (technically, a "stall piece"), nor put a good face on a bad job by official wording a yard long. Diogenes could search a good while for such a man, and be told for his pains that in a democracy respect for the opinions of others makes these practices inevitable. Where no special privilege exists, one must woo and convert the unbelievers; where funds, fame and attention are competed for by millions, we must plead and cajole and justify ourselves, in a word — advertise.

The pity is that this self-promotion soon becomes an end in itself, and then a meaningless routine. A good part of commercial advertising is not directed at the public at all and has nothing to do with selling goods. It is either institutional self-praise or virtuosity aimed by one agency of experts at those of another. And it should be humbly added that our most serious enterprises, intellectual, artistic, and spiritual, thrive on the same sort of self-conceit. Each thinks his own pretense impenetrable, his self-portrait irresistible. The man next to me in the train was reading with obvious pleasure a folder of typewritten matter in which he made occasional corrections. A writer in love with his work? Not exactly: when I caught a glimpse of the cover it bore the words: "Hypothetical Position Which Larry S. Bellows Thinks He Is Entitled to Fill." Here was Everyman: whatever the "position" sought, it is a noble one and our qualifications rise to it like water in a pump. Whatever the activity, it is not simply useful but laudable. In their Annual Report, the directors of one famous firm that sells bakery products are not content to show good management and profits; they lay claim to heroism; the public owes them gratitude for making bread — when they might, I suppose, have yielded to the temptation of making circuses.

The race for pre-eminence is run on the ocean of guff. How infinite its uses, protean its forms, encompassing every move, forestalling and monopolizing all known virtues when it is not inventing new kinds: "The enclosed railroad tickets were printed automatically at time of sale on a modern ticket-issuing machine introduced for the first time anywhere at Grand Central Terminal . . . another New Haven first designed for your convenience." Is my convenience similarly involved, I wonder, every time the *Beatific Monthly* finds a new author and underscores him as a *"Beatific* first"? Or when my FM radio station, not content with playing music, chops it up into "Roll-call of the Great," "Hour of Melting Melody," and "All-time Popular Favorites"?

A single drop of guff will flavor an entire communication, like this one, which comes from a staid old house: "Please note that the publication date for this book has been changed from the special date of September 8th to the special date of September 12th."

As good as PRE-EMINENCE is FINALITY: "The service for this mechanical pencil is guaranteed — not for years — not for life — but Guaranteed Forever." Be on the watch also for UNEXPECTED BOON: I buy an electric vacuum cleaner and lo! I find — on the box at least — that it is also an air purifier. For the SUPERLATIVELY UNIQUE, try any issue of our national weeklies, any article on any subject, and you'll soon come across "the first in six thousand years to be the only one of its kind." A trade journal, on the other hand, will afford you the BELIEVE-IT-OR-NOT DISCOVERY: "Such inventive ideas in color and weave can make textiles the main interest in a room full of people." Only the arts, though, give the BEDROCK FEELING OF REAL LIFE, say through . . . "needles which make it possible for you to reproduce the finest recorded music with such realism that all thoughts of mechanical music are forgotten and you are listening to the Artist in person." The same holds good of the movies, which sell nothing but the PROMISE OF HEAVEN ON EARTH: "Florence, Italy, where every inhabitant is a bit of a poet and a bit of a musician . . ." (Florence? — Bologna!)

But the commonest, most insidious guff is always compounded of picture and text, for which see your daily paper: "Preparing a speech — The candidate ponders over a phrase at his desk in the Executive Mansion." Or: "Puzzled — Student asks Sculptor a question on abstract art at the Modern Gallery, which opened yesterday." Don't we wish it were so, looked so! Life escapes us however hard we try to catch it and see it. We make artificial meshes and set it up in familiar poses. The very language in which our knowledge of the world comes to us is self-falsifying, whether through the quaint, never-spoken headline forms — CITY SHARES YULE JOY — or through the jargon which keeps transforming our simple feelings into things and processes: "You too can have greater-listening-enjoyment." "This special All-Expense Cruise — an unrivaled series of travel-events . . ." Or again, through the breaking up of the living self into detached functions and items: "Her back, one of woman's loveliest attributes . . ." We nominify whatever we can — it makes it more real: Wouldn't you like to know a Miniaturization Engineer? You'll find one offered in the *Times*. Are you for or against something? How old-fashioned of you! Only note this circular sent by the information service of a foreign embassy in Washington. It is headed: "The Great Historical Struggle Against Dictatorship." But struggle is subjective and some attaché has struck it out, to write above it the word "Process": guff diplomatic.

There is guff educational, too, as all parents, teachers, and children know. It tells each group in turn that the school belongs to *them*, and that criticism is desired by those in charge. Do not swallow this if you do not want your stomach turned. Nor is the school the only vomitorium. "What Can I Do About Survival in an Atomic Age?" asks the head of a great library in a printed broadside. "The staff of the —— Library found their own answer. They organized a series of public lectures on atomic problems . . . they produced a magnificently vivid and informative exhibit. . . . For their opening lecture — on a mild and sunny Sunday afternoon — the library's big auditorium was overflowing in all directions. It was the most exciting and encouraging event I have seen anywhere in the United States since Hiroshima [*sic*] — in the past ten years, for that matter.

"The answer is still unfolding. Ripples from it are rolling wider and wider. . . . Mr. —— and his associates not only realized that books mean Light. They transformed Books plus Light into *Community Action for Human Safety.* . . ." The text goes on to speak, for a dozen lines more, of "the greatest nonpartisan urgency of our times" and it ends without one clear word as to the "action" it keeps referring to. Ipecac, pure ipecac.

Guff in the name of the common good, civic guff, is in truth an endemic phenomenon. Its most usual form is the something-day or week. The Post Office has Letter-Writing Week; the Fire Department, Fire Prevention Week; the press and the theater each claim a month (theater in March, press in September); when the railroads squeezed a week out of New York's mayor, the chief radio station plaintively asked "Why not Chamber Music Week?" All this, unless we lengthen the calendar, leaves "I Am an American Day" quite lost among the other 364 or less, when one has full license to be a Patagonian and a firebug, to keep away from railroads, to listen only to brass bands, to boycott the theater, and to neglect one's correspondence.

Fortunately, the community has more sense than its leaders of thought and action; the worm turns: it turns a deaf ear. In Worcester, "after a Community Chest campaign of newspaper articles, advertisements, window cards, billboards, radio, speakers' bureaus, mass meetings, and report lunches [*sic* again], it was found that 26 per cent of the people of Worcester said they had never even heard of the Community Chest." It is too bad the deafness is to worthy calls as well as silly ones, but it suggests that advertising itself generates some antibodies.

Nor do I quote this survey to make us give our faith to the hovering pulse-taker or pollster in our midst. He too is a manipulator who will waste time and substance to proffer answers nobody could want, for example, on the great pajama issue, that (1) pajamas are worn by more than half the men in the United States; (2) that more are worn in warm climates and seasons than in cold; and (3) that rich men own more pairs than poor men. Yet where would the guff level not drop without "studies"? All the so-called branches of learning do their bit. It is hard to say whether Psychology or Sociology contributes most. At any rate the latter turns out studies of "The Relation of Marital Happiness to the Partners' Views of Each Other's Personalities," and "The Daily Movement of Population into Central Business Districts"; while the psychologists, according to the President of their Association, discover that among "the obstacles in the way of getting the proper combination of generalized thinking with observing and doing" was "the variability of complex human action and the number of diverse factors that can influence the consequences of behavior or moral decisions." Now we know.

In a still darker shade of prose emanating from the Hoover Institute and Library, we have this declaration of purpose, guff-laden beyond the dreams of avarice: "Essentially, we have tried to find means of estimating the strength of the trends of basic revolutionary forces in our contemporary period. We seek to discover how these are influencing the development of the world community as a whole, of the principal regions, and of individual nations. We seek above all to discover what is happening to three principal values — democracy, security, and fraternity or shared respect — and to show . . ." It is kinder to break off and better sense, on the whole, to believe the hat manufacturer who instanced, as the two contemporary threats to "values," Communism and the hatlessness of modern man.

Do not imagine for a moment that you have reached the end, plumbed the depths. Science and pseudo-science have not been heard from:

MAN-MADE MOON HELD FEASIBLE
TWO ROCKET EXPERTS ARGUE "MOON" PLAN
CHANCES OF ESCAPE IN SPACE HELD POOR

Or again:

NUMBER OF 4000-WORD ESSAYS POSSIBLE ESTIMATED AT 10 FOLLOWED
BY 8000 ZEROS.

If you prefer actual gadgets, you may choose among several. There is the Time Compressor, which tightens up speech and music so as to save pauses and work the human ear to capacity — "many agreed that both words and music had been improved." Other electronic devices will cook hot dogs by radio waves and dispense them at the drop of a coin (this is a General Electric invention); or again, at and by a Tennessee Engineering College, a new device will "enable the student to register an immediate protest without interrupting the Professor." Lastly, for a winter pastime: "Over the range from about 450° Centigrade to upwards of 500°, the coal passes through a phase of plasticity during which it can be molded between the fingers like putty."

After this, surely, all resistance is broken and one is ripe for believing, on the authority of "a leading canner of corn and peas" that "Freud sells peas" through the agency of "fertility symbols with a personality appeal," as depicted in a special brochure for retailers. This genteel phallus worshipper signs himself "Psychologically yours."

One ends by agreeing with Erasmus that there is in mankind a natural propensity toward and appetite for folly, a conclusion which has at least the advantage of explaining why it is so hard to accomplish sane tasks that require the co-operation of many, whereas it is easy to enlist hearts and minds for solemn foolishness, e.g. to celebrate the fiftieth anniversary of The Twentieth Century Limited by dressing people up "in the costumes of those who first boarded the train."

This example brings to mind the fact that there is also guff-in-action, whose technical name is Swash. This is luxury justified, reckless waste rationalized, the equivalent of a 21-gun salute. It makes the drudgery of business palatable and puts the high gloss on executive power. Its prime manifestation is Airport Life: the swasher is either going to or coming from the airport; it remains a mystery why hotels and convention halls have not sprung up around the signal towers of the land, to enable him and other professional swashers to gather permanently in a few strategic spots.

Swash begins with making distant reservations, canceling local engagements, knocking the breath out of family life and emulating the tornado. It requires, besides, what one supplier mysteriously calls "your Video wardrobe," some imported pigskin bags, a self-winding wrist watch, and a special style of eyeglasses which passes in a ten-year cycle from tortoiseshell to rimless hexagons. With this equipment go meals and drinks, lavish tipping and the high art of self-interruption — that is, having every activity broken into by some message, date, or duty belonging to another. Locked-door conferences are unavailing: it takes a suite of eight or ten rooms to prevent full Swash from successful interruption. The amount of paper secreted and blackened by Swash is measured in gross tons. The remainder of the expense is recorded on the well-known swindle sheet, which adds to the tax-bitten executive salary the food, liquor, bellhops, ulcers, speed, and immaterial bliss of Swash.

Erasmus could not foresee this triumph and praise it. In his time, moreover, the assumption was that folly and superstition belonged to the uneducated mass. Now everybody has his share, including the debunkers. After the Great Depression, as many will remember, some confident technologists undertook, David-like, to give battle to the Goliath of guff. Under various corporate names they issued reports on the actual properties of products and machines and sought to educate the consumers. On many points their advice was revealing and practical. But alas! these reorganizers of our daily life soon fell victims to their own special kind of nonsense. Believing in tests more than in social reality, they would, with a straight face, urge a man never to buy a shirt without first seizing collar and tail and applying a steady pressure of sixty pounds. The free-lance writer was told to refuse all typewriter ribbons that did not measure so many feet in length and to verify this *in situ.* A woollen scarf must be put through the ordeal of a lighted match. As for the housewife, she was to surround herself with 100-pound bags of innumerable substances, from which to mix her own face and tooth powder, bath and Epsom salts, shampoo, ink, and vaginal douche.

Have we not changed our whole environment by manipulating matter and inventing names for the endless ramified products? If the terms are right and rightly put together, why worry about possibility or fact? So we float down the stream of absurdities, swallowing more or less, essaying a few strokes now and then, but really at the mercy of the waves and splashes. Who has strength or judgment left to mark differences of depth and shun the rapids? Indeed, as we run out to sea, the current grows uniform. What, after all, is so reprehensible about the advertiser's parrot-cries of "pin-point carbonation" and their promises of flow, glide, gloss, and glamour, when the literary critic keeps promising just as glibly that the latest novel is exciting, stimulating, vibrant with life; or parroting jargon about architectonic, tension, focussing, and dissociation of sensibility? Disbelieve him at your peril: he will prove things by Thematic Apperception Protocols.

Our words give us away and it is apparently a world-wide phenomenon. Reports from Russia indicate that the government has reproved the naming of children Radiola, Detektor, and Elektrifikatsia. Trade marks, names of gadgets and plastics, recall the power that made the things and carry the same magic as Abracadabra: agency English is now but the vernacular writ large. In my own academic shop, though not, I may say, in my presence, meetings are held in which audience and student panel have been so enfeebled — or so exhilarated — by nomomania that they need a Speaker, a Formal Chairman, and a Clarifier. Nor is this orgy of functions simply rank Americanese: for each section of Britain's Exhibition of 1951 there was an Architect, a Designer, and a Theme Convener.

This last character was evidently the missing man at the building of the Tower of Babel, and it is a question how much he can do for us in a world where the written word is unconfined and where every activity solicits the motion of our eye toward some block of print. This is a curse, a necessity, and a reflex action. But as each new publication fills a much-needed gap, one cannot help wondering who it is that wins the William the Silent Award for Journalism that is listed in the New York phone book. There are signs, it is true, of nascent self-criticism among advertisers. The handbooks and exhortations of Mr. Clyde Bedell, insofar as I can follow them, tend in that direction. He deprecates silly pretense and mere "publicity," arguing that only "prospects" (that is, intending purchasers) should be aimed at, in a serious and informative way.

If the day comes when all business and intellectual advertising is as sober, pointed, and effective as our governmental posters on hygienic and other social issues, we shall then have the efficiently communicative advertising that we need to keep pace with novelty, bargains, and economic output — the "reasonable" advertising desired by the old *Boston News-Letter*. Meantime my candidate for the award I cited above is the well-known head of a public-relations firm who retired some years ago and took up as a hobby the marketing of liver paste and other condiments. His ads bore a picture of the jar or tin, with the legend: "It's Good — Your Grocer Has It."

PART FOUR

Winter, or Loving

16. All the Other Halves

*No Passion Spent — Episode — The Man
in the Kitchen — The Little Refugees —
A Good Society*

16. *All the Other Halves*

IF MANKIND were but a tangle of self-loves struggling for satisfaction, the political and social order might well be as precarious
as we find it, and as difficult to adjust to a changing reality, but
presumably the struggle would be seen for what it was, one identical thing throughout its length and breadth. What makes human
life so dreadful and comic, so heartbreaking and satisfactory, so
elusive and inescapably *there*, is that athwart the many desires and
interests prompted by self come the curious passions we call disinterested, the love for other selves, as well as for unseen and intangible entities that seem more than alive — wisdom, art, science,
country, divinity.

It is easy to reduce these higher attachments to ordinary selfish
ones, for we are not habitually imaginative: another man's love
affair generally seems commonplace and physically determined,
part of a statistical norm. And we are all the more inclined to such
dismissals in an age of science deficient in scientific philosophy.
Yet we know, possibly from our own experience and certainly
from any reading of history and biography, that love affairs and
religious faith and patriotic self-sacrifice are neither illusions nor
trivialities. We know moreover from medicine and psychiatry that
mind controls body as mysteriously as it is controlled by it, that
faith works cures or deaths, and that affection given or denied
shapes character. The growing complaint of the age is in fact that
individual man is "alienated," that is, feels cast out, forgotten, un-
loved, in the mass that molds him. Ever since Mr. David Riesman's
extraordinary study of *The Lonely Crowd*, we have been able to
find daily corroboration of his thesis regarding our intangible re-

lations to the group; some of us even have unconsciously altered Wordsworth's line to read:

I wandered lonely as a crowd . . .

The result of our new awareness is twofold. Still holding to our democratic conception of mankind, we are forced to recognize incommensurable differences among human beings, gaps that cannot be closed, divergences of thought and feeling that make communication pointless or impossible. By our social and political assumptions, these people are equal and must be treated alike. We judicially and judiciously ignore their differences; but they continue to live in separate worlds, worlds that square with other, neighboring worlds only for given purposes.

At the same time, all these spirits, dim, bright, narrow or spacious, seek fulfillment, connectedness, identification with some other, which to them cannot be simply another self, but must be an Idea as well, an idea charged both with reality and with ideality.

Now the viewer's paradise that industrial man has made for himself with pictures and words and colored lights, has not become a universal fact without casting strange shadows within the secret chambers of his heart. Our civilization, as I hope to have shown in several connections, tends to breed not, as is often thought, materialists and sensualists, but *voyeurs* and fetishists. And one of the immediate consequences of this is the raising of a new obstacle to the outgoing emotions, to devoted attachment, in a word to passion.

For it is one of the blessed paradoxes of existence that all ideal possibilities have their fulfillment as well as their roots in physical realities, so that the dignifying of life does not consist in sentimentally clothing grossness in "spiritual" words, but on the contrary in taking an unsubstantial vision and making it materially come true. Only a coward wants an imaginary sweetheart; an artist wants his work done that it may be seen, touched, heard; the statesman wants not a "perfect" paper constitution, but the power to make an imperfect one work; and the saint has no thought but to sit at the right hand of God. More reality, not less, is the only tenable aim of ideal hopes.

And so says our omnicompetent industrial world, which has realized — made real — a host of mankind's protracted fancies. Why then does it seem at the same time to deny the realization of the intimate hopes that earlier ages fulfilled? Why do more and more people say — whatever they may feel — that man has been robbed of his capacity to love and hence kept from sharing in the truest good of the good life? To which question one must add, Does this complaint apply especially to the United States? Our critics are sure that our lives are devoid of passion and spirit, full of sex and sadism. And our literature certainly lends color to the charge.

Here again I think our position is not unique or peculiar but merely spectacular — and as such significant for the whole Western world. To anyone who reflects on the short and disastrous history of sex, it will seem no accident that mass production, psychiatry, display advertising, and sex were invented almost at the same time, in Europe, and less than a century ago. If "invented" sounds shocking about sex, let us say: came into the common consciousness in the guise we still know it by.

Sex is manifestly an offshoot of self-consciousness and modern science. To make a part of life into the separate entity that we now imagine it to be, an old word had to be taken at the time I speak of and wrenched from its former meaning. Previously, "the sex" meant the fair sex — women. Used by itself, the word (which originally means cut off, bisected) designated gender, the distinction between male and female. It did not stand, as it does with us, for a subject of research and conversation, a pastime, a *prahblem*, a duty, and sometimes — among earnest and gifted students — a pleasure.

Yet since it is likely that some of the feelings and activities covered by our new usage existed before 1875, we can, by translation and comparison with the old-fashioned words "love" and "lust," acquire some notion of what has happened to us. To put it briefly, we got lost somewhere on the scientific road of analysis and abstraction.

We were right to become self-conscious and studious, but in the process we made an image of desire and pictured it as something outside us, a detachable, accessory quality or "appeal," which belongs to objects and lurks in formulas. In its faithful mirroring of our minds, advertising gives us back the shattered pieces of love and lust through its obsessive repetition of legs and breasts — pitiful symbols of the vanished female power. Thereupon men and women became gazers and gapers, lusting not after anything that lives and breathes, but after the unreal, unrealizable, inhuman simulacra with which we have papered our mental boudoirs.

The phenomenon is so blindingly evident among us that its strangeness passes unnoticed, but this country's verbal, visual, and "moral" preoccupation with physical characteristics that are, so to speak, standard equipment on all but a very few models of womanhood, is something that passes belief. Falstaff found that sherry filled his brain with "fiery, nimble and delectable shapes." But these were at least his own fancy, and in a liquorish mood. The ordinary well-behaved American would be surprised if told that he passed his entire life among dirty pictures publicly displayed; yet that is the fact if we regard — as one must in dealing with pornography — the intention and relevance of the exhibits.

Those we are continually exposed to are crude, intrusive, and irrelevant, and when one recently read of a charge brought in New York against possessors of obscene prints, one could only wonder at the sudden fit of morality. Perhaps the accused was a collector of ads whose taste was improving. For every article of consumption solicits our eye by an outthrust bosom half-uncovered or some other comparable summons to lust: you can't see the dogfood for the legs and the mechanical laundry proves that it stretches your curtains by showing a girl in a sweater stretching herself. The cult is desperately solemn. Not long ago, as the readers of *Life* were informed, a well-known agency was rent by a dispute over the drawing of a half-bare damsel symbolizing a brand of soda-water. Which inspired one of the boys to sing: "On the White Rock damsel, lo! Rosy nipples come and go." The final sketch, without nipples, was characterized in regard to that detail as being "less earthy." In Hollywood meanwhile, movie directors want heroines to wear false fronts — the effect of gigantism being all that seems desired. Paper-bound books must similarly have covers that gaudily uncover the same old sad parts, and respectable magazines and newspapers regularly provide "cheesecake" as if the diet would be unpalatable without it. In short, the entire American population is continuously breastfed through the eyes and lust-inspired by legshows on paper.

Because it is on paper, we are to suppose, purity reigns. A national institution regulates exposure in the movies and has rules of incommunicable subtlety about so-called seduction scenes, such as that the man must be shown as having at least one foot on the ground — common sense at all costs. Very well, we are pure — prurient-pure. And we reassert a dismal common sense after the madness of waving all these legs in the air by dwelling with equal insistence on the mechanics of standardized sex-appeal. Half our ads suggest that the delectable shape of woman was fully discovered only a while ago, and so justifies our peepings; the other half freely reveal that these fundamental curves and cushions are made with wire and rubber and silk, producing "strapless beauty," and "scientific control." This achievement is put forth as no less amazing than the other delights offered to view, so that a department store must glorify "six of the names that have done most for legs since Ziegfeld." One of these names is, pathetically enough, "Nude-Look Nylon," its effect being, of course, to make actual nudity inadequate, unappetizing, positively disgusting. But so is the demonstration, by real photographs of nymphs bending, sitting, and leaping, that somebody's girdles will conceal bulges and breaks in the sought-for line, a perfect armor for and against asymmetry.

·　　·　　·

If we ever wonder about the great change which turned the daily press and the open street into a likeness of bedroom and bath combined, we are likely to think that the same period saw an equally great revolution in sexual mores. We have the impression that we are enlightened and free, that we have sex *ad libido,* and that we not only enjoy the license we talk and write about, but that ours is the first generation to face what we naïvely call the facts of life. The exact opposite is probably nearer the truth. There is something about modern urban life and larger social equality that makes men and women peculiarly inept toward each other, so that they must actually learn from books what they profess to know by instinct. It is highly significant that in France, where according to ancient opinion love-making was supposed to be as accomplished as cookery, and no less widely distributed, the last twenty years have seen the appearance of the same dreary books that adorn our own shelves — married love with diagrams; case histories proving that you too can find happiness *à deux;* earnest encouragements of desire couched in the Body-Beautiful style of hygienic cults; complete guides that tolerantly provide for all aberrations and contingencies and that might be called "Sexual Relations, Formal and Informal" — all this flavored with physiology and pharmaceuticals. Most recently, the success of Simone de Beauvoir's large work of erudition on these matters has shown that the French public is just catching up with the knowledge vouchsafed to English readers by Havelock Ellis, Krafft-Ebing, and Freud, anywhere from thirty to fifty years ago.

Whether this knowledge helps is another question. The Kinsey Report, as Lionel Trilling pointed out in a definitive essay, usefully reminded the public that the behavior of American men was not, and probably could not be, what the laws and the assumptions of genteel fiction presupposed. But by following the modern mechanical notion of "sex," the Report re-enforced a view of life which can only demoralize us still further. It spoke, for example, of "outlets" to denote the physical act of love, and it set up industrial standards of quantity and speed to measure satisfaction. As I write these lines, Mr. Kinsey's volume of inquiries among American women has not been published, so one may speculate whether it will employ the same criteria about them — and even whether the statistics will continue, against all plausibility, to refer to "outlets." If there is any indelicacy in the thought, it comes from the initial vulgarity of the "scientific" analogy.

Our language is foolish and disgusting because, like our voyeurism, it denies all aspects of love but one and magnifies this one into an obsession, a horror — like seeing human skin under a microscope. Taken by itself the sentiment of love is silly, its physics ridiculous, its spectacles cloying, its violence frightening, its memories unbearable, its urgency irrational, its comedy cruel, and its ecstasy inexpressible. But all these together, plus what we may bring to it of natural beauty and cultivated sense, make it what the poets have said it could be.

All this we pare down to "experiences," a few minutes of timed and tabulated "sex-life." Alas for modern man! His sex life I know and wish to know nothing about, but his money life won't bear looking into, his food life is uninteresting, and his brain life, I suspect, is often nonexistent. His foot life is visibly flat and his elbow life is what has landed him in Alcoholics Anonymous. His only full life he carries with the Mutual Life, where he must have a friend, because his organic life is said by the doctor to be a poor risk, so that the poor fellow, no longer loving and lively, is only lifelike.

Everyman is in bad enough plight. But it is in women that the disappearance of pervasive sexual qualities is most disastrous and most marked. They have accepted identification with the sweater-stretching, hose-displaying images that we put up for sale, and have become persuaded that personal attractions, falsely renamed "sex appeal," is a commodity put on and off. Some forget it in the home; others always restore it after eating or sleeping or bathing. They are so busy buying it or assembling it or defending it from nature's inroads in the form of superfluous hair that the one real power of attraction, the true magnetism, is utterly dissipated and gone. They may look like the ad, having taken care to redistribute their cells into the approved forms of calves and buttocks, but all consciousness of being a life-laden creature, living by and with desire, has vanished. In our great cities, where every inch of surface seems given over to glorifying the votaries of Venus, the actual women — many of them very beautiful — go about in glazed perfection, empty-faced and sway-footed, solemn sawdust dolls with exhausted minds struggling over the implications of the latest hairtint.

To hear them discuss one another, it is clear that the old possibility of a knockout is no longer reckoned with: they win on points, which range erratically from physique to adjuncts and accessories. When one of them conveys to the rest, as to the men, some peculiar charm unexplained by anything in sight, it causes vague disquiet. For our stereotyped images of sex take little or no account of harmony, expressive play of features, modulation of voice, and the unmatchable completeness of being *some one person*. This is so far forgotten that many women disguise themselves in the common uniform so as to attract in the conventional way. One has to go through a long acquaintanceship, digging through layers of enamel, to find the woman inside the armadillo.

This complaint, which is not of women as such, but of the style our culture imposes on them, may sound as if I expected every casual encounter to lead to an embrace. Far from it. That is rather the expectation of our obsessive picture world, in which one cannot eat a cookie or buy a car without holding hands. It was obviously necessary, from the moment women entered business and industry, that the old highly charged conventions had to go. A man and a woman must be able to ride up in an elevator together without having designs on each other or being suspected of having them. But in thus sterilizing all the workaday contacts between the sexes — contacts that shocked our grandparents and still shock the Mohammedan hinterland — we forgot that we might also be drying up the sources of love.

The pros and the cons slip through the meshes of any comparison. The European assumption that every man shall be a wolf to every undefended woman is certainly tiresome, and the American Way is preferable — in fact, unavoidable, as is shown by the gradual decay of the European's automatic gallantry. To offset this, we have to recall once more that our literature high and low, and on both sides of the Atlantic, has to supply us again and again with detailed scenes of love-making, that the movie audience never tires of the glutinous kisses of movie stars, and that the respectable youth of either sex is found in clinched pairs, simulating love on every available occasion — at parties, games and boat races, in trains and theaters and parks — as if each half-hour were the last before they took vows of chastity. When one adds to this the number of those who declare themselves disheartened, "frustrated," in need of "help," one begins to suspect that something is lacking in the substance and texture of the common life.

It is depressing to find confirmation in the remark of a literary editor familiar with the facts that "the American forces abroad during the war were perhaps as erotic an army as ever fought its way across Europe, but the amorous adventures of soldiers produced only repetitious and monotonous chapters." The question here is not one of literature, art, or morals: it is one of cultural anthropology: men and women who have lost one another in life cannot find each other in bed. There is in fact nobody there but the "outlets" and other interchangeable parts that our sexologists and advertisers keep juggling with on paper. To say, then, that the most wonderful fact in a man's emotional life should be the existence of woman, as man's existence is the grandest in hers, is to say the exact opposite of what is implied by sex, sex life, and sex appeal, the opposite of all the advertisers' and fictioneers' notions; such as: that a woman (or a man) has to be young and beautiful to be desirable; that the only real satisfaction of sexual desire is possession, so that the company of a woman has no sexual meaning for a man if they do not sooner or later fall into each other's arms; from which it logically but unnaturally follows that after thirty or thirty-five a person is "through" not only as regards attracting love but even as to exerting any specifically sexual charm. By dint of believing this error and failing to cultivate, or at least free, the true sexual powers that can suffuse the voice, bearing, countenance, and mind, the interplay of mutual attractions ceases among most moderns at the point where the woman or man would no longer qualify as chorus girl or photographer's model. As a result, the atmosphere we live in is de-sexualized, emptied of both masculinity and femininity, however filled it may be with lascivious pictures, smutty stories, suggestive names of perfumes and movies, and the whole apparatus of provocative exposure and buttressed curvature.

It is not hard to guess the one outcome toward which all this tends. Reading into the future one can discern the day when, sex having become a pure visual abstraction, modern science will devise for it a simple gadget which it is easy to imagine though a little hard to describe. Remote offspring of the eighteenth-century Scotchman's kissing machine, it will supersede the Birdseye Sweetheart which has already been mooted in our day; it will be bio-electronic and will act directly, safely, on the nervous system, at little cost, no effort, and no loss of vital fluids. Small and easy to carry, it will put an end to all undesirable familiarity with persons of the opposite sex, will eliminate disease as well as disappointment, and permit the picture-ridden fancy to roam at will. In tune with every other agency of modern life, it will correct aberrations, and by reducing the violence of desire to a quiet, instantaneous change in the body's electrical potential, abolish vice and so make human life respectable at last. The only foreseeable drawback is that of allergies, which might make the sensitized organism literally untouchable. But this is something we may leave to the bio-engineers of the future. Ours only to worry about perpetuating the race till then, in a condition such that it will be able to appreciate the boon.

NO PASSION SPENT

Harsh though our judgment must be for corrective purposes, it cannot help being tempered by the recollection that all past cultures have wrestled unsuccessfully with the facts of individual passion and the needs of social order, with love and the family. It is the realm of confusion par excellence, as one will find in reading the Bible or any ancient literature or code of laws. Or else it is the realm of tyranny under moralists who can think of no other subject and thus magnify, if not succumb to, the immorality they combat. The fact that man is a creature capable of reproducing his kind at any time may be the original neurosis that makes his passions so destructive and his social life so thorny. The dawning consciousness of Neanderthal man may have been so impressed with the need to outnumber the stronger beasts or perish that now the good cause besets us fifty-two weeks a year and interferes with every other.

Each addition of thought and culture to this probably imaginary necessity has made it harder to reconcile the urgings of lust, companionship, or passion with its natural and moral consequences, that is to say, children and the strange web of feelings we rightly call attachment. What history shows, side by side with a great variety of rites and customs, is a tendency to swing from free and easy loving to a strictness that virtually banishes the reality as obscene. The Victorian moral system banked on the fact that if everyone was kept busy censoring his thoughts, words, and impulses while also busy at work, the output of goods would go up while the chances of revolution would go down. The close correlation observable in modern times between political utopias and proposed sexual liberation was verified once more, in reverse.

Victorianism crumbled at last under the impact of science, democracy, the penny press (which restored the reality of passion in the form of scandal), and fatigue. Psychiatry was devised to cope with the manifest disorders that arose with urban and factory dis-

cipline, and the twentieth century faced the task of organizing leisure, equal rights, and such facts of man's emotional life as emerged
from the welter of theories and counsels. Freud's great contribution
at the turn of the century was to show that although a large degree of
social limitation on desire was inevitable and must therefore continue
to pose moral problems, to inspire art, and to refine choice, still,
conventional repression was too great and the penalties of braving
it too harsh.

In the United States, where psychoanalysis found early defenders
and soon established itself both as a profession and as a form of intellectual slang, Freud's lesson has hardly yet been learned. The truth
is that too many old ideas and too many new undigested facts have
engrossed our attention. Busy and bewildered, we have chosen to
make of our intimate emotions a subject of routine joking and despair.
But we are not either a lighthearted or a miserable people; we are
rather a bedeviled one, much of the bedevilment coming from our
attempts to meet all the demands on our selflessness out of a dwindling stock of self. We work harder than most and adapt more readily to material change. But we are poor at balancing income and outlay in our passions and devotions. Our ideas of home and duty, love
and children, the rights of married partners and the claims of the
solitary self, are rigid and abstract, despite all our verbal emancipation.

This is why there is such a market for books on growing up and
making love in Samoa. To be sure, already in the eighteenth century,
the philosophers dreamed of the good life in Tahiti. Before them, in
Montaigne and Shakespeare, the Caribbeans were deemed to have the
simple virtues; and so on back to the various forms of the fable of
Eden. Life outside has always been hard and has always meant choosing, that is, giving up some conceivable good. That is what we find
particularly uncongenial. The discipline of practical life we accept
with great good nature and superior intelligence. But the discipline,
the flexibility touched with soberness, that is required to cope with
natural impulse, and new knowledge, and pressing duty, is something
quite foreign to our habits.

We do not yet know that sobriety is desirable in unselfishness (which is "good") and undesirable, indecent in love (which may be "bad"). Possession of one's whole being by righteousness we do not suspect enough; possession by passion we suspect too much, or fail to recognize altogether. Knowing but little about the kinds and qualities of love, we take them all on a par, or refuse them all, or more likely explain them away by physiology. The very word passion has acquired among us an old-fashioned, somewhat uncertain ring. We know about "dating" — there are courses in it. We have objective standards that we keep an eye on, so we see nothing when we look into ourselves. But since we still have somewhere in us the race's colossal background of yearning, we repeat the formulas of feeling while determined to remain "realists." The product is the tough sentimentalist of our drugstore fiction, who as man or woman pretends that the noblest thing in the world is to behave brutally and scornfully while in his heart and soul is a glowing little capsule of love.

We read other books as well, by true poets and novelists, but we do not credit what they say when it differs from the current cant. The current cant seems to spring from the tough guy's conviction that everybody else is corrupt and conspiring against him. That this belief is not an American creation born of gangsterism and callowness is shown not only by postwar European literature but also by the facts on which most of this literature is based: Fascism, Communism, and the Resistance — all of them conspiratorial modes of life based on hoarding the passions and discharging them as aggression, the simple-minded solution of a lonely crowd. But the feeling has also its thoughtful, indeed elegant, expounders, whose creed is summed up in Phyllis McGinley's line:

We two have but our burning selves for shelter.

Granted that the mood is in a sense a traditional, eternal adjunct of love, the fact that it finds no competing mood of elation, strength, or indifference to the world is the paranoid symptom. A man may legitimately think that he has enemies and that others are talking behind his back, but if he thinks of nothing else, his case is serious. So with us, who seem stuck at the bottom of the "salt, estranging sea" with Matthew Arnold's Forsaken Merman. We have not even managed to get beyond the sophomoric discoveries on which rests our emotional "realism" — that love lasts but for a time though it speaks of forever; that the perfection we find in the beloved seldom appears with such intensity to other beholders; that the sources of our ecstasy are not clear and untroubled but muddied with perishable clay. Hence even in the poetic visions of our laureates and Nobelmen, we find little but the supposedly penetrating insight of the Huxleyan couplet

> And there we sat in blissful calm
> Silently sweating palm to palm. . . .

Opening Blake and trying to discover all he meant by "the lineaments of gratified desire" would overtax us quite. And we probably would stare and faintly snicker at Stendhal's classifying of loves as lustful, heady, and passionate. None of the three is what our age calls sex, which is but a form of self-seeking or (as one desperate practitioner once said) a "nerve regulator," on a par with coffee, tobacco, alcohol, and bromides. Curiously the use of these, including sex, we do not call immoral, except when they lead to antisocial acts. They have a kind of inevitability: we have nerves and must keep them regulated, like our watches. We are nothing if not functional.

But the mysterious motions in the abyss of feeling that such a creature as man will undergo when he has not been artificially drained by mechanical tasks and thoughts — those we dare not contemplate; we haven't the language to talk about them; and when they stir somebody to notable action, society dismisses the event with contemptuous epithets. One wonders what they can be thinking of at a performance of *Tristan* or *Antony and Cleopatra* and how they interpret these works — science fiction about the Martian world, no doubt.

The love of another is but the elemental emblem of any devotion, and if the prevailing tendency is to discount both the object and the feeling, it is not surprising that the whole of life is desiccated. For it is after all an emotional destiny that anyone lives and is willing to pursue. It is fine and worthy to be devoted to the Long Lines of Bell Telephone and worry overnight about a joint-pole agreement that does not cover all it should, but there is — or ought to be — in every conscious being a center of conviction from which the world's work seems trivial, from which one's own life and self form but a freely spent particle of force serving a stronger will than the will. Such is the seat of passion, not the glands or genitalia. They also merely serve, even while appearing to serve themselves. And the proof is that passion arises as well from ideas and visions, from any burning glass concentrating the rays of desire. It must then be our loss and our error when the conventions of a culture perpetually scatter and dim the rays, in the name of any good whatsoever.

EPISODE

In a nation incessantly on the move it happens more and more often that strangers' paths recross, whether they notice it or not. One should expect it on principle, but one sees so many anonymous faces that a second meeting, if recognized, always comes as a shock. I went up to Boston on a morning train, and opposite me in the grill car sat a young couple whom it would have been hard to overlook or forget. She was perhaps twenty years old, perhaps less, and of extraordinary beauty. But it did not advertise: one had to be attuned to it. Her oval face, framed in dark hair, might superficially be called of Spanish type, with prominent cheekbones and perfectly molded chin, but a clear and rather pale coloring changed the expected effect of the most expressive dark eyes I have ever seen. Neither small nor tall, her figure was perfect in its lack of accentuation. What is even rarer, she did not trot or slink or hitch-and-drag but *walked*. She wore very little make-up, her nails were bare. When she smiled her face lost none of its symmetry or sweetness. Rounded lips, firmly tied at the corners, disclosed even teeth happily not too small, and these added a gleam of light that was like a witty afterthought. She was everything at once — pretty, handsome, lovely, and beautiful.

To see all this took less time than to describe it, and I managed to order my sandwich without holding up the waitress or staring like a cow over a fence. It was the girl's companion who required scrutiny. Perhaps he seemed younger than she because he was so weedy and discouraging to look at. His shoulders sloped like a bad coat-hanger, and the coat itself, a melancholy herringbone, covered his frame like a blanket flung over a hat tree. While his companion was neatly rather than well dressed, he was hardly fit to go out — no tie, a spotty growth of bristles, hair overlong at front and back and unkempt in between. His face was remarkable for only two features — a vagrantly receding chin and slightly protuberant eyes, of the kind that seem to have as much lid underneath as on top. I should add that his glance was very fine, deep, and dark amid long lashes curling upward. His lazy way of sweeping the air with them was only to be expected.

I watched them eat. She was cheerful, indeed gay, paying no attention to anything but her friend, as if enjoying the idea of their trip together. She always turned to him to speak and hung on the few words that he dropped. He was not sullen, exactly, but seemed vaguely annoyed at himself. In this conjecture, as it turned out, I was wrong. He did not sit straight by her side but half averted, his body at an awkward angle to the table. He looked so uncomfortable that I put him down as the younger brother or cousin, embarrassed as an ill-bred youth of seventeen can be at having to escort a full-grown young woman who is being nice to him out of kindness and good manners.

The train pulled in and I did not think of them again, although once or twice over the week end her face arose in my mind with the question, Where have I seen such a person?

Two days later I returned to New York on the Yankee Clipper.

I was already seated and reading the paper when someone, trying
to hoist a bag on the rack across the aisle from me, brought within
my field of vision a shape, a design of cloth, that made me turn
my head. It was my friend in herringbone. She was with him,
sitting in the outer seat. Neither noticed me, of course, but as
they settled down they forced themselves once more on my attention.

Though less than three feet away, I did not hear a word they said.
For four hours, they whispered, locked in each other's arms. It
cannot have been very comfortable for the girl, half reclining across
his lap, but she managed to endure it skillfully, shifting her position
now and then, being at all times completely modest. It was not a
necking party in public. No doubt the boy's lethargy contributed
to this seemliness, but the character of the occasion was really due
to her. Her face and her behavior, her visible emotion were a study
and wonder. She loved him, obviously. Anyone would rack his
brains in vain to imagine why. It could not be his looks or manly
bearing. It could not be his conversation, which was scant. It was
not money: he seemed — they both seemed — anything but rich.
For a moment the wild notion crossed my mind that he might be
of princely blood, in sordid exile. He had the tired Bourbon look.
But no, it was impossible to saddle any royal family with this creature who was holding an unimaginably beautiful woman in his arms
like a scrawny messenger boy carrying a swath of long-stemmed
flowers.

Not that he was indifferent to his burden. He held her close. He
waggled his modicum of chin among the tendrils above her brow.
He whispered, and his words may have been so electrifying that
they transfigured him. And transfigured she was. She faced in my
direction, all unseeing; I could read her quick thoughts fleeing across
her face, her smiles, her suddenly closed and reopened eyes. When
once or twice she got up and left him and brought back a cup of
water, she came down the aisle like one hastening to meet a long-
lost love. He gave her a slow beat of his eyelashes in response and
this may have been enough for her. Not for me. I wanted to yank

him to his feet, trim his head with a lawnmower, and shake him till the herringbones rattled together.

I was, once again, altogether wrong. They were certainly not brother and sister or cousins, but lovers, by intent or fulfillment. They wore no rings of any kind. Her look of the yielded heart and soul was sufficient clue. It is not rare to see women rapt with pleasure, with desire, with pride of possession or of self. One has seen the hungry mothering look and the adoring-calculating one, the eyes of reckless flirtation and the smiles of "I'm the Queen of the May." Only once in a lifetime, perhaps, one sees passion. She had it, he endured it. And what I took for negligence or indifference on his part may well have been respect or humility; I give him the benefit of the doubt. Why she chose him is nobody's business, not even hers. They understood one another and their priceless possession, however each might give or receive it. Taking in the scene, another passenger who went by winked at me and said: "Lucky guy!" But he too was wrong: "Lucky, lucky girl!"

THE MAN IN THE KITCHEN

Yes, but. From all sides, "Yes, but" speaks up with the voice of reason, or rather with reasons: to earn your daily bread, to beget and rear children, to furnish a home and give the young a decent start, to reward a wife's toil and devotion by affording her leisure, help, a career; and in addition, if it can be managed, to fulfill one's civic duty by leaving the community better or richer than one found it — what have all these difficult and indispensable tasks to do with rapture, poetry, and passion? We are a Baconian people and it was Bacon who said that "the stage is more beholding to love than is the life of man." Our Professors of Human Relations agree that "love alone is no basis for marriage." But then, still professing, they go on to list half a dozen requirements for "marital success" which imply "harmony at all levels, physical, mental, emotional, and spiritual"; this, moreover, is explicitly for the benefit of the children to come, since out of a happy home will come no warped characters, no delinquents, sadists, fascists, or un-co-operativists.

Of all the mad utopias, this delineation of marriage is undoubtedly the maddest. On its plain face can be seen the unmistakable asylum smile. Whatever else it be, marriage is a practical arrangement, and it is clear that in order simply to find out whether all those required compatibilities exist one would have to be married and taking notes under test conditions. To insure, moreover, that physical and emotional "adjustments" should be present soon enough to make life tolerable would demand a preparation reaching back into infancy. The efforts to enlighten and correct and patch up existing marriages are certainly praiseworthy. But the institution as such is not susceptible of radical improvement, first because what brings people under its sway is in any event largely chance, and second because it is not really one institution but many. As in disease each case is in certain ways unique, so each marriage is an unrehearsed and never fully told tale. It should be our duty, therefore, to regard marriage with the awe and respect we accord the Unknowable. As an institution, it is one of those about which we must preserve extreme sobriety, neither loving it, nor hating it, acting neither impatient with it nor indignant, nor know-it-all, making it yield, where possible, as much as we yield to it.

The reverse of course prevails. We have no manners toward marriage and no shame about our coarse intrusive behavior. All the world loves an engaged couple, and makes them pay for their privilege right through to the tearstained, nerve-racked, wickedly tedious and outrageously expensive wedding day. All the world loves a married couple and tells them how to live. All the world loves a divorcing couple and repays itself for earlier smiles and favors (not to mention silverware) by telling tales about what cannot possibly be known. And all the academic, legal, and medical world digs into the mess to come up with five rules and ten norms of the most one-sided, irrelevant, and platitudinous kind, whether they be perfectionist or commonsensical.

The only platitude that really applies is "You never can tell," and Shaw said the last word about it for our benefit in his comedy of that name. The only perfectionism we are entitled to propose is that which would make our own behavior more discreet. It is just possible also that in situations of which we have more than casual knowledge, we may be able to modify usefully the assumptions or expectations of the friends who confide in us.

At this moment of time in the United States, with mobility and powers multiplied, every young person is likely to believe the gospel of opportunity which tells him or her to develop the gifts that nature supplied. But each also feels the pressure of the competition thus generated, and all end by following the forms and fads that sweep mysteriously over the crowd. No doubt these differ from group to group, yet almost anywhere one may observe the effects of the hidden force which seizes the children — especially the girls — almost ahead of puberty and makes them struggle for they know not what: popularity, success, something which is not the attention of this boy or that boy, but an abstract prize. For this, the half-grown, ill-balanced creature will make efforts and concessions and endure pain and grief that have all the impact of tragedy, save for the triviality of the cause and the low envy which makes not blank verse but gossip. Trade and advertising, the movies and popular fiction, the newspaper clichés and the press agents of jazz singers — all help re-enforce these rigid exhibitionist standards which American youth imposes on itself, and which produce the popular or pin-up type. When a little more developed, in high school or college, she struts about as in the ads putting forward her two little bundles as on a peddler's tray — pathetic and profoundly modest, since it is evident she thinks this is the best she has to offer.

Such is the preparation, apparently, for "What It Takes to Catch a Husband" as this is disclosed every few years by some article in a national magazine. We do not have to take literally the mixture of cynicism and anticynicism, feminism and antifeminism, that we can find in these reports of interviews with wholesomely photo-

All the Other Halves 317

genic girls. The significant thing is that regardless of individual sweetness and good sense, a dozen people taken at random from time to time will give lip service to the prevailing ideas about marriage. If no more than imitation, it is still indicative, the counterpart of the mass impulses that sway the children and that for instance made one hundred and sixty-five girls under eighteen faint at a football game in Mississippi two years ago.

What the "mature" idea comes down to is to make one last competitive effort which will put an end to one's struggling and competing. That looks, quite understandably, like happiness. Catching a man means the ultimate success; make-believe ceases and real life or possibly the good life begins. The hunt is therefore deliberate, painstaking, and economically alert. Compared to the forethought that goes into selecting the most likely male, a man's choice is indeed cavalier; and it becomes just credible that the shirt advertiser is right when he displays nine imprints of female lipstick with the legend "This is what women put on men when men put on Arrow Shirts." It may take a moment to puzzle out why women would want to kiss the shirt, but as a symbol the act does seem perfectly logical.

In counterpoint with this desire of a woman to be settled and have a place of her own, one hears the feminist note of equal rights to a career. In the last eighty years the world has found out that women have talents as varied as those of men; they are not all born housekeepers and mothers. And they can now get training and positions, though it appears that measured in money their success is limited — very few earn as much as six thousand dollars a year. This is probably an artificial limitation. Either the career woman has not married, in which case her employer feels she may leave at any moment; or she has, in which case he unreasonably feels that her loyalty and energies are divided. In either event, she is less valuable, less in demand than a man.

If she has married, she discovers that a career is not an easy third party to accommodate in the home. It is already a legitimate complaint that the modern man's job — unless it is manual labor — takes up too much of his waking life. He carries it home and neglects his wife. To compete with him in the outside world, she in turn should be as much absorbed: where then is the home life? In a briefcase built for two. To this must be added the danger of competition within. In my own profession, I have again and again seen bright young couples break up because of the wear and tear of adjusting rival claims on time, energy, and opportunity: if she is finishing a piece of work it is sensible that he should do the washing up for a while, but this doesn't help him get on with his research, and vice versa. If a good offer comes from the West — to her, does he pack up and tag along? If she earns more than he, or if in fact she supports the whole ménage, how long can he work in peace of mind toward his degree? They may be quite united on their common plan, but life does not follow plans; relatives, outsiders interfere, comparisons are easy and odious, the future is uncertain and hard to gauge; they are both young, not fully formed — it is very hard, even if there arise no doctrinal differences when both are writers or architects.

Nor should one forget the influence on human relations of character and type of work, success or authority. Feminist opinion says that women are "the same" as men, or different but equal, or equal but with additional rights by virtue of motherhood and the long injustice practiced on them by men. In a marriage this admitted legal and social equality is necessarily modified by actual traits, traits that probably keep changing till middle age, and that take no account of mutual expectations. The feminist view used to express indignant horror at the idea that so many men want a "plaything," something soft and frilly and caressing — a mistress, in short; whereas the New Woman offered herself primarily as mother, alpinist, and lecturer on eugenics. There is no right or wrong to the issue; it merely states a fresh difficulty. For if it is woman's prerogative, decreed by nature, to procure herself a husband and provider who will help her perpetuate the race under the best conditions, then it is nature's inducement to him that he should see her as an object of desire and protection. He too may want to settle down and have children, but why a man should want to live with a sort of militant business partner, whose chief concern is either her profession or her babies, has never been explained by those who propound high-minded views of love and parenthood. More than likely, the notion has seldom become fact. It exists mainly in the pictures and statuary of totalitarian regimes — two profiles with but one jaw, striding toward the future with leg outstretched and distinguishable as to sex only by minor details of drapery. As long as women continue to curl their hair and wear little bowknots in odd places, to call other little things hats, and favor *lanjeray* generally, they may and must expect to be taken by men as something else than comrades in pro-creation and domesticity.

This is not to say that they were created to feed and amuse men. On the contrary, the chores of domesticity are as great a curse as the ignorance and idleness of the harem, and the greatest danger to marriage today is the encroachment of domestic duty upon every spare moment of life. Not the statute book but the greasy dish is woman's enemy, rising to smite her thrice a day every day. A truly modern society *must* bring into being the expendable plate and fork, and then go on to tackle the other ills in the new woman's bur-densome round: not enough space, no help to speak of, never quite enough money for ever-expanding needs that do not bring ease or pleasure but merely "safety" and the maintenance of the common standards of health, insurance and recreation — all of which makes nervous, harassed, short-tempered, illiterate wives and mothers, and fathers too. The refreshment of mind that comes from sociability is cut down by the inexplicable lack of time and quite explicable lack of service. Man and wife barely suffice to take care of the house, the children, and the bills without adding the burden of visitors, or of visits. For it is no pleasure to park oneself on friends who toil behind the scenes, and only a little better to share the kitchen-and-bedroom drudgery that everyone is so well trained in. As the host said to his housebroken guest at the sink-side: "Another set of dishes, Harry, and my house is yours."

The point is not that there should be a race of helots to wait on their masters hand and foot and free them from conversation, but that some portion of any life should be led disinterestedly and *as if* the hungry generations were not treading us down. This is only to say again that modern technology is only beginning to be applied to living; it has been too busy securing our existence and spreading the means of it as broadly as might be. The spread of prosperity is in fact what causes the dearth of more elegant leisure: the baby sitter is the last of the retainers as well as the hardest to retain. Even the occasional workman is disappearing: a kindhearted plumber in New Jersey taught the ladies to do their own repairs because he *could not afford* to answer their calls. The man of the house is all the more called on to be a Jack-of-all-trades, as well as baby feeder, diaper changer, shopper for groceries, and part-time cook. When he has to sit and rest, like his spouse he knits.

In a word, we all belong to the upper masses; the social pressure is all from side to side rather than from top or bottom, and thus not so easily reduced. It is therefore time for us to take thought in order both to simplify and to diversify the common life. The symptoms of distress are all too evident: alcoholism is only the most showy. Not material hardship but excessive moral constraint sends the best and most sensitive to the psychiatrist and the divorce court. The rest are supposed to divert their minds with movies, anodynes, cabarets ("Irma, the Body Beautiful: 130 pounds of Sophisticated Dynamite"), or a subscription to *Esquire*. And all of this, poor as it is, addressed in the one-sided old way chiefly to men.

For both sexes, the rigid social edict to marry young — as if temperaments and opportunities were cut on a single pattern — puts the best of life at the service of the Bitch-goddess Success without even defining her attributes, and then casts off the obedient in mid-career as useless. We are quite surprised, then, when a great wave of disgust overcomes the middle-aged man who has been toiling since college (he probably worked his way through) as he finds his brood fled and a strange, stout, nervous woman on his hearthrug, to whom he has nothing to say. He is of no more use to her than she to him, but his chances of escape seem better, by social convention. He will become an unattached man and be asked to dinner parties, whereas his wife will scarcely be asked by her own friends — no use. Yet by the same inexorable system he is driven into the toils of an identical though younger woman who has been in business too — the business of waiting for him or his like.

We are not surprised but shocked when on a lower plane the flight of men toward liberty takes place en masse, away from home, at a convention. The Legion is proverbial but significant, and its actions should be pondered even while being controlled: TOSSED GIRLS FROM MEZZANINE said a report from Chicago a few years ago. The Bacchanalian urge is strong and it will not be damped by sermons or arrests. It is in fact a national tradition in the form of revivalism, and its sexual character was noted long ago in Mrs. Trollope's book on the *Domestic Manners of the Americans*. Our history in regard to outbreaks of mass hysteria is no worse than that of other Western peoples, but like them since the passing of the Middle Ages we lack a Feast of Fools. Christmas is not enough, as is shown by the popular, the universal response to such substitute orgies as the recent Coronation. When it was all over, the British papers had the impudence to rebuke the people for enjoying the event that the press had done everything to turn into a jamboree. Even in wanting it both ways there is such a thing as discrimination.

The wisest man would be a fool if he thought he could propose a remedy to civilized anarchy and rigidity. But discrimination, differentiation, may suggest a state of mind in which to look for solutions. For the trouble starts with not asking: "Who am I, what do I want?" or with giving the wrong answers. It is utopian to wonder whether any civilization could ever become so temperate and just as to regard with equal favor several kinds of arrangements in love and marriage, but it is surely no more utopian than the unique matching of bodies and souls that our assumptions demand and that our "experts" dither about. We are in fact pluralists in our arrangements and do not recognize it; if we did, the need of deliberate choice might have in that realm the same beneficial effect — to provoke thought. Children would be accustomed to Possibility, and would not start at the age of eight with the sole ambition of being on the Tigerette Pep Squad for the sake of that gold-and-black uniform which slays the boys.

Men and women do not sufficiently know what they want, being hypnotized by what they ought to want. Most men are unaware, for example, that a great many young women have a quasi-religious regard for babies, and will quite honestly use any means to become mothers: the man they marry is simply part of the necessary equipment for their creative work. Some men share this feeling and it would certainly be desirable to match these two by two, instead of making them unhappy by fours. Something very like this applies in reverse to intellectual men, whose clear demands since Milton's day have seldom been credited by women. This is not the old principle of congenial tastes, it is the free acknowledgment, with no penalties attached, of different types.

Once this variety admitted, we face a question which is not to be blinked by any student of history and biography, whether the bourgeois principle of one man, one vote, and one wife produces by and large greater order and happiness than some other established system. I speak for no vested interest, but I can conceive a philosophic American of the year 4000 regretting that his remote ancestors had prohibited the Mormons' polygamy. Millions of good men and women have lived under that moral code, the patriarchs of our Western religions among them. And it should be remembered that our monogamy in the past was curiously amended, not only by upper-class privilege and lower-class casualness — but by unlimited births and the resultant deaths of the mothers. The most respectable seventeenth-century Judge Samuel Sewall, of Massachusetts, had three successive wives and sixteen children. Let us not envy rashly, but rather consider that we do everything to encourage a multiplicity of attachments among the courting young, only to precipitate them into a state where monogamy too often comes to mean monotony. We are then surprised at the results, which we "study" without ever going back to first principles. Surely, a world that includes Islam ought to be ready to consider mankind's experience entire and perhaps arrive, for the sake of various temperaments, at diversity within unity.

For example, to continue the fantasy, it would in fair play extend the Mohammedan allowance of four mates to women as well as men; and a devotee of the exacting or absent-minded disciplines, such as art or mathematics, would say that the system ought to be tempered by its opposite — micropolygamy, or the right to have but one-fourth interest in a wife. His difficulty would be, not that of engrossing more than his share, but in keeping her from being exclusively fascinated by him, which is to say, by the other three fourths of his life.

As to the problem of children, which is what this imaginative flight was aiming at, it would not be so great as in previous times. We are today quite civilized, partly because the old considerations of inheritance by the eldest son no longer apply: there is no fixed piece of earth to inherit and little else to replace it. We have accordingly given up many of our shameful jests and attitudes toward illegitimacy, and have lost some of our prejudice about "one's own blood." The fact that blood now comes in a bottle has also helped destroy a grisly superstition and the proverbs that go with it. But more important, the mixing of the peoples by war and social revolution has enlarged our thoughts about what a child is. More and more people in this country adopt foundlings and foreigners, and care for them because here are orphans and they, the adults, are intending parents — the most sufficient of reasons.

THE LITTLE REFUGEES

A justly famous woman said it more than fifty years ago: ours was to be the Century of the Child. Had she known our jargon, she might have said "of the common child," for in America at least we have, as I suggested a moment ago, almost wholly recognized the claims of the newborn member of society as such. We still have to fight against child labor in certain states, but in the main we teach, feed, nurture, and doctor our children better and more systematically than any other people. This is admirable democratic logic. If children have no minority rights, who has? Of all the dependent groups they are the least able to organize and fight for rights: they can hardly formulate them. Yet it is plain that any dumb sense of injury inflicted in their bewildered years will stay with them and plague society to the end of their days. So much we have learned and made a national conviction — to the point, indeed, of being blamed for our "irrational accent on youth" and excessive compliance with its whims and follies.

It cannot be denied that among a certain group of the American population, the most conscientious and intelligent, there has grown up not merely a worship of the child but a positive dread of somehow inadvertently desecrating the little god. A psychiatrist and pediatrician had to write a book entitled *Don't Be Afraid of Your Child* (though he *will* bite!). If parents now have the jitters, it is in part due to previous expert advice. We read, for example, in the work of another widely read pediatrician: "The death of a parent during infancy is almost always interpreted as a betrayal and creates strong guilt feelings in the child. . . . No matter how unhappy parents are, they should try not to get sick or die until their child has developed a capacity to find his own path through the world." This advice has undoubtedly kept many a father from catching cold, but the clue to the prevailing state of mind is given in a later sentence, in which the parents are asked to ponder "what stresses you may have added to the child's already sufficiently difficult task of growing up, and try to relieve its pressure."

What the psychiatrists have done is to reword and transmit as science the bourgeoisie's feelings of distress, oppression, and self-conscious distaste for their own lives. This is the emotion of "statistical living" borrowing ideas from Freud and from revolutionary politics, and serving them up in jargon sauce to sustain the ill-housed, overdriven and possibly sex-ridden pair in their struggle with the little innocent in the bassinet. An exaggerated concern with his innocence is the basis of our child worship. Everything he does is right because he has no ulterior motive: he is not selling anything. So if we want a better world, let's keep him in that pristine state — where he wants what he wants and yells like a maniac when he doesn't get it.

There's the rub: if he is not always the blissful babe of Madonna paintings, the fault must be ours; we're frustrating him, denying him love, complicating his complexes. It's my fault and my mother's before me; thumbsucking and bedwetting are the curse of Oedipus: oh, to be a child and not have the responsibility of setting it right! Our novels sing pretty much the same song, lodging innocence in different symbols but agreeing that not to know is the beginning of wisdom. After this, one sees the dramatic point of the event reported by the *New Yorker*, that a dressing-up party was held somewhere at which the guests wore diapers, engaged in sucking contests, and the like. Clearly, the only salvation for the modern adult is to have died in infancy.

Is not this the worst of our paradoxes, then, that we have made life better for the child in order to achieve a better society, but saddled the grownup with such a sense of responsibility to the future of the community that he wants to change places with the young, the licensed hedonists?

Our error is to have had such vaulting ambitions — lack of soberness again. It was admirable to stop beating children, to dress them in loose short clothes, acknowledge their penchant for mud and water and climbing, and refrain from hectoring them into grownup behavior — to follow, in short, every one of the precepts Rousseau expounded two hundred years ago. But it was a mistake to turn the home and the school into factories of progress, imagining we had the formula for it. Not only did the formula vary from expert to expert, and from year to year, as well as multiply through the distortion of every user, but the conflicting counsels were also vitiated by the fact that they were based on observations of existing children — so-called norms that statistically neglect the infinite play and whimsy of nature. What a child "takes" from the bookish handling he receives no one can predict or should presume to. When one gets tempted here, one's duty is to recall Francis Place's autobiographical remark that he did not remember ever seeing his father without the man's being drunk and knocking him down. Yet Place grew up to be a philanthropist of great practical ability and well-balanced mind. The elder Place will not be set up by anyone as a model parent, but he should stand as a warning that an angelic father may have the same reverse effect as he, that is, produce a devil of a son.

The vice of the whole child-rearing racket is its abstractness. It teaches the primacy of emotion in character development, which is sound, but it is itself feelingless in its verbiage, and it ignores the patent fact that every emotion from birth is attached to some idea or image. Food, play, "I won't," are thoughts as well as passions. Manipulating the passions in a vacuum of thought ends in futility. By the same token, the injunction to give children plenty of love, for the good of their souls, has no meaning if one is not ready to give it before the advice is uttered. What kind of love is it that is turned on like a tap? Again, the vague proposition that children will be happy if their parents love each other is as foolish and contradictory as the summons to stay alive *on purpose* for the child: it is easy to imagine a child legitimately jealous of parents who were madly in love with each other. And what could be worse than to grow up in a home where so much harmony prevails that only one unshakable view is taken of every subject — a perfect brick wall without a crack for difference to slip through?

In bringing up children, circumstance is all. Anyone who has ever really looked at a child while fathering or mothering him knows that the concrete instance and the passing moment outwit every generality. Forethought and calm are indispensable, but unless one acts also from spontaneity and true feeling, one is deliberately (though unconsciously) making a little artifact out of a living being. Who has not heard of the model parents, modern style, who do everything right, but the child has nightmares? There may be many explanations, but a simple and possible one is that if the parents were at times sterner with the child, he might feel he had sterner defenders against his hidden fears. "If they tiptoe around *me*," thinks the poor mite, "they won't be much use against dream bears."

In other words, while we run after recipes diluted from Freud, we forget some of the obvious facts of life as they strike the child. It is hard to remember that from lack of size and strength, all children belong for many years to the downtrodden: everything is too high, too heavy, too distant, too obscure. Their world, as they can't help noticing, is not real; the real one goes on above their heads, in every sense. Hence they should without exception be considered not as miniature human beings who will fill out and fill up with our notions, but as refugees from another planet whom one is slowly trying to acclimate to an alien culture.

It is amazing with what tireless will the poor things try to make sense out of the overwhelming nonsense in which they are plunged. "George Washington would rather die," dutifully repeated one little boy, "than stretch his ribs to tell a lie." The original read: "stain his lips," but the emendation is surely an improvement in the direction of reason. Another, having had (at his own request) a little lesson on what made things fall to the ground, was overheard teaching it to his younger brother: "I'm telling you, it's the Law of Droppity."

Our death-disapproving pediatrician was right on one point: growing up is hard, but the young soon learn to lead a double life. Questioned as to his future plans, the child admits that he would like to be a cowboy "but I guess being a doctor would be more sensible." And there are inevitable moments of revolt, exasperated declarations of independence severing all connections: one New

York mother whose children occasionally play on the street nervously calls them in about six, just as I happen to walk past. They protest "Ah, no, Mother, we're playing! Yes, on the sidewalk. Sure you can't see us, but we're right here, on *your* side!"

The lunacy of the adult world has long been the theme of "cute" fiction about children, but it takes endless vigilance to preserve our relation to that world and to theirs, to lead *our* double life on their behalf. Little Jim wants me to go out to his house in the country, sixty miles away, to see his new wallet. From a strict point of view he is obviously crazy, he has "no sense of values." Now if it were a new horse or swimming pool, I'd be interested and even flattered by the invitation. So far, any adult easily makes the adjustment to the little lunatic. But how many grownups keep from laughing or exchanging glances about the wallet? They laugh also at certain things they can't or won't explain: "We'll tell you when you're older." You get patiently older — dutifully eating all their queer food — and when you're older they've forgotten what they were laughing at — they can't tell you — so you never know. . . .

Emerson said the definitive word when he remarked that to bring up a child properly would take all one's time. It would also take the combined imagination of ten geniuses. For the little refugees are given us quite passionate and restless, many-gifted and full of ambitions. They have it in them to become Shakespeares and Newtons, if only — if only we did not whittle them down to our own size by our stupidity, inattention, or misplaced conceit. This does not make them our betters; we were cut down, too, from our possible scope. And if as adults we are to have lives worth *our* living, we cannot enslave ourselves wholly to childish needs. It is in any case impossible to do and say the right thing, faultlessly, all the time. In a bus last winter there was a lively child of about ten, who wore a hearing aid and talked incessantly to his intelligent-looking mother. Their dialogue, which I set down verbatim immediately after getting off, perfectly sums up the unconscious war of two worlds:

BOY. How long have I been going to school, Ma?

MOTHER. Two years.

BOY. Two years? TWO YEARS! Gosh! (*Pause*) How long have I got to go?

MOTHER. How do you mean — this year or all told?

BOY. All told.

MOTHER. About twelve years more.

BOY. I can't do it. I'm gonna bust. I know too much already.

MOTHER. Don't be silly.

BOY. I can feel it.

MOTHER. You're not talking sense; you can't tell how much you can learn.

BOY. Yes, I can. That's one thing I can tell about. (*Pause*) When are there going to be mosquitoes?

MOTHER. Why do you want to know?

BOY. 'Cause it's the time I like.

MOTHER. You like mosquitoes? . . . Why, they won't be here till summer.

BOY. In vacation? I thought we'd have some before and get out of school before vacation. We did before, get out of school before vacation, didn't I?

Here he caught sight of an ad showing a green snake labeled "In-flation" and held under a cleft stick. He read out loud the words printed in red: HOLD IT DOWN! Then he said: "Mother! What are they doing to that snake?"

MOTHER (*looking up at the ad, then around her, as for help*). They're — it's — it has to do with keeping prices down.

BOY. Prices? What's prices? (*She gives him a sweet smile and says nothing. He smiles too, but with an indescribable expression of puzzlement and pity. He gives it up. Soon he is chanting absent-mindedly*) "I know too much! I know too much!"

Imagination, the modern school would say, is precisely our forte. We have banned the rigid ways of our ancestors, treat each child as an individual, and attend first to his needs. This is largely true and wholly praiseworthy. Children now like to go to school (a good and sensible one is meant) and they learn there how to make their own strangely rational ideas conform to our less symmetrical civilization. They learn democracy in action — committee work, elective choice, co-operation on projects, and tolerance of the mentally or physically handicapped. The progressive school in America is a very close approximation of American society, and I intend no mockery when I say that after working on a project in noise and confusion with the aid or hindrance of ten other children, a boy or girl is ready to fill a job in journalism, advertising, hospital work, or the civil service.

But for that very reason it is idle to pretend that the school is remaking society or that it is of imagination all compact. Schools are better or worse along many scales of merit, but the school as an institution is not capable of improvement: it will always be molded by the surrounding culture; it will always be in partial opposition to that culture; it will always be staffed, in the main, by ordinary minds; and it will always impose some arbitrary scheme on its pupils. The modern school is justly proud of its success with hard cases and with bright children, but it is unreasonably vain when it comes to claiming absolute and generalized success. It does not see that to be "creative" and "free" and to "take leadership" and be "full of initiative" are also tyrannical demands that some children cannot fulfill and that others see through as self-righteous pretensions.

Moreover, if growing up is difficult and runs the risk of injury, to feel that one is being brought up is an insult. For this defect the school should blame its involvement in the toils of the doubtful sciences. It applies quite breathlessly all the "findings" — "Our experience with the three-year-olds whom we have observed in our own Nursery School during the past twenty-five years or so has shown us that three-year-olds are extremely susceptible to the use of certain 'key words.' Three-year-olds have not, in our experience, changed very much in these last twenty-five years, and during all this time these have been the words that have served us best in getting these children to do what we want them to. 'Surprise' and 'secret' both tend to work like charms. 'As soon as you put these toys away, I have a surprise for you. . . .'" This is no doubt better than scolding and beating, but what one would like to know, after another twenty-five years, is what surprise is in store for the manipulator. Owing to the tests, there seems to be an approved mode of behavior for each age, less room for diversity than the catalogue promises, no regard for time, and too great a heat of anxiety generated in parents over the illusion that little Peter will enter Harvard still sucking his thumb. If children could form a union and strike for their rights they would want longer hours and wilder play; since for practical reasons these can't be granted, the least we can do is give them their share of intelligent neglect.

But the word neglect is one no school can stomach — perhaps rightly so. The school is possessive, creative, and wants to turn out an ideal product. If we yielded to its siren lure "How can the school be more useful to child and parent?" we would see prospective couples urged to conceive the child on school premises, a committee aiding, and all the subsequent steps taken in co-operation, so as to make the offspring fit in both with the program of his entering group and with the needs of the school in giving instruction-by-example to its older boys and girls. The ideal citizen of the future would have been a pupil, an alumnus, a trainee-parent, a delivered parent, and a model parent of one and the same school.

Possessiveness is indeed hard to fight where children are concerned. Their helplessness seems to be asking for it, but this is an illusion, and it would be well if we could train ourselves to use the pronouns "my," "our," as little as possible in connection with children. They are "they," semi-independent creatures like ourselves, with different tastes and hopes, a different pace and rhythm of life, and an attachment to us which must be treated not as a right or an opportunity but as a gift of which we want to increase the value — by making it as genuine and disinterested as it can become. In a very few years, thanks to orange juice, these helpless crawlers are six feet two regardless of sex, and able to look down on you in more ways than one: it is good then to have their affection for what we are worth — and who can love another who is in his pocket or on his neck? This is, incidentally, the best reason for teaching one's children some manners, to be used toward oneself as much as toward strangers. No reason exists why parents should be doormats, or should condone bad language and behavior because it is their own silly flesh and blood that is guilty of boorishness.

For our children are not an extension of ourselves, a second chance for us to be brilliant or successful, this time by proxy: they are precisely what my little niece said at four when her mother was explaining to her why her brothers were bigger than she: "I get you — I'm new." The habits of an older generation will not have it so. This same child when newborn was lovingly examined by her grandmother, who finally said to my sister: "I don't understand it. John and Timmie look like our side of the family and Ann takes after her father, but this one doesn't look like anybody." To which one felt like asking, with a slight stare, "Isn't it a relief seeing a little variety?" Children in fact resemble everybody in turn and are at the same time nobody but themselves. They should be so inside and out.

Part of the inside is the mind, and over the filling and training of the mind there now rages in our midst a battle which will not soon be ended. In the name of intellect and moral absolutes, critics have attacked our entire system of public education and attempted to blacken the reputation of John Dewey as its sole inspirer. This is giving Dewey both too much and too little credit; he has nothing to fear from wild words. The greater danger is that in the present lining up of forces, no true position is likely to be attacked or defended by either side.

The modern school undeniably misses many chances to train the mind. It is extremist — like its advisers in psychiatry — in the faith that love is enough, or adjustment, or even happiness. The modern school moreover raises strong suspicions that it dismisses brains because it hasn't got any; that it cannot think seems to be proved by what it says in print and from the platform. And this progressivism is endemic, it covers the country, covers it with paper, reports, studies, findings: the mind is lost among findings.

But when this has been duly said, there remain two other things of equal weight and importance. One is that the culture as a whole is not enamored of intellectual pursuits as such. Some excellent reasons for this I have advanced earlier. The culture as a whole entertains itself with books, movies, newspapers, and broadcasts that also betray the same lack of precision and literacy deplored among teachers. If galloping TV is fatal to the young, it is not because the school likes or condones it, but because the parents are content to have it so. The culture is in these matters quite consistent; the school is not and cannot be an island of special refinement for it is not supported or attended by an elite. The school is, after all, run by ordinary citizens, tied in with political machines, and staffed by very representative men and women who, amid their gruelling, underpaid, and multitudinous duties, make not the slightest pretense at being intellectuals.

Yet from their position close to the grass roots the teachers see very clearly one thing that their critics overlook, and that is the need to teach the modern population how to live under modern conditions. It is no doubt absurd that history and English literature should make way in the curriculum for courses on How to Shop, Date, or Select a Dentist. Yet if the ignorance of those elementary routines exists, it has to be dealt with. We may grant the clumsiness of the remedy, but we cannot deny the necessity. Nor is the dilemma a simple one: we have too many teachers poorly trained to teach the old academic subjects, pupils consequently bored by things that do not touch their own lives, and "real life" programs that satisfy common interests through field trips, movies, and discussions. It will not do simply to assault those who run the system as best they can from day to day as if they had deliberately chosen to make American schools bull-session centers instead of little replicas of foreign lycées and gymnasia.

The illuminating thing is that as foreign lycées become democratized, the "American" phenomenon is reproducing itself abroad. After listening for half a century to Europe's rather blind critique of our educational system, we are now going to have to listen to their amazement at what happens when you push every child through one identical school system and keep him there till sixteen. The lycée merged with the common school will no longer be an elite institution producing distinguished minds. As for the German gymnasium, the best students of the subject blame it for contributing to Germany's inner strain and lack of political wisdom. It did not "keep in touch" as our berated American schools certainly do, possibly to excess. In any case, both experiences, here and abroad, show the delicacy of the relation between school and society and the danger of overvaluing, hence of overdriving, the educational system. In the school as in society, there is a point beyond which one dare not mortgage the future in hopes of revamping the present.

THE GOOD SOCIETY

Just as in dealing with the young one should never reprove without giving encouragement and seldom approve without casually pointing out defects, so in thinking about society we should bring to bear at least two contrary perceptions or ideas. And this, not in order to conciliate others by tempering criticism with insincere praise, but in order to guide our hands in either demolition or reconstruction. We cannot raise an arm without making two muscles work opposite to each other; our minds should be able to hold two opposite ideas and use them both at once. This principle secures the very point of government by discussion, but its translation into parties and schools of thought easily leads to the deplorable habit of being always of one's own opinion. If, as must have happened in the course of these chapters, I have contradicted myself, I hope that some at least of the instances have been of the kind that strengthens judgment and gives action a surer touch.

It may have seemed, for example, that although I began by finding our country admirable in every respect, superior to others in energy, variety, political intelligence, social adaptability, and generous impulse, I gradually shifted my ground from praise to fault-finding, and in recent pages have steadily advocated a "soberness" that is the reverse of wholehearted admiration. I would interpret my own presentment, or at least its intention, quite differently; first reminding the reader of the reservations expressed throughout, whether in the midst of praising and blaming; and second, offering the double movement pro and con as an example of the frame of mind I think best suited to our tradition and our situation.

This is not the middle-of-the-road position nor the passive acknowledgment that there is much to be said on both sides; it is rather the habit of acknowledging that contradictories co-exist and make valid claims that cannot be dismissed without taking precautions or paying ransoms. Too often we prefer to enter the cycle of illusion, disillusion, and despair which makes us embrace Saint Thomas after Karl Marx or nudism after Victoria's petticoats; which replaces foolish sentiment with tawdry sex, and battle-and-king history with formless social studies; behaving in each phase as abstractionists committed to a so-called idea instead of pragmatists keeping an eye on the ball.

At the moment, under the impact of world events, Americans have so violently put aside what they have been taught to shun as "wishful thinking" that they have taken up "dreadful thinking." They think they will surely be right if they predict the worst; they groan at every mishap or misdeed in the country; they exalt the power of those whom they declare public enemies, saying that all is over, the forces of darkness are closing in. At the same time, they grant foreign nations every right to be peculiar, and will explain others' blunders by ancient cultural privilege, meanwhile denying us a comparable latitude. All they ask of their country is perfection and absolute justice. Indignation is of course their natural element, heavily fortified with ignorance.

To them as much as to the super-patriots it is necessary to recommend soberness and the observation of facts. It is a fine thing to have the imagination of disaster if one is a Henry James, or even a Henry Adams; but it is as rare a quality as the imagination of love, and the substitutes for either are simply conventional sentiments, more or less shabby for having passed from hand to hand.

One may concede that in this convention the impulse is good. It is our American pride that wants things fair and free; we growl or splutter when they aren't. Reform is our middle name and progress our sign manual. Perhaps so, but we should by now have a clearer conception of what progress is than that which animates our doomsters. If progress is our specialty, let us for God's sake know what it is we are so good at. With us — and with any people that shares in modern civilization — it consists of two parts. One is to keep pace with changing fact so as to conserve what we think good. The other is to spread, to generalize, whatever gains we make.

Let us not think we are the first to have civilization nor that ours is so perfect that we can offer it as a model to others. Every civilization could justify itself in part and often outstrip us in that part. The Aztec nation, which gave its chosen youth a year of bliss before sacrificing them to the gods, provided something equaled nowhere else. It was wonderful while the year lasted. The "chosen" of other systems could boast of more lasting privileges. But they did not last forever, and our understanding of civilization, our definition of progress, lies in that perception. If we do not perish for violating the third commandment with our image-making, we shall deserve the glory of having seen that a social good cannot remain a good, it will fester, unless it is distributed as widely as possible. That is the meaning of equality — a deliberate undertaking to behave as impartially as we know how towards all men, not a silly and impossible measurement of their deserts.

This, if anything, is the explanation of our giving and sharing and lifting ourselves out of the scarcity, drought, malnutrition, and other evils that have immemorially been "accepted." We don't accept them. Half a million dollars an hour are given in this country for charitable purposes, most of them not mere alms but permanent salvage work on bodies and souls. The result of our efforts is progress on the simplest numerical, material basis. There is no other, for everything else is imponderable. We may be stupider than other peoples, or more nervous or less artistic or farther from contemplation, but this we have done and are doing. A second Rome, let others call us a she-wolf: we begin by giving suck to little boys.

Some of our unlovely traits follow as a necessary consequence. Emancipation emancipates and what is let out is not always Little Lord Fauntleroy or Patience sitting on her monument. We are brash and make much noise on this windy continent, talking as we do all at once in a hundred tongues. But so must it seem to any well-placed observer over any comparable portion of the planet. We are not seemly, because we are less a nation of classes than a people of peoples.

This spectacle is the result of a religious, not a moral idea, if by moral we mean dividing sheep from goats and by religion the inclusive fatherhood of God. The fact that with us "the people" means everybody is what distinguishes us historically and what makes it imperative to train on any of our deeds or institutions the double vision I tried to describe above. That is to say that we are bound to keep in mind the "religious" intent of American civilization even as we take the "moral" attitude of criticizing, rejecting, condemning. Thus we deplore the evils of trade and want to diminish guff; we want more intellect, better manners and conversation; more passion and spiritual freedom; but we cannot pass sentence without appeal; for, on the one hand we are committed to inclusion, not exclusion; and on the other, the thing condemned still fulfills a function and will need some sort of replacement. In this regard, no clearer demonstration of our organic wholeness could be desired than the investigation of our corrupt city machines: to houseclean we do not burn down the house.

Our impatient friends who look to other systems or past eras as a blessed place or time make the obvious mistake of supposing that they can carry with them on their journey to Utopia all that we have in the way of benefits. They want all this plus the fruits of the unrealized ideals they covet. Or else, frankly giving up inclusiveness, they scheme to restore special privilege for a class they think deserving and great, and to which, by a striking coincidence, they invariably feel that they belong — be it agrarian, intellectual, aristocratic, or theological.

Faith in the gospel of mankind is seemingly very hard to keep strong and clear. No sooner is one excluded group at last accorded its "rights" than it wants to pull the door shut behind itself. When recently an American writer referred to minorities in the United States and mentioned criminals and homosexuals among them, there was an outcry from the proper, the noble minorities, who found the conjunction "unfavorable." But if there is one thing that needs doing at the moment, it is a thorough reform of our prisons — *before* the riots occur — and a revision of our legal codes so that homosexuals may no longer be an easy prey to blackmailers and other persecutors. And while on the subject of persecution, one might add Indians and conscientious objectors as groups we are committed to defend.

Our approval or disapproval is irrelevant. These are practical problems and we are nothing if not practical. Put down "Good out of evil" as Emerson did when he wrote in his diary: "One must thank the genius of Brigham Young for the creation of Salt Lake City and Walt Whitman for service to American literature in the Appalachian enlargement of his outline and treatment." Good out of evil is still too narrow a formula for what actually happens under the "religious" view and its permissive habits. The better way to describe it would be infinite creation, unimagined novelty. A modern example, purposely chosen for its social immediacy and cosmic unimportance as well as its characteristic American simplicity, is that of the Hot-Rod Club in Glen Cove, New York. Instead of being a menace to life and sanity, this organization governs itself by strict laws which include safety and the literal observance of traffic rules. It uses the highroads on stated occasions under the protection of the police, whose approval it has earned by reducing delinquency through its turning of youthful spirits into constructive channels.

Now all this to a German-trained "thinker" is nothing but *echt amerikanische Getöse* — nonsense and confusion. Kant's categorical imperative requires us to decide whether hot-rodding *as such* is good or bad, and the decision depends on what would follow if the whole universe became one vast souped-up engine driven by a boy. The conclusion must then be *Verboten!* Every prohibitionist and denouncer of our age fundamentally shares this weed-and-flower view of human society. It has just enough truth to seem incontrovertible. But it leaves out the alternative which is so often found here — the transformation of wildness into order through self-control.

But here again we want the double vision, the two muscles of the arm working together in antithesis. For no society can be good that is all society, all community interest and control. The great problem of the century is the ancient philosophical problem of the One and the Many, for our machines have given overwhelming reality to the Many and mankind must perish if it cannot hold both ideas at once. Whitman's "Appalachian enlargement" meant both to him, even though in his day one had to vindicate the anonymous mass.

It is hard to remember that less than sixty years ago, the employee wherever he worked was a kind of serf: on the job at a quarter to eight — to take the clerk's routine in a fashionable shop — and out at 10 P.M.; more than fourteen hours on one's feet, with only two twenty-minute rests for munching a little food, though even then the clerk might be called to wait on a customer. To the dwellers in that world ours might well seem a utopia. We know it is not, for we know where the shoe pinches us. Our demand is for room to breathe among the liberated mass. Clearly, it is our capacity to see ourselves both as ones and as groups of many that will test our political genius — *E pluribus unum* in very special sense.

The justification is of course that mankind contains everything we desire — heroism, genius, saintliness — and we can never tell where each will spring up. We increase our returns in these goods by broadening the opportunities for talent; and this quite logically makes us choosier. The seesaw here is between the "religious" and "the moral" views of any one candidate for our approval. It is in our tradition to combine them. The democracy of Mark Twain, we know, does not prevent him from observing "what a dull-witted slug the average human being is." The tradition should similarly keep us from pinning all our hopes on one earthly savior — in any realm — and from plunging into despair at the thought of those we confidently designate as dull-witted slugs.

Failing the double vision, the American critic of America ought at least to temper his own brashness, which is up in arms against the national brashness, by a touch of what the Greeks called *hubris:* when at the top of your lungs, think how far you may fall. If our very numerous leaders of opinion cannot take time to differentiate between one error and the next and suit their language accordingly; if they do not care enough for their country to learn about it from other sources than obvious and congenial ones — for example by reading some of the admirable trade-union journals; if they will not be at pains to discover what purposes are served by some of the institutions they attack, let them at least have *hubris*, a twinge of apprehension, now and then, lest they pull the edifice down on their heads.

For America is noticeably changing as regards ideas, the critiques of foreigners, and the variable merits of self-investigation. The tendency is to take systems seriously, with or without previous study, and to strike attitudes in keeping with some new-found rule of life. The man of ideas is rising among us as a power: that is why he is being attacked. Henry Adams, who complained that he had published articles all his life but could find no evidence that anyone had read them, would be aghast at his morning mail — insults and congratulations daily, from strangers, often written before they have finished reading page one. This, once again, is good-and-bad. When the innocent become embattled it is time to run for cover, and when the Texas drawl puts on speed about ideologies, responsiveness ought not to go much further. But its presence makes the weighing of words more than ever a professional duty.

Fortunately, if our surveyors are right, the waves of stormy thought that agitate our intellectual surface still take a good long while to reach the depths. However much we may deplore it for certain purposes, the body of the nation is not instantaneously moved by its mind. The entire press, as we have seen these last fifty years, may reflect some current of feeling which has no counterpart in the population. For editors live in cities or in touch with cities, and the nation still lives closer to the big open space it overran and settled on. The continent is still half wild, not in area, but in atmosphere. This influences every American mind, for not being separated into groups to any marked extent, everything takes effect on us sooner or later: folly, wisdom, jokes, error, truth, nature. One has to go to South America to find genuine isolation — horizontal and pseudo-intellectual — and to see the incapacity of another wild continent to revivify the civilization of Europe. This may possibly excuse the rudeness of seizing for ourselves the name America when we are only a fragment of its northern half: if there is a new world it is here.

The single name, whichever it should be, is a misnomer, for it is one and the reality is manifold. None of us knows more than a fraction of a fraction, clinging arbitrarily to remembered names and broken sights and linkless memories: the word "wild" brings up Tupper Lake and Raquette River and Follansby Clear up in the Adirondacks — was that camp named Moneysunk, or did I dream it? At any rate the Indians' mark is everywhere: Patchogue, Copiague, Ogunquit, Winnetka. And no less repeated, like dots on an epidemic chart, are the new beginnings: New Hope, New Enterprise, New City; but not cut off from the best of the old. Within a radius of less than fifty miles in Maine are Norway, Sweden, Paris, Denmark, Naples, Poland, China, Mexico, and Peru. Athens, Georgia, has airy houses no less fine than Aspasia's; which, taken with the grand colonnade at Columbia, Mo. (the remnants of a great fire), atones for Nashville's Parthenon, cast in concrete in a park, disillusioning about all concerned, yet nobler than the bull on the tobacco factory at Durham, N.C., which bellows at an unpastoral hour to summon the people to work.

Everybody knows Tombstone but they ought to know Barstow, about which Harry Partch has written a great song, and they ought to go to our Western Sacrobosco (Hollywood) and see for themselves that even though larger than Midwestern cities, it is not uglier or more deplorable: the contempt is a cliché. Wilshire Boulevard breaks out into hills and ocean that make one forget the art of photography and acknowledge that there is more ugliness between New York City and Bivalve, New Jersey, than between Vine Street and the sea.

San Francisco I will not name. It is loved and praised on principle because it is cramped like a European town, and Fisherman's Wharf smells of the Old World. I like it well enough, but Palo Alto more, and Raton, New Mexico, where the summer heat makes you think of Dante — and think that he was wrong to call it punishment. More heat in Pueblo, Colorado, where a royal Korean leopard rug came momentarily to rest, or in Portland, in the same state but farther west, where even the lampposts are of cement. One has to reach Aspen to be cool and think of Goethe, whose bicentennial was honored there — fittingly, since almost his last words were: *Amerika, du hast es besser.*

By association with him, who wanted to cut a Panama Canal, the great dams come to mind — Norris, Shasta, Grand Coulee — the only architecture that truly merges with the landscape and measures it. Or you can stand on the heights of Alton, Illinois, looking down the great river and thinking of the sea captain who founded a girl's college there because, said he, educating a man was shooting at a single target, whereas educating a woman was like grapeshot over a whole brood. This thought recalls Jane Todd Crawford, for whom there is a highway named in Kentucky, along the trail she traveled to reach the surgeon who first made a hysterectomy. Unlike other peoples we do not only name for killers and saviors: we have Lawyersville and Cattleman Corners, and Helper, Utah. But Gambier is not a profession and Oliveburg does not celebrate either a tree or a trade.

For higher things, go to Lawrence, Kansas, where the Massachusetts abolitionists, amazed to find a ridge, decided to stop and found a university. South again to Greenville, S.C., where another, the unique Bob Jones University, sits a hundred yards off the four-lane highway, all modern buildings, all fundamentalist teaching, plus a picture gallery full of old masters. Next, to Williamsburg, the town restored by the Rockefellers and declared by Mr. Lewis Mumford to "smell of embalming fluid," yet all the same one of the first towns in the United States where Mumfordian principles of city technics and civilization were carried out two centuries ago; Pigeon Forge, Tennessee, and its charming hand-made pottery; Antietam — just a name, and what had McClellan's horses done there? Lincoln doesn't say. But he makes one think of Illinois again — Chicago, the maligned, for it knew better than New York how to deal with its God-given waterfront; Joliet, Marquette — Jesuit names, one a prison; Champaign-Urbana a twin city half departed, Urbana left with its flat campus, long fraternity row, and brown soil in which it is dangerous to drop seed, for it sprouts and the world market hears of it at once.

Farther north another pair, Minneapolis and St. Paul, which being a match won't talk to each other, sitting on minerals less interesting than the waters that divide them, but which bring the vision back to the dark regions of Pennsylvania, darkly named: Shamokin, Scranton, Oil City, and the City of Dis, Pittsburgh. Wash off the smog in the waters of Big Moose, or better, in the ocean off Gay Head, or in the quiet bay of Cotuit, about which Francis Thompson (who never left London) ridiculously complains of Henry James: "He throws off Cotuit with a pen-scratch or two." What good would it have done Thompson to know that Captain Myles Standish had bought Coa-tuet (Broad Fields) from the Mashpee Indians, with never a thought of oysters, and that it is a quiet village of ancient mariners? One has to smell Cape Cod to value it; even Thoreau, magician that he is, cannot bring up its image from cold print, though he makes Walden and Concord visible enough. Walden is now a swimming park, but Concord is the same — the bridge, the manse, the burying ground; no movie house for little men and women, but a big white building which people will tell you is "Mr. Emerson's church."

Vermont is greener, Peacham gay; and a famous judge, eager for home, wrote a satire in verse about Essex Junction. In York state (the country name), Moody Arab ought to be a junction too, but it is only a con-junction of names on the railroad map, the same which tells you that South Byron is still a stop, the parent town disregarded or dispersed — *sic transit*, but Ypsilanti will do if Byron's gone: the West is rich in memories, or would be, if we remembered what it knew. . . .

We don't because the meaning has not changed in a hundred and fifty, in a hundred, or in fifty years. Dickens made fun of us in the person of General Choke of Edenland: "What are the great United States for, sir, if not for the regeneration of man?" But at that very time Henry James, Sr., was saying the same thing in less arrogant, more humorous tones. Fifty years later his son William would say: "One loves America above all things for her youth, her greenness, her plasticity, innocence, good intentions, friends, everything." Another quarter century, and Scott Fitzgerald put the meaning in an epigram: "America is a willingness of the heart." After his death, a hundred thousand more Europeans, forlorn, fleeing wanderers, found out what he meant.

To us who came before them, the meaning is not fainter, though more familiar, and we scarcely need Emerson's gentle reminder and advice: "The ear loves names of foreign and classic topography. But here we are, and if we tarry a little, we may come to learn that here is best."

August 9, 1952–July 15, 1953